# NATURALISM
# AND
# SUBJECTIVISM

Publication Number 367

AMERICAN LECTURE SERIES®

*A Monograph in*

The BANNERSTONE DIVISION *of*
AMERICAN LECTURES IN PHILOSOPHY

*Edited by*

MARVIN FARBER, Ph.D.
*Distinguished Professor of Philosophy*
*Chairman of the Department of Philosophy*
*University of Buffalo*
*Buffalo, New York*

The following books have appeared thus far in this Series:

Causality in Natural Science — V. F. Lenzen

Emotions and Reason — V. J. McGill

A Good and a Bad Government According to
the New Testament — Jean Hering

The Phenomenological Approach to Psychiatry
— J. H. Van den Berg

Operationism — A. C. Benjamin

Psychoanalysis and Ethics — Lewis S. Feuer

Culture, Psychiatry, and Human Values — Marvin K. Opler

The Origins of Marxian Thought — Auguste Cornu

Metascientific Queries — Mario Bunge

Anthropology and Ethics — May and Abraham Edel

It is the purpose of this series to give representation to all important tendencies and points of view in Philosophy, without any implied concurrence on the part of the Editor and Publisher.

# NATURALISM

## and

## SUBJECTIVISM

*By*

**MARVIN FARBER**

**CHARLES C THOMAS · PUBLISHER**
*Springfield · Illinois · U.S.A.*

# CHARLES C THOMAS • PUBLISHER

BANNERSTONE HOUSE

301-327 East Lawrence Avenue, Springfield, Illinois, U.S.A.

*Published simultaneously in the British Commonwealth of Nations by*
BLACKWELL SCIENTIFIC PUBLICATIONS, LTD., OXFORD, ENGLAND

*Published simultaneously in Canada by*
THE RYERSON PRESS, TORONTO

Library of Congress Catalog Card Number: 59-11896

With THOMAS BOOKS careful attention is given to all details of manufacturing and design. It is the Publisher's desire to present books that are satisfactory as to their physical qualities and artistic possibilities and appropriate for their particular use. THOMAS BOOKS will be true to those laws of quality that assure a good name and good will.

*Printed in the United States of America*

ONULP

*To the Memory*
*of my Parents*

# PREFACE

The present work is scheduled to appear in 1959, which is notable as a centennial year for a number of reasons: among others, as an anniversary of the appearance of Darwin's *Origin of Species* and Marx's *Critique of Political Economy,* and also of the birth of John Dewey and Edmund Husserl. It is concerned with the tension between naturalism and idealism in its historical outcome of subjectivism, as developed in the phenomenological movement.

Great interest attaches to phenomenology because of its strategic position as the last stronghold of idealism. The old opposition between naturalism and supernaturalism, or between materialism and spiritualism, has been superseded by a conflict between naturalism as a philosophy based upon the findings and methods of the sciences, and subjectivism as a general tendency, with its principle of the primacy of the experiencing being. The practical importance of this principle is seen in its use for numerous philosophies of man and existence. That makes it all the more pertinent to examine subjectivism in juxtaposition with its major antagonist—naturalism.

The criticism, at times severe, which is offered by the present volume, will be sure to meet with hostility in some quarters. To those who demur in the name of a "pure" philosophy, or in the name of a vacuous philosophy of existence, it may be said simply that fidelity to the cause of truth is alone at issue.

The writer acknowledges his grateful indebtedness to

the University of Buffalo for a sabbatical leave of absence and a research grant-in-aid, which made possible the completion of the book at this time; to the Husserl Archives of Louvain, for authorization to use materials from unpublished manuscripts of Edmund Husserl; and to the Macmillan Company, for permission to use the writer's chapter on "Experience and Subjectivism" in *Philosophy for the Future* (edited by R. W. Sellars, V. J. McGill, and M. Farber, 1949). Portions of the second, seventh, and ninth chapters have appeared in *Philosophy and Phenomenological Research.*

                                                    M. F.

# CONTENTS

# NATURALISM
# AND
# SUBJECTIVISM

*Chapter I*

# EXPERIENCE AND BASIC FACT

## A. THE ISSUE OF NATURALISM
## VS.
## SUBJECTIVISM

The reader of philosophical literature must be impressed above all by the warfare of the "schools," by the conflicting tendencies in philosophy. In the great tradition, spiritualism and materialism were the leading contenders. In recent years the chief actors in the professional field of philosophy have been naturalism and subjectivism, with the issue defined in terms of rival types of method. This is not to imply that traditional spiritualism disappeared from the scene, for it did not; nor that materialism, especially in the form of dialectical materialism, was superseded by naturalism, for it has had its own continuous development.

The term "naturalism" is sufficiently broad and tenuous to comprise all varieties of materialism, and also to allow for more cautious points of view, qualified by agnosticism and even pantheism in some conspicuous cases (Spencer and Huxley illustrating the former, and Haeckel the latter). It has had the advantage of providing a marginal academic respectability. In general, the definition of "naturalism" by Ralph Perry is useful: it is "the philosophical generalization of science," and its various forms are determined by the content and the method of the sciences. The rapid development of the special sciences,

and especially the impact of the great evolutionary movement, in the nineteenth century, brought on a violent
reaction in the interest of traditional beliefs and institu-
tions, a reaction which became a prime motivating force
in the world of philosophy. The "containment" of the
sciences was a major objective for a generation of philosophical writers.

Traditional empiricism and psychology had led to a
psychologistic philosophy of logic in England (J. S. Mill)
and Germany (Sigwart, Wundt, and others). Allied with
evolutionary concepts, this view of logic appeared to
threaten the objectivity and rigor of formal science—as
though logic were conceived as being a chapter in the
natural science of psychology. The criticism of this faulty
and one-sided view of logic was one of the steps leading
to the exclusion of the scientific method from philosophy.
The original motivation for Edmund Husserl's phenomenology was thus provided. When the consequences of
the evolutionary naturalistic movement for ethics are considered, the motivation for Husserl's associate, Max
Scheler, is also seen. In the name of "pure" philosophy,
these scholars, along with many others (Rickert, Dilthey,
*et al.*) sought to oppose the growing scientific movement in
philosophy. Certainly the latter was inadequate in some
important respects. But the issue should have been viewed
constructively, the correction of a poor scientific philosophy being made by a better one, and not by means of
an antiscientific point of view. That is to say, if it were
only an intellectual issue, which was not the case. In
Husserl's hands—and he was one of the ablest of his
generation of opponents of the scientific philosophy—the
issue became clearly defined in terms of subjectivism as
opposed to a naturalistic objectivism. Only his version of

subjectivism was intended to be fundamentally different from the ordinary psychology of the time, and of the tradition. Above all, he sought to rise above the "naïve natural attitude," which covered evolutionary as well as Marxian thought, in his usage.

The central theme of the subjectivist is the analysis of experience. Naturalists, pragmatists, realists, and positivists have also devoted much attention to this theme. The present study will include consideration of the analyses by conceptual pragmatism (C. I. Lewis), naturalism (John Dewey), and subjectivism (Edmund Husserl's phenomenology and its sphere of influence). The latter is of unusual interest because of its elaboration as a universal philosophy of idealism, and as a forerunner of "existentialism." The task of a complete and consistent scientific philosophy, whether it be called "naturalism" or "materialism," and "critical" or "new," is made more clear by determining the limits of a subjectivistic procedure, and by examining closely the arguments marshalled in support of subjectivism.

## B. THE HISTORICAL AND SOCIAL CHARACTER OF THE ANALYSIS OF EXPERIENCE

The choice between rival philosophies may be decided on the basis of their treatment of experience. Now the appeal to experience is invariably an appeal to an experience defined in terms of a given theory, to an "interpreted" experience. The "atomic" experience of Locke conforms to the pattern of individualism of his time, and is different from the rationally conditioned experience of Kant, or the socialized experience of more recent date. The very statement of the problem of analyzing experience, in particular the "given" in experience, is thus historically conditioned. In view of the fact that scholars of divergent tendencies appeal to "experience," as well as the fact that all philosophical problems can—and must—be traced back to their locus in experience, this theme is of primary importance.

The "appeal to experience" is ostensibly an appeal to observed facts, and to the use of logical methods. In the wrong hands, especially when made by a philosopher rooted in the tradition of idealism, it proves to be a trap for metaphysical purposes. If one begins with the mind, he rarely gets beyond it. A "great mind" is frequently the outcome. That is because of initial dogmas, or initial assumptions, in the use of the concept of experience. Whose experience is meant? One's own? If one proposes to restrict himself to his own experiences, he has still to take account of other persons, as well as the natural world. The *basic fact* for all philosophizing which aspires to be true to experience is the fact of the natural world and its priority to man; and also the priority of a cultural tradition to each individual man. The latter is what he is because of the tradition which produced him. In other words, no treatment of experience may disregard the fact that experience is an event in the natural world, any more than it can disregard the fact that it is a cultural product.

The question of the nature of experience is far-reaching enough to call forth the familiar alignments of standpoints. The survival and continued activity of the various historical traditions is sufficient to bring that about. It does not matter that the development of science has outmoded many of the traditional views, for in philosophy death is no guarantee of disappearance, and even the unreal may "come to appearance." If one reads philosophy on the surface, taking statements at their apparent face-value, many of the differences of views appear to be trivial or senseless. But philosophy should never be detached from its social-historical context, in terms of which its significance is to be sought. These considerations help to explain why such a seemingly straightforward theme as the analysis of experience is still in a state of dispute.

Finality in the analysis of experience is never to be achieved, unless one operates abstractively with a limited view of experience, limited in its historical extent and with respect to the person making the analysis. If the knower plays a role in experience, and if the cultural group to which he belongs conditions and influences the process of experience; and if, furthermore, there are "meaning-sediments" of past generations, of an intellectual, aesthetic, etc., type—then there can be no finality. That there must be certain "structural" features of experience, man being what he is and in view of his relationship to his fellow men and the rest of nature, will be granted, while recognizing the unavoidable openness and incompleteness of experience. It follows that the analysis of experience must be undertaken again and again, in each cultural generation at least. That is always necessary, if only because of the added advantage of the later perspective. There is also the factor of scientific progress; for obviously, a number of sciences cooperate in the understanding as well as control of experience. In this sense, the analysis of experience will never disappear as a problem, or as a theme for philosophic inquiry. It is not a matter of a stubborn problem which resists all attempts to solve it, as in the case of the historical "problem of knowledge."

In recent years considerable attention has been devoted to the question of what is "given" in experience. The very expression "the given" is assumptive—as though there were an independent, fixed mind, opposed to the world, so that one could ask what is "given" to it. If one adopts a subjectivistic method in philosophy, or a transcendental method, in conformity to the Kantian tradition, the nature of the "given" is an important problem. That problem may be said to be "methogenic," or to result from the method adopted, in contradistinction to "empiriogenic" problems, which are real in experience. If one views the evidence of experience objectively, he realizes that man, and consequently the mind, is the result of a long process of evolution; that man is a part of the world and of society; and that it is a strange aberration to ask, as Schelling did in his program for transcendental idealism, how the mind comes to present a world. Only a historical account of the social and religious motivation can explain such a fantastic position. The objective point of view in philosophy does not ignore or falsify the established results of the sciences. It is determined by them, guided by them. It seeks to analyze experience and its conditions *within the framework of physical nature.* The *basic fact* of the priority of nature is not construed as something "given" to a mind, and an archaic mind at that. The understanding of man as a part of nature is an accomplished fact, even though it is necessary to recognize distinctive organizations of existence, from the inanimate to the social and intellectual. Man has been parceled out among the various sciences, and the mind is treated in terms of behavior. It is a quaint matter, then, to ask how nature comes to be presented, in the fashion of the transcendentalists or subjectivists; or indeed, what is "given" to a mind viewed as already on hand. The methogenic problem of the "given" is seen in proper perspective by an analysis which is abreast of the scientific development of the present era.

The question of the "given," while an important historical problem, is, strictly speaking, a false one, the result of freezing the mind into a formal agent which somehow conditions experience. The *analysis of experience,* on the other hand, is a real problem, truly "empiriogenic." Now experience is in nature, and not nature in experience. There was a time when there was no experience, meaning human experience; and human experience may eventually disappear. The independence of the world, with respect to the knower, is a brute fact which no philosophical arguments can alter. These considerations are commonplace in our time, but they are by no means accepted by all philosophers. Their consequences would make spiritualism impossible in all its forms.

Having made clear the assumptive use of the expression "the given," it will be instructive to examine its use in some prominent examples of contemporary philosophy, both non-idealistic and idealistic. In the name of the systematic analysis of knowledge and experience, some philosophers have made the individual thinker the point of departure, and have sought to determine what he "contributes" to experience, and what is "given." But what is "given"? For some, it is a formless, nameless "stuff"; for others, it is a world of things; and for still others, the mind (a "great" mind) does all the "giving"— it gives the "given."

Man constitutes a part of his own environment, a fact which is fully recognized by cultural scientists. To go still further and to speak of constituting the "material" of culture, and the world of nature itself, is to substitute dogma for the recognition of a patent fact. But it is not enough to grant a "constitutive" activity of man in his

process of experience. The nature of that activity must
be determined truly. It is seen that there is always a
"standard equipment" of the mind for a given time and
place, and that that equipment changes historically. There
are no fixed forms of the mind, any more than there is
an unchangeable physical nature. The concepts and explanatory principles are different in ancient India, ancient
Greece, and in the modern world.

The varied interpretation of the world itself requires
an explanation. In part, the differences in interpretation
are due to the self-corrective and cumulative efforts of
scientists to understand and control the world, and in
part, but more fundamentally, they are due to the nature
of human activity, to social factors. In a significant passage,
Engels has pointed out[1] that the alteration of nature by
men, not solely nature as such, is the most essential and
immediate basis of human thought. Because of human
activity, there is very little left of "nature" as it was in
earlier periods. But if one abstracts from such changes,
the physical environment may be regarded as a "constant."
The "variable" human environment is then seen to condition the intellectual changes; the dominant world-view
pattern for a given period is closely related to the leading
social interests. While allowing in turn for the influence of
scientific progress on the social order, one must recognize
that the social environment has exercised deciding influences, and has determined the "given" in its most
important sense.

For one who is a Catholic, the philosophy and theology
of the Church are more potent factors in his "given"
than the sun and the seas. The worker who enters a mine

---

1. Cf. *Dialectics of Nature*, New York, International Publishers, 1940,
p. 172.

daily in order to support himself and his family must surely assign a position of central importance in his "given" to the mine and all that it entails. To the youth who thinks of marriage there are still other facts, organic and social, which are conspicuously "given." In short, experience and its world, in its most comprehensive sense, constitute the "given."

To limit experience to one segment or stratum is justifiable only for a particular purpose, as in the use of a subjectivistic procedure for the analysis of experience. Thus, one may restrict his consideration of the "given" to his own conscious processes, to what may be called "methodological solipsism," which is quite different from the absurd position of genuine solipsism. The convinced solipsist, if such there be, and if he is really sincere and wishes to be consistent, is doomed to silence and inactivity. To think or reflect must be perpetually embarrassing to him, because his thought and linguistic system are social in their significance and reference. This does not apply to the "methodological solipsist," who is not "convinced" of solipsism, and who, perhaps, should therefore not be called a solipsist. That is the case with the phenomenological method in its initial "egological" stage, at which the experiences of an individual knower are considered in provisional isolation from all other knowers. But no assumption concerning the privacy of an individual mind should be injected. That an individual mind can only occur as a member of, or in relation to, a group of minds is an immediate fact that must be accepted by everyone, including the phenomenologist. The recognition of the "intentional" character of experience (meaning that experience refers to an objectivity) alone may not save the phenomenologist from accepting a general philosophy of "immanence," which is merely a form of idealism, depending upon the well-known assumptions.[2] More must be allowed for in characterizing experience.

It would be better to speak of reflectively viewed experience in its first stage, as limited to an individual, and in its second stage, when extended to comprise social experience. The first stage carries through a "suspension" of beliefs (an *"epoché"*) concerning the world and other knowers as far as possible, and it operates with a highly restricted "given."

## C. PHILOSOPHIC "IMMEDIACY" AND THE POINT OF DEPARTURE FOR PHILOSOPHY

Interest in the "given" is often motivated by the aim of determining an "immediate" fact for philosophical analysis, which could provide a point of departure, basic criteria, and a secure support for the whole structure of philosophy. There can be no question about there being *something* immediately given for any point of view, whether subjective-idealistic or materialistic. Its precise nature is what presents the problem; and the greatest difficulty turns out to be due to the standpoint that has been adopted beforehand. The identification of what is taken as "the immediate fact," for a particular point of view, with the total "given" as such, has been the source of much confusion.

---

2. For the critique of idealism, cp. R. B. Perry, *Present Philosophical Tendencies*, New York, Longmans, Green, and Co., 1912, pp. 113 ff.; and V. I. Lenin, *Materialism and Empirio-Criticism*, New York, International Publishers, 1927, Introduction. Cf. also the present writer's criticism of idealism in *Philosophic Thought in France and the United States*, University of Buffalo Publications in Philosophy, 1950, pp. 428 f. Prominent in the tradition of idealistic reasoning is the "cardinal principle of idealism," that "consciousness in some form . . . is the one necessary and universal condition of being" (Perry, *op. cit.*, p. 155).

When Whitehead begins the exposition of his "Method of Extensive Abstraction" in his *Concept of Nature*,[3] he takes "Something is going on" as the immediate fact, for his point of departure. But this immediate fact is not taken in isolation. It is included in a "duration," which is a "concrete slab of nature." This applies very well to the present discussion of experience. No individual perception in a specious present can serve as the immediate fact. Every perception involves a past and a future; it retains from the past, and anticipates the future. Furthermore, it involves a physical and a social environment or context, and therewith it takes its place as an event in cultural history. An isolated perception cannot be an ultimate unit of experience, any more than there can be an isolated physical fact. Such units are provided by retrospective analysis.

The immediate facts, for the basic natural attitude, are above all the stubborn, unavoidable, or challenging events and conditions so abundantly illustrated in ordinary experience—the joys and sorrows, births and deaths, the cases of hunger and frustration. What Dewey has gone to pains to emphasize, in his *Experience and Nature,* as the "precariousness" of life may serve as a title for some of the foremost immediate facts. In this sense one *participates* in the general process of experience; one is immersed in the world of experience, and can never *really* get outside it. One likes the things to which he has been conditioned — food, clothing, entertainment, etc. Both with regard to feeling and thinking one is the product of his time, even in his negative reactions against some of its features. In the struggle for survival and mastery over nature, it is

3. Cf. A. N. Whitehead, *The Concept of Nature,* Cambridge, The University Press, 1920, Chapter III.

not "man against nature"; it is man as a part of nature attempting to adapt the forces of nature to his own ends. It is even less meaningful to suppose that one gets outside his cultural system when criticizing it, no matter how fundamental the criticism may be. And finally, it is if anything still less possible really to get away from or "behind" experience in general. One does not accomplish that feat by calling the latter "natural" experience, which is then to be viewed from another, allegedly superior vantage point. It is simply impossible to remove oneself from his natural and cultural setting, which is the *basic, immediate fact* for philosophy, just as it is for everything else, for all analyses and inquiries in the special sciences.

This general thesis should be borne in mind throughout the discussion of subjectivism. It would be a simple misunderstanding to suppose that one in the process of pure reflection leaves behind the field of experience. It should also be emphasized that an actual experience, or even the stream of experiences, is not regarded as the immediate fact for the natural view of the world. They are immediate in a specially defined sense, within the limits of an explicitly defined, subjectivistic point of view. The *abstractive* treatment in phenomenology of the stream of experiences, with the objects referred to as such, is a stage in the reflective analysis of experience for which there is ample justification. But it should not be confused with the immediate fact for man the organism and man the active knower, finding his way in a hostile world, or in a world of social conflicts. The reflective analysis is intended further to serve that knower, and it is only folly resulting from wishful thinking, aided and abetted by fallacious reasoning, that can bring about the dissolution of the real immediate fact in an idealized pure consciousness.

## D. THE MIND AS CONTRIBUTIVE AND THE ERROR OF IRRATIONALISM

No account of experience can be true which does not do justice to the contributing activities of the mind. That the mind is not purely passive in experience was recognized by Locke, who pointed out that the mind is able to perform operations of its own. No better evidence for the contributiveness of thought is needed than the amount of nonsense there is in the world. To what extent thought is contributive is another matter, of course, and there the claims of the idealist must be examined carefully—both the part-idealist for whom something is given to mind and by mind, and the whole-idealist for whom the mind provides all reality, and sometimes more besides.

To point out the fact that the knower (and, indeed, the whole tradition of knowers) "contributes" to experience, is not to suggest that the knower makes anything out of whole cloth. He is a product of his time, and what he does is conditioned by the existing scientific level, the motivation of his social system, and his aptitudes. He may seek to transform society, but he does not "constitute" or "create" society; although he may devise new theories, or new concepts, some of which may radically change past views. The nature and degree of any "creativeness" is determined by conditions beyond the control of any individual thinker. The kinds of innovation which are possible depend upon the nature of the tradition, as well as the existing social system.

The fact that the mind contributes meanings and interpretations to experience can be ascertained descriptively. That does not mean acceptance of the Kantian principle that form is contributed by the mind. The Kantian view can only be made workable with the aid of the "Absolute

Mind" that hovers over the Kantian system, giving it the necessary support, and that assumption is itself not supported by evidence. Nothing is left of the arguments for the transcendental ideality of space and time. The mind has a history, and there are no demonstrated eternal, fixed forms. To recognize the "contributiveness" of the mind is not to imply that any ideas or conceptual forms can be genetically unrelated to the causal order of experience. The truth that Kant himself recognized, that, in point of time, there is no knowledge before experience, applies generally.

The mind is contributive on the perceptual as well as on the conceptual level.[4] Illustrations of its contributive function on the conceptual level are most readily seen in its idealizations, which are not merely reports of what is found in the natural world. Philosophers in all ages have found it tempting to hypostatize the idealizations and to assign them a being of their own. The reflective description of the process of idealization tends to dispel that dogma, and shows that the function of constituting ideal forms, and, indeed, the entire process of ideal identification, of the recognition of sameness, is not only necessary for theoretical purposes, but also for the most fundamental activities of experience.

A well-known type of question will be suggested at once. If to know is to know meaningfully, and to apply conceptual forms and schemes, then it will be asked whether it is possible to know "truly," i.e., whether there

---

4. Cf. E. Husserl, *Erfahrung und Urteil*, Prague, Academia Verlagsbuch-handlung, 1939, for a detailed descriptive analysis of such contributions. This little-known treatise merits the careful study of all students of philosophy. In this work Husserl undertakes to do what Kant failed to do, in showing the actual part played by perception and the understanding in the process of experience. The acceptance of his descriptive findings in no way commits one to his systematic idealism.

may not be a falsification of experience due to the employment of a falsifying scheme. In other words, are we in a "predicament" due to the very fact that the mind contributes to experience? The very formulation of this question is assumptive. It disengages the mind from its natural framework, and supposes that the conceptual productions are regarded as substantive, ideal entities which somehow are capable of shutting us out of the correct view of an independently real world. Indeed, the supposed independently real world is assumed to be already interpreted truly, i.e., it is "in itself" the object of a true interpretation which for some reason the mind is forbidden to realize in experience. If one considers the actual function of the process of idealization and the constitution of ideal conceptual systems, he will see that they are proved or disproved in experience, that they are verified or invalidated in practice, so that it is misleading to ask, in static terms, whether it is possible to know reality truly.

The verification of some of our conceptual schemes becomes a mystery, or at best a matter of good fortune, on the view that the mind is a falsifying agency. There cannot be a complete falsification, in view of our practical success in solving our problems. The alleged falsification can at most be partial, and it is not to be identified with the cases of false statements or incorrect hypotheses which have to be abandoned. The remedy for the latter is more and better knowledge. There is no remedy for the alleged evil besetting knowledge essentially, due to the use of static concepts, other than use of some other means than the intellect in order to experience reality "truly." Instead of speaking of "truth," it would then be more appropriate to speak of the night in which all cows are black. To look to "intuition," in the sense of Bergson,[5] would be to abandon all hope of objective truth, and to forget the painstakingly acquired lessons of scientifically controlled inquiry.

It would certainly be a strange situation if the mind should "falsify" reality by means of devices proved valuable in practice. But even if it is granted that there is no necessary falsification, it will be admitted that there are difficulties in the way of descriptive analysis in reflection. One's vision, reflectively directed, is itself conditioned by the scientific and philosophical level of the time, and also by traditional ideas and schemes. Personal factors may also be of influence. It follows that the desired complete descriptive analysis is an ideal which is largely realized only in the best examples of philosophical analysis, i.e., when care is taken to reflect upon the reflective process, including the investigator and all the conditions that bear upon him.

### E.  THE "GIVEN" ELEMENT IN EXPERIENCE ACCORDING TO LEWIS

This function of reflection is recognized by Lewis,[6] although he is concerned with the purely epistemological rather than with the sociological conditions of experience. In his view, "it is the business of philosophy to analyze

---

5. Cf. H. Bergson, *Creative Evolution*, New York, H. Holt and Co., 1911. Bergson's logical shortcomings were effectively exposed by contemporary critics, including Santayana and Perry; and Whitehead has shown how a constructive answer can be given to the criticism of intellectual devices. Their improvement, and not the abandonment of the intellect, is called for. For a recent French criticism of Bergson, see Politzer, *Le Bergsonisme: Une Mystification Philosophique*, Paris, Éditions Sociales, 1947.

6. C. I. Lewis, *Mind and the World-Order*, New York, C. Scribner's Sons, 1929, p. 36.

and interpret our common experience, and by reflection, to bring to clear and cogent expression those principles which are implicit because they are brought to experience by the mind itself." Philosophy is thus "the study of the *a priori*," its aim being "to reveal those categorial criteria which the mind applies to what is given to it"; and thus "to define the good, the right, the valid, and the real."

Historical considerations are obviously excluded by this type of analysis. What is here called "our common experience" is already interpreted, and bears the imprint of countless past generations. Then what can be meant by the interpretation of the philosopher, who has the role of interpreting "our common experience"? Can the philosopher do that by means of certain ultimate, intuitively "clarified" concepts? Descriptive analysis without interpretation, i.e., without the use of concepts and explanatory principles, is an ideal impossible in practice, and it is well to recognize this fact explicitly. That the pattern of interpretation used in an investigation can itself be examined in reflection, and thus be "clarified," disposes of the danger of a "predicament."

Philosophers have become so accustomed to regarding the analysis of experience as falling to them that they for the most part fail to inquire wherein their procedure differs from that of the psychologist and social scientist. It must be possible to draw the line clearly between them, or else philosophy must surrender any claim to independence, or even partial independence. In the case of prejudice, for example, the logician's interest in exposing the errors in reasoning can be readily distinguished from that of the psychologist. As for the epistemologist, his attitude or point of view, his method, and the character of the evidence will distinguish his interest, which is specialized.

This is clearly expressed in the literature of phenomenology, which is, in its best sense, a descriptive theory of knowledge. The attitude is one of "universal questioning," with logic and naturalistic psychology "suspended" as a preliminary step, so that there is a minimum in assumptions. These considerations are not incompatible with Lewis's position, as quoted above. They underlie his position, and call attention to the need for a still more explicit and thoroughgoing methodological study of the "conditions of experience" that are due to the activity of the mind, or to the contributions of the mind. The descriptive procedure that has been indicated can only be one phase of philosophic inquiry, but it does play a necessary part in the analysis of experience.

Lewis distinguishes two elements in knowledge: the concept, which is the product of the activity of thought, and the sensuously given, which is independent of such activity. His analysis is a "logical" one which involves ideal conditions never met in experience. To that extent it is non-empirical. There is always a mixture of the two factors—which Lewis recognizes, of course—and he is interested in "cognitive experience," in which the immediate sensuous data are given to the mind, and a form, construction, or interpretation is present as a result of the activity of thought. This distinction is sound as far as it goes. But lacking in Lewis's analysis is a detailed descriptive account of how the mind actually performs its "constructive" activities. Elaborate descriptive-philosophical as well as psychological studies are called for. It is necessary to point out the truth of the causal-genetic view, as to the conditions underlying the activities of the mind—the dependence of the mind on nature and on society, and the way in which the mind may be said to "reflect" the world. Analysis in the theory of knowledge can only suffer because of detachment from such basic facts. This is shown, for example, when Lewis holds the "given" to be "ineffable," to be that which remains untouched and unaltered, however it is construed by thought (53). The term "given" may be used in this ideal, limiting sense for purposes of analysis. It names a limiting, conditioning element in experience, abstracting from the interpretation of the mind. But there is also the more inclusive sense of givenness, according to which the world of experience as a whole is "given"— the physical and the cultural environment, with their "deposits" of meaning. The "given" in the full sense really includes the domain of nature; the society into which one is born; the language which he learns; the intellectual, moral, and religious traditions; and, fundamentally, the very likes and dislikes which one has.

It is the "thick experience of the world of things, not the thin given of immediacy" that constitutes the datum for philosophical reflection, in Lewis's view. "We do not see patches of color, but trees and houses . . . . Such initial data of object and fact set the problem in philosophy and are, in a measure, the criteria of its solution" (54). The use of the term "immediacy" to name the "thin" content of the "given" is not altogether fortunate, since the total situation and things are "first" for actual experience, as Lewis himself indicates. He points out that the "given," as he conceives it, is an abstraction, even though it is not an "unreal" abstraction; that the "given" is *in*, not before, experience; and that it is an identifiable constituent of experience (54, 66). He is right in defending the use of abstractions. So long as one recognizes the actual total nature of experience and avoids confusing products of analysis with real elements, it is a proper procedure to carry through an analysis from the point of view of a knower who separates his meaning-activities from that which is sensuously "given." That is one level of analysis which may be accepted as such. But it is society that is prior to the individual in a naturalistic, genetic sense, i.e., *in reality*. What is called "first" in an analysis depends upon the purpose of the analysis and the frame of reference. If it is the actual knower and his actual experience, the immediate fact is that whole objects and their relationships are there, in their natural and social setting. If it is a physical-psychological inquiry, the sensuous basis of experience is fundamental. For the phenomenological investigation, the objectively directed experiences themselves are taken to be "first." This does not mean, however, that the judgment of what is fundamentally real is arbitrary. Alternative procedures for special purposes, involving abstraction as they do, should not be taken to imply that alternative views of reality are equally justifiable.

Lewis's analysis makes it impossible to construct or constitute all the elements of experience on the basis of the mind and its contents. The basic pattern which he lays down, the dualism between "what the mind brings to experience" and "what is given in experience," bears a resemblance to the Kantian analysis. But it is advanced without the Kantian dogma of a fixed, unifying self and the categorial forms, and without the Kantian pretense to *a priori* knowledge, meaning universal and necessary knowledge. Lewis's construction is a pale shadow of Kant's enormous claims. The mind brings alternative concepts, theories, or interpretations, and a choice is made from among them, in order to make application to situations in experience. The name *a priori* for such concepts is thus hardly appropriate, in view of their modest status as possible patterns of thought, which may or may not find application in experience.

It is always desirable, in undertaking a systematic analysis of knowledge and experience, to remind oneself of their physical, organic, and social conditions. That would prevent errors from arising due to the "static" treatment of the mind—as though it were a finality, without beginning in time, and a long history. In short, such a reminder is like providing ordinate and abscissa to establish the proper locus of the discussion. Its preventive value is very important. A philosopher should not be vague or noncommittal on the basic questions of metaphysics. An analysis of experience and knowledge should not neglect to indicate the basic facts which, if recognized, would make agnosticism, skepticism, and spiritualism untenable. In other words, the epistemologist has no right to forget the place of the knower in reality, or to forget the knowledge forced upon us by ordinary experience, let alone science. The content of established knowledge is relevant to an inquiry into the nature and structure of experience. One errs in his analysis, if these facts are not made explicit. Healthymindedness is at issue.

It would be best to designate the "given" in Lewis's sense as the "sensuous given," so as to distinguish it from other "givens," such as the cultural whole of experience. The stratum of the "sensuous given" can only be provided by an analysis which introduces ideal conditions. The "empirical given" for any person consists of things, of interpreted objects; and the alleged "indubitably given" of phenomenology (or the "given" *qua* indubitable) consists of an actual experience with its object "meant," but not posited as existent.

## F.  DEWEY ON IMMEDIATE KNOWLEDGE AND
## THE NATURE OF THE "GIVEN"

As a representative of the tradition of naturalism, Dewey endeavors to hold to the truth that man the organism strives to preserve himself in a hostile environment, and to represent it unflinchingly in all its consequences. Extensive consequences are determined by it, positively as well as negatively. Inspection shows, however, that even the most resolute naturalistic inquiry which favors the use of organic categories meets with difficulties in the context of social science, where clear, concrete reference must be made to basic problems in terms of concepts appropriate to the social context. Precisely this point is a characteristic distinction between a cautious naturalism (an incomplete materialism, really) and a thoroughgoing materialism applied to all regions of existence.

Dewey undertakes to give an account of experience which does justice to its naturalistic character and conditions, and which at the same time recognizes the difficulties caused by the interpretations of the mind and the construction of theories. He calls attention[7] to the frequently occurring and perhaps inevitable practice of the philosopher "to mix with his reports of direct experience interpretations made by previous thinkers." The tradition of empiricism is cited as a striking illustration of this danger, so that empiricism faces the objection that it is not true to experience. By experience Dewey means "something at least as wide and deep and full as all history on this earth, a history which, since history did not occur in the void, includes the earth and the physical relations of man" (8). It would be better to say "involves" instead of

---

7. *Experience and Nature*, Chicago, Open Court Publishing Co., 1925, pages 3 f.

"includes," and to make sure that the definition of experience makes it clear that the natural world antedates the
emergence of human experience. This would effectively
avoid any suggestion of idealism. The concept of experience, as construed by Dewey in all its comprehensive-
ness, is intended to provide philosophy with the advantage
of "the method of pointing, finding, showing" (11).
"Reality" is held to include "whatever is denotatively
found." "Experience" is thus a "directive" word, and it
appears to be all the more useful because the unfavorable
and the hateful will therewith receive the same attention
usually accorded to the noble and honorable. However, if
"reality" is taken to include that which is "found," it
must be explicitly pointed out that the field of reality is
antecedent to any process of "finding," i.e., if the narrowness of positivism is to be avoided.

In his treatment of experience Dewey does not consider
that *true* and *adequate* knowledge will not give a false
emphasis to the intellectual elements, and do an injustice
to the nonintellectual elements. With the use of the
"denotative method he proposes to go "behind the refinements and elaborations of reflective experience to the
gross and compulsory things of our doings, enjoyments,
and sufferings—to the things that force us to labor, that
satisfy needs" (16). The recognition of such things certainly
belongs to the program of the descriptive analysis of experience, beginning with the "natural" view of the world
and man. The truth of the "natural" view of the world
must be accepted and done justice in the reflective analysis
of experience. It is concerned with temporally and causally
prior facts which provide the material and the primary
occasion for reflection. Dewey's admonition that we go
"behind the refinements . . . of reflective experience to

the . . . things" recalls Husserl's famous slogan, "Back
to the things themselves." For both thinkers, direct seeing
is held up as the basic method. Dewey's observation (26)
that the things which a man experiences come to him
clothed with meanings which originate in custom and
tradition, brings to mind Husserl's discussion of "sedimented meanings," and also his apt figure of the "garment
of ideas" thrown over the data of experience. But there
are also differences—above all the basic difference that
the "things" to which Dewey refers are social, physical,
biological, whereas Husserl's appeal is to direct experience,
his best examples being in the field of logical experience;
and he did not speak as a naturalist. It will be sufficient
at this point to mention one further difference in the
analyses of the two thinkers. For Dewey, experience is
history (29 f.), and it is a method, not a stuff. The "taking"
of some objects as final is itself declared to be an episode
of history. Husserl, being interested in finality, in ultimate
and eternal truths, endeavors to rise above history and
time in their naturalistic sense. Dewey, on the other hand,
regards the "assumption that the ultimate and immediate
object is timeless" as responsible for an insoluble problem. In his view, anything denoted is found to have
*temporal quality* and reference.

Dewey's reflective procedure goes back "to the primitive
situations of life that antecede and generate" the reflective
interpretations, "so that we re-live former processes of
interpretation." Thus we go "knowingly and cautiously
through steps which were first taken uncritically" (31).
The resemblance to Husserl's general pattern of inquiry
is apparent. The "naturalistic" program for reflective
analysis of Dewey seeks to probe to the "elementary
building-stones of experience." But much more should be

said regarding the mechanism of the procedure to be followed out. Dewey is cautious in his claims for his empirical method. One may show the way to others, so that they can see for themselves. Moreover, the findings of one person may be rectified and extended by the findings of others. In this way cooperation for philosophical reflection resembles the cooperation seen in inquiry in the natural sciences (35).

When Dewey speaks of experience, in the complete sense in which he means it to be understood, as the *method* of philosophy, he is doing little more than providing emphasis in a desired direction. Negatively, it aids in combating one-sided and artificial methods. But positively, it does not furnish precepts for procedure, or anything more than a general appeal for the use of empirical description as a method subject to the confirmation of others. In other words, the method of philosophy is conceived as being like that of any descriptive discipline, and as merely being more general. In the present context, Dewey does not clearly distinguish *philosophical* inquiry from common sense or science. In the main, he sketches a naturalistic genetic method which runs parallel to the "pure" genetic method proposed by Husserl. He fails, however, to point out adequately the procedure which he must use as a philosopher, and the conditions under which it must be used, *qua* philosophy. The main lines that philosophy has to take are indicated by him, as follows: "It has the task of analytic dismemberment and synthetic reconstruction of experience" (40). Surely that must include the attempt at a thoroughgoing reflective inspection of all the activities and contributions of the mind, of all the conditions that bear upon the experience of the group and the individual, the challenging of every belief and judgment with respect to its foundation in experience, and the systematic "questioning" of all items of knowledge in terms of one's own direct experience ("reflective experience," which "reactivates" the original presumed experiences)—in short, an attempt at a complete analysis of experience, in connection with the findings of the various special sciences which show the place of man (and experience) in nature, and the mutual relationships between the knower and his environment.

The parallelism with Husserl should not be overdrawn, however, in view of the differences in dominant aims and premises and the emphasis upon testing, upon experimentalism, especially as shown in Dewey's philosophy of logic. If a subjectivist sees clearly and truly, in his descriptive analysis of experience, his findings can and must be ordered in the naturalistic account of experience. But it does not follow that all idealistic *theories* can be translated into naturalistic terms, e.g., those involving the alleged "supertemporal" elements.

Distrusting any flight to a realm of certainty which is removed from the realities of experience. Dewey never loses sight of the "outstanding fact," "the evidence that the world of empirical things includes the uncertain, unpredictable, uncontrollable, and hazardous" (42). It is the "predicament of the inextricable mixture of stability and uncertainty" that gives rise to philosophy, and that is reflected "in all its recurrent problems and issues" (45 f.). Even a cursory inspection of the historical problems of philosophy will convince the reader that this thesis could not be sustained. It expresses a limited truth merely, and will not apply properly to such thinkers as Hobbes, Spinoza, and Hegel. Dewey goes so far as to state that "variant philosophies may be looked at as different ways of supplying recipes for denying to the universe the character of contingency." This view of philosophy will hardly apply to the major issues of the tradition. The medieval conflict of realism and nominalism, for example, had objective historical significance for the Church and its opponents. In Dewey's view, however, "quarrels among conflicting types of philosophy are family quarrels." For many philosophical disputes that is undoubtedly true. There is indeed "warfare of the schools," and sometimes it seems as senseless as a feud that is continued by the descendants of the original combatants. But the most important historical conflicts in philosophy cannot be disposed of so easily. Thus, the words of William of Occam to the emperor Louis, who was opposed to the Pope, may serve to indicate the historical vitality of his "terminism": "Thou defend me by the sword, and I will defend thee by the pen."

In accordance with his empirical method, Dewey recognizes "the contextual situation in which thinking occurs," and notes that "the starting point is the actually problematic." For a naturalistic empirical philosophy, the work of thinking goes on within the same world of experienced things, and not as "a jump from the latter world into one of objects constituted once and for all by thought" (68). He is thus opposed on principle to a constitutive, transcendental idealism, with the usual fixed, supertemporal structures. When he goes on to ascribe the general, basic error involved to the imagination influenced by emotion, he is neglecting history and giving only part of the explanation. To pair spiritualistic idealism and materialism, as he does (72), is to commit an error of historical shortsightedness. As Dewey views them, "one doctrine finds structure in a framework of ideal forms, the other finds it in matter. They agree in supposing that structure has some superlative reality. This supposition is another form taken by preference for the stable over the precarious and uncompleted." Why there should be two rival parties over a period of so many centuries, or why they should function differently in different historical periods, is not answered in this way. The abstract opposition between the "stable" and the "precarious" is really empty until tested by actual historical examples, and defined concretely in terms of real, social forces. Insisting that incompleteness and precariousness be given footing of the same rank as the finished and the fixed, Dewey regards philosophy as concerned with the "proportioned union" of the safe and sane and the hazardous. But he does not point out just how philosophy adds to the sciences in determining the desired "proportioned union"; nor does he consider that such a union must be undertaken repeatedly and endlessly, because of the varying factors requiring unification.

Dewey is right in calling attention to the importance of the "precariousness" of the world. That is a factor of permanent importance. But so far as intellectual history is concerned, the precariousness of *social* life is far more important. It is necessary to be quite specific, and to point out what is "precarious," especially in relation to the given system of society. The term "precarious," so characteristic of Dewey's usage, is not an apt one in all cases, and it may tend to obscure some facts. Whereas earthquakes and hurricanes are examples of present unavoidable "precariousness," social conflicts, strikes, unemployment, wars, etc., may well be examples of avoidable "precariousness." The opposition, as well as harmony, between man and nature is indeed an ever present fact. The element of antagonism will not explain the diversity of systems of thought, however, for it is a constant opposition.

The facts requiring explanation are not simple, and one must be on his guard against oversimplification. Certainly some have sought, and others will seek, a philosophy of eternalism in compensation for the evils of temporal existence. But still others revel in a temporalistic view. How can that be explained on the basis of the precariousness of "the world"? Differences of temperament, or of insight, or of knowledge and ignorance play their part in individual cases. Thus it may not be possible in a given case—e.g., Parmenides—to assign a complete social-historical explanation on the basis of the available evidence. But it could well be that the philosophy of "Being," which excluded change, represented a vested interest in stability, in preserving the existing social system. The all-sided and logically weighted development of this line of thought is sure to be fruitful in its bearing upon philosophical movements and thinkers.

## G. THE PRINCIPLE OF THE COOPERATION OF METHODS

It will be well, finally, to look again at the reasons for the controversy about the "given" in experience. Some of the disputants simply philosophize past one another, or hardly touch one another. If there is a survival of a historically obsolete theory of experience, say an atomic view, or a transcendental-absolute view with the traditional trimmings and trappings, there is clearly a basis for opposition. But there may be "tolerance" apart from such objectionable views, and the concept or stratum of experience that is designated, its extent and nature, will depend upon the kind of question which motivates the inquiry, i.e., subject to the requirement that the concept of experience is descriptively sound so far as it goes. The motivating question requires a procedure for its answer; and the procedure adopted in connection with a naturalistic view of experience, for which there are real temporal events, evolution, and causal relatedness, is not inconsistent with the procedure for which the initial subject matter is a stream of phenomena for an individual knower. One does not have to choose between them as some people choose a religion, or a Greek-letter society. The logical controls involved, and the recognition of the physical basis and hence unity of existence, are sufficient to allay fears about cutting up experience into real and unreal (or "irreal") types. The basic realities of experience are not affected when "attitudes" or procedures are changed. But a theory which aims to do full justice to experience in all its fullness must recognize that experience is also cognitive, and that as such it exhibits great complexity upon analysis.

## Chapter II

# NATURALISTIC AND PURE REFLECTION

## A. ON SUBJECTIVISM AND THE MEANING OF REFLECTION

Every philosophy that is concerned with experience is reflective. But there are different kinds and degrees of reflection. A thoroughly reflective philosophy is an ideal, in the sense of inspecting all aspects of experience. That would mean the complete examination of the contents, grounds, motives, and aims of experience.

The term reflection is often used more narrowly, with the emphasis upon "inner" experience, or the "subjective conditions" of experience. According to Locke, reflection is the knowledge which the mind has of its own activity, whereby these activities arise in the understanding. For Kant, reflection is concerned with the determination of the subjective conditions under which we are able to attain concepts.

In recent Philosophy Shadworth Hodgson was among those who attempted to elaborate a pure philosophy of reflection. In his *Philosophy of Reflection,*[1] philosophy is distinguished from science by the "inner and indelible characteristic" of reflective perception or self-consciousness, which he holds to be the central and cardinal feature in philosophy.[2] The method of reflection "consists in a repeated analysis of phenomena as they are *in* conscious-

---

1. London, Longmans, Green, and Co., 1878, two volumes.
2. Vol. I, p. 49.

ness . . . and not in their character as objects outside consciousness" (99 f.). The latter may be treated *also* as objects *in* consciousness, so that this method is more general, being applicable to *all* phenomena. Hodgson's procedure is to trace consciousness back to its "sources," and to come to primary states which are "undistinguished into objective and subjective." Psychology assumes a world of "things," and "supposes them to impress another 'thing,' the sensitive organism, with primary feelings" (116 f.). Hodgson asks how the world of "things," as we know it by science, has grown up out of the world of primary feelings as we know it at the beginning of our knowledge. The subjective method which he proposes is characterized in the following passage: "It is a reexamination of the phenomena of primary and direct consciousness, under the guidance of the principle of examining their objective and subjective aspects in conjunction with each other, which is a method only possible in reflection. Reflection first makes the discovery of the double aspect and then applies it and the continued and methodical application of it is metaphysic" (133). There are no "new or transcendent discoveries."

The program proposed by Hodgson has important features of similarity to Husserl's early formulation of phenomenology. Husserl did not know of Hodgson's work until after the appearance of his *Logical Investigations* (1900-1901), when W. E. Hocking, who studied with Husserl early in the latter's Göttingen period, brought it to his attention. In a general way, Hodgson anticipated the idealistic leaning of the later Husserl. Maintaining that only philosophy can answer the question as to the nature of existence, if an answer can be given at all, he defines existence as "presence in consciousness" (49). For all the modes of existence, such as actual existence, imaginary existence, and necessary existence, "there are corresponding modes of presence in consciousness, and without a corresponding mode of presence in consciousness we should have no knowledge whatever of any mode of existence. In short, consciousness itself is the subjective aspect of existence . . . . We know existence as consciousness, and to know that we do so is self-consciousness" (50). The argument that we should have no knowledge of any mode of existence without a "corresponding mode of presence in consciousness" is really tautologous: one cannot *know* without experiencing, or knowing. But this line of thought had a widespread appeal. Thus Josiah Royce, America's foremost idealist, offered a reward to anyone who could produce an object that was not known. It is difficult to understand how able thinkers could be convinced by such an argument, even in the 1870's; and still more difficult to understand how that could happen in the present generation, as is the case. Only an antecedent will to believe that warms the heart and dulls the mind can explain such a curious circumstance.

Hodgson would be right in regarding philosophy as being reflective in character if he construed reflection broadly enough. His view that philosophy has a distinct method and a distinct and positive content (30) ought to be extended to comprise all devices that may be required for philosophical purposes. There is over-simplification if one speaks of "a distinct method," construed in subjective terms. A subjective procedure, while useful for special philosophical and psychological purposes, must be aligned with the other procedures used in philosophy as well as in the special sciences.

## B.  THE FUNCTION AND AIMS OF REFLECTION

Just as there is no one meaning of the term "reflection" — indeed, some of the crucial issues of philosophy turn upon the different meanings and conditions assigned to "reflection"— there is no general agreement on the function and aims of reflection. The reasons are only in part due to the difficulty of getting others to understand one's point of view.

But there is a real problem of philosophical intelligibility, which has received serious attention. The use of one of the major philosophies of the past, the philosophy of Kant, for example, as the means of communication among philosophers would hardly be a solution. That would only add one more difficulty to an already admittedly bad situation, for an initial agreement on the interpretation of the chosen philosophy might well detain scholars indefinitely. No doubt that could be a way of disposing of the problems of philosophy, pending progress beyond the point of clarifying the Kantian terminology. The difficulty would be even greater if Hegel, Husserl, or Whitehead were selected. But there is a point here anyway. Philosophy cannot be a monologue; it is social in its conditions and reference, and must be communicated. Complete and exact understanding is an ideal which need not be realized, even for philosophical purposes. An approximation is sufficient here, just as it is in the special sciences. On the other hand, should general agreement be set up as an aim of reflection? Demonstration, validity, and correctness should be the aim. General agreement is hoped for, to be sure. But a minority of one may be right, which is the important thing.

Dewey speaks of reflection as follows:[3] "Empirically, all reflection sets out from the problematic and confused. Its aim is to clarify and ascertain. When thinking is successful, its career closes in transforming the disorderly into the orderly . . . the unclear and ambiguous into the defined and unequivocal . . . ." The need for reflection is a general one in experience. It is prompted by the occurrence of problems which require reflection for their solution. Philosophy shares that with the sciences, and with thinking in all regions of experience.

Reflection need not be "autobiographical" in the sense of reviewing the events of one's own history. Its aim need not be to give an account of one's own conscious processes. On the other hand, the subjective process of reflection must use the conscious experience of one subject as the medium for the analysis. How could it be otherwise? It is an individual subject who reflects and describes what is observed. He may check his results—either factual descriptions or "essential findings"— with the experience of other persons, and thus seek to avoid mistaking invention and wishful thinking for observations. The phenomenologist proposes to reflect with the greatest possible thoroughness, and to question his experience about the evidence for other persons, so that he feels compelled to begin as an individual. Unless he is careful to acknowledge clearly the factual and *real* priority of nature and society to the individual, he is apt to become involved in archaic nonsense, no different from the speculative excesses so prominent in the tradition of philosophy.

One describes in reflection. It may be supposed that one can "see" correctly, at least most of the time. But does one see with Humean eyes, or Kantian eyes, or a

---

3. *Experience and Nature*, pp. 65 f.

Gestaltist's eyes? It is clearly important to attempt to "get back of" the interpretations and theories in terms of which we view the world of experience. Thus reflection itself must be examined, in the hope that an interpretation which appears to be a datum will be revealed as such. The "given" in experience comes to us as already interpreted, unless one uses the term "given" in a special sense, as the ideal limit to be determined by an exacting process of analysis. But the latter is an ideal which may well never be realized completely. This should not be construed as being in any sense a concession to the anti-intellectualistic view of experience, or of the mind. That experience occurs as interpreted will always be the case for us. The point is, that a deepseated problem is engendered therewith.

The guiding precept for a thoroughgoing philosophy of reflection must be: *Question everything*. The alleged "self-evident" is not exempt therefrom, but, on the contrary must be scrutinized all the more carefully for its evidence. The universal process of "questioning" challenges the very problems of philosophy, and all traditional philosophy. Thus one endeavors to probe to the "ultimate grounds and elements" of all knowledge and experience; and these are naturalistic and social-historical as well as logical and epistemological in character. To illustrate the latter, Husserl is interested in determining "what is presupposed in all presupposing." "Radical" and complete understanding constitute the ideal goal. That involves an analysis of experience, which must be undertaken periodically because of changing objective and subjective conditions. If it is granted that the mind contributes interpretations to experience, then it clearly follows that finality cannot be expected in the case of any one analysis of experience. The reflective analyses themselves must be dated.

In addition to the theoretical aims that have been indicated, there is also the goal of constructing a logical theory of values. Whether a philosopher must also consider the means of realizing his ideals has been debated. Professor Ralph Perry restricted the *philosopher* of values to the formulation of criteria, leaving it to others to find ways and means for the realization of values. That he did not shrink from the arena of practical affairs is well known, however. In taking a stand on this question one should bear in mind the fact that when a man becomes a philosopher he does not therewith cease to be a man, or a citizen. The disciplines making up the philosophical enterprise, including phenomenology (meaning the descriptive analysis of experience as viewed in all its modes and structures), logic, and value theory, by no means forbid the inspiring spectacle of a philosopher in action, rare though that happens to be. They require practical activity for their realization in experience.

## C. TYPES OF REFLECTION

The style as well as the aims of reflection have their history. Thus Locke was determined by the science of his period, by the concept of atomism, and also by the prevailing social and political motivation. The promotion of the welfare of mankind was an aim of his *Essay*, in which he expressed the hope that his analysis might be of some use to man. Consider his questions and what he tried to achieve, and did achieve in his way. By means of his critique of innate ideas and principles and his positive empirical program he helped to undermine the authoritarian tradition. Disclaiming the ideal of knowing all things, he was interested in the truths which concern our conduct.[4] Although his program was empirical in its intent, it was not realized correctly, the data for reflection being in part the products of theoretical thinking. The dogma of the simple idea as a unit of experience, and the ill-fated definition of knowledge as the discernment of the agreement or disagreement among our ideas, were responsible for much confusion, and soon bore fruit in the subjective idealism of Berkeley. Locke may be criticized for his errors, which were serious and important; but there is also a basis for the tribute James pays him (in his *Principles of Psychology*), as "the immortal Locke."

We, too, have our style of reflection, an improved if not a completely satisfactory psychological theory, and our historical motivation. Do we, like Locke, want to contribute to the good of man? If so, then a "pure" philosophy cannot be adequate, i.e., one for which the actual empirical world is irrelevant. One cannot then retire to a detached realm of essences or "Ideas." We also have the task of sweeping away and combating traditional errors. The development of the special sciences, as compared with Locke's period, reacts upon philosophy, changing its form as well as content. When the great diversity of social-historical motives is considered, in connection with the question whether there is one unitary aim for philosophy, the historical character of reflection is clearly seen.

A few illustrations will be pertinent. (1) There are new types of error, as well as familiar old ones, already prominent in Locke's time. Authoritarianism persists, and adds to its forms and types. Relativism appears in new forms, more formidable than the earlier types advanced by skeptics. A narrow pragmatic relativism in the phil-

---

4. Cf. Locke, *Philosophical Works*, London, George Bell & Sons, 1894, Vol. I, p. 133.

osophy of logic and the confusion of truth with validity are examples. (2) The fact that the special sciences now cover so much more territory than in the seventeenth century has important consequences for philosophy. The progress of the sciences renders obsolete the dualism of qualities and the dogma of the simple idea as the unit of experience. That the task of philosophy is not lightened, but is, on the contrary, still more exacting, is due to the necessity of acquiring an understanding of the most important findings and principles of the sciences, an achievement which ought to be made a professional requirement. (3) Philosophy in the abstract cannot be considered apart from its concrete embodiments in the various systems of thought. Such systems are incomprehensible unless their historical progenitors and contemporary social and scientific influences are known. That being the case, how can one speak of a unitary aim of philosophy? One philosopher defends religion, and regards philosophy as the handmaid of theology. He has his passing historical function, especially in the medieval period. Another philosopher champions the rights of the individual by way of an attack upon the dominant realism of the Church, defending the thesis that only individuals are real. Philosophy was conspicuous in the eighteenth century preparation for the great French Revolution, from Voltaire to Holbach, in recognizing the interests and extolling the virtues of the bourgeoisie. Responding to conditions developing after the revolution, Comte tempered his program of scientifc philosophy by calling for the perpetuation of the "natural" hierarchy of classes in society (he speaks of the employers as the "natural leaders" of the workers). The social function of Utilitarianism, and of materialism and idealism in various historical periods, are further examples of instructive themes deserving more attention than they have received by professional philosophers.

The classification, already mentioned, of philosophies into philosophies of renunciation and of participation, is suggestive. Otherworldly, ascetic, and mystical philosophies practice or eventuate in renunciation. The Cynics' contempt for worldly goods and cultural pursuits; the mystics' ecstatic experience as a means of salvation; the scourging of the flesh and the devaluation of this life in view of the belief in a better life to come, in the Christian tradition; and the restriction of philosophy to a purely descriptive program, or to purely logical processes—these are some of the ways of practicing renunciation of social issues. Vastly different though they may be among themselves, they all agree in one respect: they do not attempt to change the *status quo* of society. Philosophies of participation, on the other hand, comprise conservative and reactionary as well as melioristic and revolutionary types. The Utilitarians were interested in social reforms, within cautious limits, and in extending the suffrage. Early English materialism, as illustrated by Hobbes, was a means of combating the Church in its struggle for supremacy over civil society. Similarly, French materialism in the eighteenth century was directed against the feudal-ecclesiastical tradition. At other times, however, materialists may be seen to be socially conservative, defending the existing economic system while rejecting supernaturalism. Because they aim to transform the existing social system, the dialectical materialists may be regarded as broadly similar to the French materialists, although, to be sure, their historical derivation is not accounted for thereby. As for idealism, it may be noted that German idealism from Kant to Hegel had its progressive as well as conservative features, whereas their idealistic followers illustrate ways in which philosophy has been reconciled with prevalent social conditions.

Historically, it is true that most philosophers have assumed the task of defending and justifying values. If that task is made subject to logical standards and viewed systematically, it may be used to unify all the activities of the philosopher. The concept of value, broadly conceived in terms of human interests and their fulfillment, embraces the descriptive program that is peculiar to philosophy, a program which is universal in its possible scope and comprises all "phenomenological" or "purely reflective" descriptions. Logical activities are similarly embraced by the concept of value.

Philosophical reflection must be distinguished from ordinary common-sense reflection, and from psychological reflection with a "natural attitude," or a "natural view of the world." If the natural view of the world is simply taken for granted, with all its theoretical elements, one's point of view is uncritical to that extent—uncritical philosophically, that is to say. It does not matter if the principles involved are not given up following a reflective inquiry. The term "uncritical" simply means that they are taken over without question. Because it is the concern of philosophy to examine the supposedly self-evident all the more carefully, the natural view of the world must come in for a searching analysis. It turns out to be permeated with interpretations, and with "deposits" of meaning going back to bygone cultural periods. Since naturalistic psychology assumes whole groups of sciences as well as the prevailing view of the world, it does not provide reflective analyses that could satisfy the philosophical requirements, in the form in which they are carried through.

It was a great weakness of the psychologistic type of philosophy to have failed to recognize that fact.

Philosophical reflection must furthermore be distinguished from scientific reflection in general. Every science is critical to a certain extent; it "questions" a certain set of beliefs, and is reflective in a field of inquiry which is marked off. The philosopher undertakes to carry the process of analysis as far back as possible. Everything must be placed in question, including the procedure itself. That is what is meant by the term "radical" in this context. It must be "all-sided," in the sense that the natural view of the world is examined from the point of view of critical (or "radical") reflection, and the latter is viewed in terms of its status and function for the interests of the naturalistic view. Philosophical reflection thus requires a distinctive "attitude" and a well-defined procedure. Neither Hodgson nor Dewey provide the latter adequately. Hodgson's choice of subjectivism doomed his procedure to one-sidedness and falsification. Dewey does indeed contribute significantly by his emphasis upon the cultural conditions and aims of reflection, and also by some notable examples of reflective analysis. Husserl's program for a reflective philosophy, while defined in great detail, is advanced in an idealistic setting, like that of Hodgson. As a result, he fails to remember the indebtedness of pure reflection to the naturalistic view, in the course of his later development. But his elaborate formulation of a procedure for philosophy is an important contribution to philosophical method, despite the critical reservations that must be made in appraising it.

Described very briefly at this point, it begins by submitting the natural attitude toward the world, as well as the theoretical, valuational, and other types of attitude, to an examination *in toto,* from a carefully defined subjective point of view. All other views concerning the world and knowledge may be "suspended" for the purpose of questioning them. No "denial" is involved. Perhaps the term "suspension" is an unfortunate one. All the activities of experience and their objects as meant must be capable of being brought to view. Just as an official can be "investigated" while he still holds office and is actively engaged in his duties, so may the natural modes of experience be viewed in reflection. The ideal of examining every belief and construction is brought to emphatic expression in the procedure of "suspension." There are dangers and excesses to be avoided in the presentation of this procedure. Thus, there is the misleading use of metaphorical language, and modes of expression such as "only by *leaving* the natural point of view or attitude can you become aware of it." The Germanism "in the reflective attitude" or "in the natural attitude" *(in der natürlichen Einstellung)* may suggest that one has gotten into a special kind of container.[5]

The first stage of this reflective procedure, the suspension of belief (the *epoché*) appears to be negative in character. But there is a positive descriptive program which develops in phenomenology, once the critical ground has been prepared. The means to the end, the procedure itself, must be inspected, in accordance with the requirement, emphasized by Husserl, that everything be questioned for its justification. Everything must be "seen," must be brought to view. General objects, conceptual constructions, and relationships can be "seen," just as particular objects in sensory experience can be observed. The logical and conceptual structures which are of interest

---

5. Cf. M. Farber, *The Foundation of Phenomenology,* last chapter, Cambridge, Harvard University Press, 1943, for a criticism of such errors.

in philosophy can thus be described and analyzed. In addition to examining every step of the reflective procedure in its own terms and in the light of its own precepts, it is necessary to consider its social-historical significance and its relationships to the sciences.

## D.  CONDITIONS BEARING ON REFLECTION

How important this initial stage of reflection, the suspension of beliefs, is as a condition for philosophy may be seen in the case of such a writer as Urban, whose curious distrust of "modernism" is expressed in his book, *The Intelligible World*. But the full list of those conspicuously in need of an *epoché* would make an impressive volume—whereby it is not implied that any philosopher may feel free to ignore the *epoché*.

The philosophical process of reflection upon experience and knowledge is a never-ending task, and must be undertaken again and again. The changing cultural conditions forbid finality, so that the efforts of the most gifted thinkers are unavoidably incomplete and historically conditioned. It is not enough to point out, as Schopenhauer did, that experience is the object of philosophy. It is necessary to recognize the *conditions* of experience. As Schopenhauer expressed it,[6] "The object of philosophy is experience, not like the other sciences, this or that definite experience, but just experience itself, in general and as such, with respect to its possibility, its domain, its essential content, its inner and outer elements, its form and matter." As the history of philosophy shows, there is a danger of subjectivism in making experience to be the theme of philosophy, the danger of restricting the interpretation of reality to a specified set of forms of experience.

---

6. *Sämmtliche Werke*, Vol. VI. p. 18, Leipzig, F. A. Brockhaus, 1922.

To speak of the "possibility" of experience is not necessarily to say much, unless *real* conditions of possibility are understood. Such conditions are neglected by the representatives of the idealistic tradition. The "essential content" of experience is of course structural in character, so far as philosophical analysis is concerned. To settle upon the general nature of experience is a major problem in itself, as shown by the varied views in the tradition. How the treatment of experience differs from that of the special sciences, as well as "common sense," must be indicated clearly.

The basic conditions for reflection are twofold, and two important types of problem are determined thereby. There are philosophical conditions, such as a well-defined language, and an understanding of the ways in which the mind contributes to experience. Furthermore, there are the conditions under which the philosopher lives, which act upon him. He must understand his social system and the factors of temperament and personal bias, so that he may critically examine the traditional categories and theories. The analysis of the contributions of the mind to experience and the consideration of historical conditions are of the greatest importance for the achievement of objectively valid knowledge in philosophy, although personal factors may at times be decisive.

To begin with preconceived ideas and beliefs, or with prejudices, is to violate the very first precept of a sound procedure. Should "the whole man, with heart and head," come into action, as Schopenhauer advocates? Or should the "heart's desires" be consulted, as was the case with Lotze, and so many others? The intrusion of the heart can act in either direction, as an aid for the realization of a great purpose, or as a deterrent from objective inquiry.

A. E. Taylor[7] is more frank than most philosophical writers in admitting his motivation. "The one thing I have had it long on my conscience to say, is that I have always wished my book to be understood in a definitely theistic, indeed, in a definitely Christian sense. I have never disguised to myself that when I speak of the 'Absolute' I mean by the word precisely that simple, absolutely transcendent source of all things which the great Christian scholastics call God." Philosophy therewith becomes a matter of faith, and of loyal adherence to one particular fideistic tradition. Taylor's helpful statement may be compared with Feuerbach's declaration in his *The Philosophy of the Future,* to the effect that Hegel, in his philosophy of spirit, made the last grand attempt to restore Christianity through philosophy. For a rational inquiry, statements expressing articles of faith should be treated as conclusions that are judged logically, rather than as premises or unclarified preliminary motives.

Prejudgments are by no means restricted to those who belong to the prominent historical traditions. They are illustrated readily enough in the schools, the sects, and even by those who disclaim prejudgments and seek to chain themselves down to the "given" in experience. The term "naturalism" meets with hostility, or as is also the case, with emotional warmth, depending upon the conditioning of its hearers.

The ideal of "freedom from presuppositions" includes the elimination of prejudices and the programmatic suspension of all assumptions. The universal abstention from belief would guarantee negatively the desired "beginning." It is clear that a strict logical procedure with strong safeguards is necessary to prevent the old prejudices from returning.

---

7. *Elements of Metaphysics,* London, Methuen & Co., 1924, p. xiii.

Such a precedure must at the same time provide for the examination of all hitherto accepted principles, and must make clear by detailed descriptive analyses how the mind contributes concepts and interpretations to experience. Only then can one hope to have a sound basis for achieving objective truth. Just as reality is temporal, so all items of experience are historical and belong to a definite cultural period. The passing, historical factor belongs to the content of the descriptive inquiry which is concerned with it; and a correct description of something historical is not therefore a passing description. It may be said: Once true, always true, if only in the modus "having been" (to use one of Husserl's expressions). There are no fateful or insuperable difficulties in the way of achieving historical objectivity.

In designating a procedure as "subjective" one must recognize its limitations in addition to crediting it with the merit of helping to make complete reflection possible. It might be well, however, to avoid the use of the tradition-laden and highly ambiguous term "subjective" and to speak of "pure reflective analysis," in which full justice is done to the activities of the knower. The "subjective realm" has been so much misused that logical abuses appear to many to be self-evidences.

A treatise might well be written on the theme, "The Reasons for Differences among Philosophers." Such a factual study would provide many pertinent illustrations for the present discussion. "What should be" may not be considered apart from "what is the case." The problem of the achievement of objective truth in reflection is raised when one considers the motives that actually impel philosophers and the social-historical significance of philosophy in general. The frequently disdainful treatment of dialectical philosophy by representatives of opposing movements illustrates the force of extra-philosophical factors.

Dewey has made much of the influence of social-historical conditions on the thought-systems of the philosophers, although mainly in a general manner rather than with specific references to economic and social conditions.[8] The "social-historical" study of philosophy brings many revealing facts to light. In ancient Greece the philosophers enjoyed the necessary leisure for their way of life because of the existence of slavery. Their status in social life clearly molded their thought, and predetermined their point of view in important respects. The attitude of Plato and Aristotle toward slavery is a case in point. Aquinas in relationship to the medieval church, and Hobbes as a defender of monarchy, are pertinent illustrations. The words of Shakespeare in *Timon of Athens* will also be recalled: "The learned pate ducks to the golden fool." Such considerations indicate obstacles in the way of the attainment of objective truth. How can one know whether he is, or is not, prejudiced, or how can one know the extent to which he is led by motives issuing from his status in society? The question at issue here goes beyond the psychological process of rationalization, for one may act and think in accordance with his own interests and still speak the truth. The problem is simply the establishment of truth.

This question may be subsumed under the larger theme of the interpreting activity of the mind in general, which has already been considered in connection with the error of irrationalism. Just as there is no general cognitive predicament, in the sense that the mind, despite all its virtues

---

8. Cf. his *Experience and Nature, The Quest for Certainty, The Influence of Darwin on Philosophy, Reconstruction in Philosophy,* and *Logic, The Theory of Inquiry.*

and powers, shuts us off from the "ultimate" truth, there is also no special predicament which deprives us of objective knowledge for social and individual reasons. The assumptions underlying the alleged general predicament are responsible for an artificial problem. An untenable view of the mind, and of experience, is at the basis of the difficulty, and that view predetermines the conclusion. But the mind is not outside nature; and there is no evidence for a "general" or "absolute" mind. Hence the conception of the ordering of nature by the mind is at best a sterile hypothesis. The nature of the mind, its practical function for living beings, guarantees that it is capable of achieving objective truth. Experience shows that in innumerable ways, and it is a condition of survival. There is no need to doubt it as a matter of principle, even for the most exacting philosophical purpose. In special cases, methods of proof must be devised, but there need be no proof for the capacity of the mind for truth.

Can the more specialized question regarding private and socially induced motives also be answered, as a matter of principle? Motives that operate include fear, religious hopes, class interests and private advantage, and temperament. There is no available method which would enable us to guarantee the achievement of "objectivity" in every single case. There are however safeguards to be observed. The process of reflection must be extended to include a view of the thinker in his historical conditions. There must not only be an *epoché* with regard to concepts and principles; the thinker must be viewed in his position in society and in cultural history. What are his interests? How do they bear upon the questions at issue? He may indeed, and with right, be led by his interests. So long as he does so explicitly and announces that fact, he is not guilty of the usually covert error of being influenced by his interests while claiming personal detachment and social "neutrality." It is necessary to reduce all normative statements, all preferences, to theoretical and factual propositions, so that they can be tested. The philosopher who has no preferences, no interests of any kind, is a fiction.

The problem of the attainment of objective truth requires all-sided consideration of the individual, social, historical, and existential factors involved. The naturalistic reflection which is "radicalized" and added to in pure reflection must in turn be supplemented by the inspection of social-historical significance. The alternative would be to rest in the "pure immanence" of a subjective realm with the aid of an absolute consciousness that is removed from all problems of matters of fact. The procedure of pure reflection is a stage in the complete process of reflection. It is sufficient for one dimension of problems—the clarification of basic concepts and structures in terms of direct experience—and is thus an important auxiliary method. But it should not be used exclusively, beyond its proper range of application.

According to a naturalistic metaphysics, reflection is itself "a natural event occurring *within* nature because of traits of the latter."[9] One underlying condition for reflection is correctly described in that way; but it is also essential to point out the social-historical conditions of reflection. It is certainly true that all types of reflection are "natural events," just as it is true that they cannot occur without the human organism. But that is not to say that one has to accept the basic assumptions and concepts of the current sciences as unquestionable in reflec-

9. Dewey, *Experience and Nature*, p. 68.

tion. Their philosophical examination is a supplement to their scientific criticism. Those philosophers who think that they are rising "above" nature, however, exhibit incredible naïveté, surprising even if that is maintained as a mode of response to religious or vested academic interests. That reflection is itself an event in existence is a statement of simple fact. All "purely reflective" procedures and analyses of abstractions, etc., are natural events. In a very real sense, one cannot get himself, or his thinking, outside the natural order. The "questioning" of all our knowledge of the natural order as such is still a "natural" process of questioning. That fact should not be lost sight of when one introduces a special terminology to name the new attitude that is systematically adopted for "questioning" not only the natural order but all the provinces of experience, "ideal" as well as real.

## E. THE IDEAL OF CERTAINTY

Exponents of the subjective tradition maintain that the procedure of pure reflection provides certainty, in contradistinction to the doubts, the "mere probability" of "natural experience." This thesis is of crucial importance for subjectivism and requires careful consideration. Two questions are involved: what are the motives for the interest in the ideal of certainty; and is the claim to certainty tenable, on the part of subjectivism?

Dewey's extensive criticism of the goal of certainty bears mainly on the first question. The first chapter of his *Quest for Certainty*[10] is significantly entitled "Escape from Peril." He suggests that man's distrust of himself has caused him to get beyond and above himself by means of "pure knowledge." Activities in the sought-for realm

---

10. New York, Minton, Balch & Co., 1929.

would not be overt, and would have no "external consequences." It is Dewey's thesis that the notions about
"certainty and the fixed" flow from the separation, set
up in the interest of the quest for absolute certainty,
between theory and practice, knowledge and action. He
charges that "in the absence of actual certainty in . . . a
precarious world, men cultivated all sorts of things that
would give them the *feeling* of certainty." In his view,
"no mode of action . . . can give anything approaching
absolute certitude"; and "since no amount of pains and
care in action can ensure complete certainty, certainty in
knowledge was worshipped as a substitute." In his *Experience and Nature,* Dewey observes that philosophers have
set out with data and principles sufficiently simple to
yield what is sought, in this case absolute certainty in
knowledge of things. He sees philosophy used as a substitute for religion, when the latter ceases to give men
the sense of certainty and security they want. The element
of truth in this thesis may readily be confirmed by the
history of philosophy. But such reflections do not give
the whole truth concerning the goal of certainty by any
means. The appeal to the absolute reliableness of the
"inner life" was a convenient way of disposing of the
factors of doubt and incompleteness which make the empirical knowledge of the world more or less probable, and
of supporting the position of religious faith. It is sufficient
to refer to Saint Augustine, and the principle of Catholic
philosophy that it is possible to achieve "certitude."

It is necessary to devote more attention to the social-
historical factors underlying ideas and beliefs than Dewey's
analysis provides. An important perspective is opened up
when one considers the role of science in economic
development. Modern science, as a basic factor of the

Industrial Revolution, has made "certainty" a reality in the sense of making possible the conquest of nature by man. The causal understanding of natural phenomena, the striking degree of success of scientific prediction, and the great progress in the field of social science, all argue against the rejection of "certainty" in all senses. The universal determinism of Spinoza reflects the confidence of the early period of modern development, the exuberence of scientists who first found nature to exhibit laws. With scientists aligned against the feudal-ecclesiastical tradition, there was no motivation to plead limits to the human mind, or to experience. The situation becomes more complicated when the religious tradition, adapted to the new economic and social conditions, makes itself felt in philosophy; when more complex intellectual conditions result from the fact that thinkers motivated by the interests of the rising bourgeois class find it desirable to restrict the program of science, to soften it by reconciling it with religious interests, and to safeguard itself against the findings of social scientists. Various modes of compromise result at different times: Hume's skepticism and ultimate doubts, and Kant's agnostic dualism in the eighteenth century, both circumscribing the validity or extent of scientific knowledge; the agnosticism of evolutionary philosophers and of some recent scientists; the cautious temper of recent empiricism and pragmatism; the distrust of laws and generalizations in the literature of social science.

C. I. Lewis's cautious temper of mind is seen in his defense of the thesis that all empirical knowledge is probable, never certain. Any number of perceptions may be cited as "certain"— or at least as certain as our knowledge that $2 + 2 = 4$. If one asserts that the proposition

$2 + 2 = 4$ is "certain" deductively, but that one's actual judgment of it may not be infallible, the same thing would apply to empirical knowledge. Is the proposition "I am an American citizen" merely probable, i.e., less than the limiting case of certainty? Or, let us fancy a factory worker to be doubtful about the relationship between his "take home pay" and the rising cost of living. Even if he were doubtful, on the ground that a mistake is possible in a great number of instances, his wife would clinch the argument with all the desired "certainty." There is a point beyond which one should not press his doubts—the point of adequate practical verification.

"Man's distrust of himself," which is deplored by Dewey, is hardly an explanation of the retreat to "pure knowledge." That retreat may well be, in effect, a device for safeguarding vested interests. "Certainty" need not be paired with "the fixed," or regarded as "absolute," as seen when one considers the nature of scientific progress. Obviously, different concepts of certainty are involved. It is interesting to note how apparently diverse forces cooperate in opposing a thoroughgoing scientific view of the world. Partisans of religion in philosophy withdrew, via the idealistic tradition, to an "inner life" which provided certainty in a specially defined sense; while philosophers of various schools and tendencies made concessions to it, whether consciously or not, by arguing that science cannot provide certainty, in another sense.

"Certainty" may be construed subjectively in terms of feeling, as a kind of inner illumination; or objectively, as the upper limit of probability; or as indubitability with non-contradiction the final criterion. Formal knowledge, which is independent of the course of real events, may be said to be "certain," in the sense that it could not be denied without contradiction. So far as our general purposes are concerned, "certain" means "certain enough," just as "clear" means "clear enough," as Whitehead once put it. The subjective meaning may be dismissed, as leading to an impasse, in which each individual is the absolute authority, so that only objective meanings can be considered. The procedure of systematic doubt as initiated by Descartes and appropriated by Husserl is intended to eliminate all possibilities of error, and thus arrive at a point, or region, of certainty. It proves to be a revealing approach to the last stage of phenomenology, which may well be the last stronghold of idealism.

### F.  THE SUBJECTIVE PROCEDURE OF PHENOMENOLOGY

The phenomenological method is designed to apply to all phases of experience. That its limitation to a subjective context prevents it from realizing this aim, and that it was an irresistible temptation to Husserl to adopt a general idealistic philosophy, is made clear by a study of its development. Husserl is pre-eminent in the phenomenological movement, for his type of analysis has yielded results which command the respect of other investigators most widely. Like some of his predecessors in the idealistic tradition (Hegel, for example), he was able to achieve valuable results despite the restricted and ultimately repressive setting of his philosophy. The means to an end which he originally adopted—a subjective procedure for reflection—which yielded analyses of interest to psychologists and logicians, proved to be a fatal limitation to his philosophy.

As a continuator of the empirical tradition, Husserl aimed to analyze experience. The method of philosophy was declared to be descriptive, direct "seeing" being the ideal. The field for description proved to be in need of extension, even on that level, and Husserl in his early period emphatically argued for the direct observation of "general objects," discussing at length the immediate apprehension of them in his first published work, *Philosophy of Arithmetic* (1891). He was careful in this period to accord full importance and value to the various scientific methods, in keeping with his own excellent scientific training.

The original aim of phenomenology was quite different from that of Dewey, or from that of any of the philosophers deriving from the natural and social sciences. It led Husserl into the ranks of the opponents of the scientific philosophy developed at the close of the nineteenth century. As for his own conscious motivation, his primary aim was to overcome logical psychologism, or the view that logical validity can be construed in psychological terms and derived from psychological principles. In other words, an admittedly erroneous position taken by logicians who were reacting to naturalistic and empiricist influences became the target of Husserl's initial criticism, and led him first of all to a "neutral" position on the issue of idealism and realism. The phenomenology which was first formulated in his *Logical Investigations* (1900-1901) was concerned with direct description, and was even called descriptive psychology. Some years later the "phenomenological reduction" (i.e., to "pure consciousness"— the restriction to conscious experiences and their correlates) was formulated, and it was advanced as the first prerequisite for philosophical analysis. It was intended to define the field for philosophy to begin with, and it defined the setting for a transcendental philosophy. In Husserl's exposition, there was a strong feeling of opposition to naturalistic procedures.

It is possible to construe the "reduction" in non-idealistic terms, as an auxiliary method in philosophy, and to align it with other methods, under the general heading of methodology. It should be regarded as one type of reflection among others, with its own peculiar value for philosophical understanding. Representatives of the last stage of Husserl's development have objected to that, however, maintaining that the subjectivistic procedure of phenomenology is something *sui generis,* absolutely unique, different in principle from all other ("mundane") methods. Such claims could hardly promote sympathetic understanding, or even an attempt at sympathetic understanding; and they are as unnecessary as they are unwarranted. It is hardly helpful to portray Husserl after the fashion of Porphyry's treatment of Plotinus. To make phenomenology ineffable and indescribable (in "natural" terms) would be to deprive it of all scientific interest. The analysis of "intentional" experience in all its types constitutes a self-contained study. The phenomenological datum for analysis is my-experiencing-the-object, whether the latter be real or fictive in character. That there should be a temptation to constitute *reality* out of the experiences is understandable, but none the less inexcusable. That has had the unfortunate result of tending to discredit phenomenology as a whole. The subtle arguments in question[11] are no better basically than Berkeley's well-worn argument for subjective idealism.

---

11. Cf. Husserl's *Formale und Transzendentale Logik,* Halle, M. Niemeyer, 1929, e.g., especially the argument for idealism, pp. 205 ff. Husserl's exploitation of his method for idealistic purposes is shown by his conclusion: "There is no conceivable place where the life of consciousness could be pierced and we could come to a transcendence, which could have another meaning than that of an intentional unity appearing in the subjectivity of consciousness."

The descriptive analyses of phenomenology are intended to be independent of the question of the demonstration of reality or unreality, and independent also of all causal-genetic considerations involving "natural" time. Thus the description of the content and structure of experience shows how an experience of reality is incompatible with one of illusion, for example. It portrays the structure of each type of experience. But it does not give us a test of reality. There is no "pure phenomenological" way to reality in the sense of a being independent of the knowing of it. The analysis is concerned with the context of the knower and his objects, everything being viewed from the perspective of its being known or experienced, so that there can be no talk of being apart from knowing, from that point of view. The analysis is confined to the determination of general structures, and it does not deal with factual situations except as exemplifying such structures. They are described as they are manifested in experience, where they are found. So are all the constitutive activities of thought seen in operation, through reflection. They are studied in their "essential" types by means of re-enacting and re-activating experiences such as remembrances, conceptual abstractions, and recognitions.[12] The experiencing of evidence, of truth, of

12. Dewey's distinction between "having" and "knowing" is therewith taken account of. Certainly the phenomena must be experienced, in order to be described. How the description can be carried through without introducing a classificatory scheme presents a difficulty for *any* method or point of view. In the case of phenomenology, however, the unusually thorough effort to suspend assumptions for the sake of a complete inquiry, the systematic effort to distinguish between interpretations and the "primitive" elements of experience, brings us closer to the ideal of sheer description, an ideal which may perhaps never be realized completely. It will be recognized, of course, that phenomenological description is by no means the only kind of description.

adequacy, can be contrasted with the experiencing of error, of inadequacy, etc. They are seen to rule one another out "essentially." One may be quite wrong, however, in his descriptive analysis of an "essential" structure. On this level one is no more secure against error than he is on the "naturalistic" level of scientific description, say in the description of an ant colony. Thus the vaunted superiority of "inner" over "outer" experience is seen to be unfounded. But both types are necessary.

If, as the present writer maintains, Husserl's idealism is untenable, and violates his own explicitly formulated precepts, the really challenging question that must be faced concerns the fruitfulness of the entire procedure. That every sound descriptive proposition in phenomenology can be asserted in objective terms within the framework of a naturalistic (realistic, or materialistic) philosophy has been indicated. One does not leave nature when holding its concepts in question for the sake of analysis. It is appropriate to point out its contribution to the understanding of the structure of knowledge and experience, and to the clarification of basic concepts.

Generally speaking, it is safest to welcome any and all descriptive findings, just as it is best to allow "pure" scientists complete freedom of investigation, without continually raising the possibly myopic demand for direct results. This is well illustrated in modern pure mathematics. The fundamental studies of the philosopher, *qua* descriptive investigator, affect the entire structure of knowledge. They represent a necessary dimension of inquiry which may well be endless. They can never be the whole story for philosophy, but they are an important part of it. It remains a function of philosophy to call attention to neglected facts, and if necessary, to include them in its field of inquiry. That applies to the analysis of experience by means of "inner description," from which psychology has turned away, leaving it to philosophers and novelists.

No descriptive work in that area should be ignored. The phenomenological method is not the only way of clarifying the basic ideas. It is one way, and it adds to the understanding of their meaning and structure. The social-historical interpretation or explanation of an idea also "clarifies"; and so does a simple historical account. All who contribute parts of truth should realize that they can coexist. Standpoint commitments and conflicting interests should not be allowed to obscure that fact.

*Chapter III*

# BEYOND NATURALISM

From the very beginning of his philosophical output, Husserl was affected by a grave and fundamental difficulty. This could be seen in his *Philosophy of Arithmetic* (1891), in which the subjective and objective orders appear at times to be confused. Frege called attention to that weakness, which was promoted no doubt by the use of the infelicitous term "content" to name an object of experience. Husserl's "original problem," which set the pattern for his entire subsequent development, was forced upon him by his studies in mathematics and psychology. How could he satisfactorily reconcile the methods and results of both types of inquiry? To make psychology fundamental (i.e., as psychology was then understood) was to go the way of "psychologism," with the principles of logic interpreted as actual laws of thought processes. On the other hand, to use deductive methods solely, without regard to the intellectual activities involved, might well lead to a narrow formalism, or to a form of conventionalism. Husserl turned away from "psychologism" in his *Logical Investigations* (1900-1901), and did his best to refute it in all its important formulations and arguments. In rejecting a "naïve" and "skeptical" form of psychologism, Husserl did not close the door to a new type of experiential approach to a philosophy of formal reasoning. The definition of a "transcendental" psychology, a discipline emancipated from all the conditions of naturalistic psychology, was to be one of his important steps toward the desired synthesis of experience and formalism. This amounted to a kind of systematic rationalization of an early predicament. The method of correlative analysis, the dual point of view, was to be the outcome.

The element of confusion now shifted to the area of naturalism in a new way. The problem was to attain to a "pure" realm of consciousness, while placing in obeyance all our judgments about existence or reality. "Suspending" the realm of existence in a well-defined manner, the term "existence" could not be applied in any new sense to the realm of conscious experience which remains as the subject matter of "transcendental" inquiry. There is a strong temptation to assign metaphysical status to this "pure" realm. That should not be done; and it is not done overtly, in a forthright manner. Instead of that, there is a strange mixture of remarkably penetrating methodological insights, and awkward reversions to the very type of dogmatic metaphysics and unwarranted epistemological arguments which Husserl officially condemns and disdains. The world of nature is "bracketed," as a matter of method. Within the pure phenomenological realm, a meaning-world is to be "constituted." To one who stands in the great tradition of German idealism, it is sorely tempting to go the whole length, and to forge and fashion a "new" type of a long-familiar idealistic metaphysics. A decisive stage in that process is taken up by elements of instability and confusion. Close and critical scrutiny of Husserl's presentation of phenomenology in his *Ideas,* the first volume of which appeared in 1913,[1] is particularly called for.

---

1. *Ideen zu einer reinen Phänomenologie und Phänomenologischen Philosophie,* first published in Husserl's *Jahrbuch für Philosophie und Phänomenologische Forschung,* Vol. I, 1913; English translation by Boyce Gibson, *Ideas,* New York, The MacMillan Co., and London, George Allen and Unwin, Ltd., 1931.

Husserl often complained that he was misunderstood. "Only in Freiburg can one come into phenomenology," he once said, in his characteristic language. It is true that many writers misunderstood his intentions, and his very text. It may also be recalled that Husserl himself was unable to make his thought understandable to his old master, Franz Brentano, when he visited him. To guard against misunderstanding as much as possible, it is advisable to adhere closely to Husserl's text; and care must be taken to understand his language in the intended sense. The following discussion will be closely connected at all times with Husserl's actual presentation.

The recently published new edition of Husserl's *Ideen*[2] includes a group of notes by Husserl, written in later years. They are revealing and to some extent illuminating, and it was unquestionably a valuable service to the student of phenomenology to make them available in the form of supplements to the volume. It will be sufficient to take account of a few of them in the present context. Although the notes do not upset any of the basic views of Husserl, they reveal him as a self-critical and self-questioning investigator, and as a man with a passion for completeness of understanding in a chosen direction. He had his periods of insecurity, but the outcome was always to be a still more determined sense of finality. It was characteristic of Husserl to view himself as continually developing, so that he could well afford to look back at earlier inadequacies in thought as well as in language. As for those hapless persons who remained on the "ground" of some of his earlier work, Husserl could observe understandingly, "They have not gone along with the development."

---

2. Edited by Walter Biemel, Haag, Martinus Nijhoff, 1950.

## A. FACT AND ESSENCE

In the course of his discussion of "Fact and Essence," Husserl speaks of "sciences of experience" as *"sciences of 'fact.'"* The acts of cognition which underlie our experiencing are said to posit the real in *individual* form, as having spatio-temporal existence, as something existing in *this* time-spot, and having a real content which in its essence could just as well have been present in any other time-spot. Furthermore, the same real being, so far as its essence is concerned, might just as well be present at any other place, and in any other form, and might change otherwise than the way in which it actually does change.

Husserl's view concerning essences should be tested by reference to a human being who is historically conditioned. Could a particular human being have appeared elsewhere just as well, and at another time? An affirmative answer would have to postulate the same historical conditions. A human being's "essence" is bound to the particular circumstances of time and place. Similarly, great care must be taken with respect to such examples as rivers, hurricanes, or a garden. Each of them "could be elsewhere" if all the requisite conditions were met. That is close to saying "A is A," and is still far from suggesting the present concept of essence. But if one is to suppose that "this particular garden" could be elsewhere, he should delegate his phantasy to make sure that he will not be infringing upon property rights. Examined carefully, with respect to all details, could this garden, in its particularity, be anywhere else? Or could it be different? The whole causal order would be unhinged, if the answer were in the affirmative. Moreover, one could never prove the affirmative, and all the available evidence is against it.

In general, one must be wary in the presence of the

effort to emancipate an order of essences from the realm of facts. The concept of essence has been useful, but also fraught with mischief. There is danger that usefulness in the context of definition is taken in time to lend support to a speculative theory of supertemporal objects of a higher order.

Does every fact have an "essence"? It will be recalled how uncertain Socrates appeared to be, in the *Parmenides,* on the question whether there is an "idea" for everything, including things the mention of which may provoke a smile—such as hair, or dirt. Challenging examples are close at hand. Is there an essence of war? Belief in anything fixed in the procedure of warfare might well be dangerous. There are undeclared wars, wars called "police actions," and "cold wars." The general class of "conflicting interests" would still require a differentia.

Husserl is sure of himself, however. Thus he reasons: "If we stated that every fact could be 'essentially' different than it is, then we stated therewith *that it belongs to the meaning of everything accidental, to have an essence . . . .*" But the reader will insist upon asking whether every fact could be "essentially" different than it is. The meaning that is to be attached to "essence" is not clarified by Husserl. From the questionable statement that every fact could be "essentially" different than it is, one cannot derive the statement that everything accidental has an essence in the sense of "essential being."

Husserl maintains that "an individual object is not simply an individual, a 'this-there,' a unique object." In his view, it has its own peculiar nature, its own *essential* predicables which must belong to it ("as a being as it is in itself"), so that other, secondary, accidental determinations can belong to it. Thus, every tone is said to have an essential nature, with "the acoustic in general" as the uppermost essence. For the purposes of definition, or the analysis of meaning, one may be interested in deriving a phase or aspect intuitively from an individual tone, or in the determination of a "common element." But to talk of an "essential nature" does not add anything to the physical or psychological determinations of the sciences.

According to Husserl, everything belonging to the essence of an individual can also belong to another individual. "Belongs" is an assumptive term. It would be better to say something like "may be ascribed to" or "may be said about." Perhaps the latter would be a better mode of expression. That would help to prevent one from supposing that something could be found "in" one object which could also be found "in" another object. The danger of the reification of essences must be forestalled by all available means. That danger is by no means discouraged by Husserl's mode of expression, as when he speaks of "essence" as designating that which in the peculiar being *(im selbsteigenen Sein)* of an individual discloses to us "what" it is. Terms such as "peculiar being" and "what" are potentially mischievous. Whether the individual in question be an automobile or a particular human being, we come to know "what it is" by the methods of the natural and social sciences, and by an account of the relevant causal circumstances. Individuals are members of classes, and one can make use of the recorded and general knowledge supplied by the sciences and experience. Whether the term "essence" is more of a liability than an asset may well be asked, in view of the tendency to pretentious overstatement which usually goes along with its use. There would be less danger in speaking of structures, relational patterns, or conceptual forms. It would still be true that we must allow for the experiential process of observing such abstract, or ideal, or conceptual objects. Husserl was right in recognizing the need to analyze and describe all the elements in cognition and experience, on the side of the knower as well as on the side of the known. But two types of error must be avoided: (a) "the general" which one "sees" is not to be taken as something in existence, whether substantively or as a framework; and (b) the "seeing of the general," or "general seeing," is not to be regarded as the latest in psychological equipment, with a basic patent going to phenomenology for its "essence-seeing." "Essence-seeing" beckons seductively to philosophers resting none too steadily on the fringe of logic, and to those who wish to accomplish by seemingly rigorous methods what was formerly achieved by a simple "leap of faith." There can be no objection to speaking of "seeing of the general" as "general seeing," if it is made clear that by "general seeing" is meant "seeing of the general" —and also if no reified type of being is meant by "the general."

In 1927 Husserl wrote an "objection against the entire first chapter of the first section," i.e., his discussion of "Fact and Essence" (Cf. Supplement VI in the Biemel edition of Husserl's *Ideen* I, pp. 389 f.). He observes that his discussion there had proceeded from natural experience, and was based on natural ground. The universe of existence in general, of something in general, is the world, and all eidetically ideal objectivities are related to the world, or to a possible world. Hence formal logic is the general formal logic of realities, as for Aristotle. Husserl now thinks it necessary to consider carefully, whether that is really carried through. He asks about the evidence for this presupposition, and whether the "unclarified presupposition" occasions vacillations and difficulties. Can one know that all existence fits into the indicated regional distribution, and that sciences are to be based thereon? The regions are the universal world-structures, but the concept of a world-structure does not come up for discussion. Husserl speaks of "the great error" of making the natural world to be the point of departure (without characterizing it as a world) and going over directly to the *Eidos,* as though one could come at once to the exact sciences. Appropriate discussion of the process of idealization is called for.

So it is "a great error" to make the natural world the point of departure without characterizing it as a world. Would the proper process of "characterizing" it make it more acceptable? As Husserl expressed it, the world as a unified universe is not "prepared in advance." His removal from the naturalistic view of facts is total. Whatever dissatisfaction he felt, in his retrospective reconsideration of his *Ideas* of 1913, it did not affect his basic position and his preference for idealism as a general philosophy.

## B.   THE QUESTION OF NATURALISTIC MISINTERPRETATIONS

### 1. The Philosophical *Epoché* and the Danger of Hostility to Ideas

Husserl maintains that he has presupposed nothing in his basic point of view, and that even the concept of philosophy is not presupposed. The "philosophical *epoché*" which he undertakes requires that one completely abstain from judgments concerning the doctrinal content of all previous philosophy. In truth, however, this is an empty ideal, a philosophic fiction. The philosopher undertaking the *epoché* or abstention in question is quite a sophisticated person, very much determined, positively or nega-

tively, by the general tradition of culture. Usually he is
very much a son of his time; and he is never wholly free
from the motivations and important interests of the social
system to which he belongs. Husserl may avoid "dependence" on the traditional philosophy, for one thing,
by placing it in abeyance tentatively, while carrying on
the process of "questioning" that is so characteristic of
phenomenology. But he could not begin with nothing,
and hope to arrive anywhere. The philosopher who disdains the entire tradition back of him would be much
like the aviator who set out on a rocket-flight with contempt for the earth and all physical realities. There are
grave limits to be observed in any kind of talk about
"rising above" the level on which one lives.

What does one hope to achieve by performing an
*"epoché"* with respect to the evidence and principles of
the sciences? Are their findings first of all to be validated
philosophically? We shall have the occasion to return to
this theme, and to point out the danger of disregarding
what we know as a matter of fact—a danger the present
writer calls the error of illicit ignorance.

Husserl proposes to enter into a controversy with
empiricism, within the limits of the *epoché,* "since what
is at issue here may be established by immediate experience." The denial by empiricism of "Ideas," "essences,"
and "essential knowledge" leads Husserl to accept the
challenge. He is aware of the fact that the victorious
advance of the natural sciences has favored empiricism,
while calling attention to the indebtedness of the natural
sciences for their high scientific level, as "mathematical,"
to "eidetic foundation." "In any case," he goes on to state,
"in these circles, and therewith also among the psychologists, there is a hostility to Ideas, which must finally

become dangerous to the progress of the empirical sciences themselves." Why this is dangerous should be pointed out. It must be ascertained in what respect this omission is of a *logical* type. Husserl envisages the necessity of new essential sciences as indispensable for the progress of the empirical sciences. This claim must be justified, of course, and only concrete results will be convincing. This also applies to what Husserl calls "the eidetic foundation of these sciences, which is by no means already completed." The approach to mathematical formulation, and the degree of use of the model of deduction, are familiar ideas in the methodology of the sciences. Just what "eidetic foundation" is and precisely what it commits one to accept, must be made clear. If the expression "essential sciences" *(Wesenswissenschaften)* is rendered as "sciences dealing with Essential Being," in recognition of the ontological drift of pure phenomenology, the critical reader will be sure to ask, *"Why being?"* Perhaps no one really would object to climbing upwards. It would be well to be cautious before undertaking such a journey, however, and to make sure about the goal and the equipment for the journey. If words could facilitate matters, the linguistic inventiveness of the philosophers would be entirely adequate for any purpose. For the rest, the "immediacy" to which an appeal is made is found on inspection to involve the whole world, past and present.

## 2. Concerning the Narrowness of the Historical Types of Empiricism

In the course of his critical discussion of empiricism (in § 19), Husserl attempts to acknowledge the merits of "empiricist naturalism." He recognizes that "it arises due to the most estimable motives," and that it is a "practical radicalism," which defends the right of an autonomous reason to be the only authority on questions of truth. To the empiricist, however, genuine science and the science of experience mean just the same thing. "Ideas" or "essences are regarded as "scholastic entities," or "metaphysical apparitions." If Husserl has appeared to be fair, if not magnanimous, up to this point, he quickly reveals his feeling of hostility and devaluation when he has the empiricist state that delivering mankind from that kind of philosophical spook was the chief merit of modern natural science. How sensitive Husserl felt when confronted with a basic challenge to the legitimacy of "Ideas" and "essences" is indicated therewith. In view of what the natural sciences had contributed to human progress, no well-educated person could find the chief merit of the natural sciences to be the dispelling of metaphysical apparitions. Instead of resorting to irony, it would be in place to clarify and justify the "phenomenological" conception of "Ideas" and "essences."

The narrowness of the historical types of empiricism will not be defended here. The correction of that narrowness will take the form of a more complete methodology and theory of knowledge. Does that require the abandonment of naturalistic empiricism? In keeping with the warfare of the schools, Husserl's opposition to that point of view is so deep-seated that it becomes necessary to leave the "dogmatic" level and to set out for the realm of pure phenomenology. He speaks of "new data," which are "eidetic in nature," of "objects which are irreal," which become accessible through an "essential seeing." But why should one speak of "data" here? In phenomenology, one discerns features in objects, including relational and structural patterns in experience. If "eidetic data" are designated as fictions, and are acknowledged to be "irreal objects" in that sense, there need be no charges of "ideo-logical extravagance" or of "a reversion to scholasticism." A theory of knowledge according to which such items are *instruments* without metaphysical import, to be tested by their value for experience and for thought, would be free from such objections.

In opposition to the empiricist's limitation of facts to experience, Husserl contends that facts *(Sachen)* are not necessarily facts of nature. The extension of the field of facts to comprise facts about "ideal" relationships—as in pure mathematics or in formal logic—must be allowed for. If it seems necessary to do that by means of a special terminology, it might be well to avoid traditional terms such as "eidos," which is reminiscent of Plato's meta-physical heaven, "essence," inviting metaphysical fixation as it does, and "irreal objects," a usage which may offend rational understanding.

"Immediate seeing," not merely the sensory seeing of experience, but "seeing in general," is taken by Husserl to be the ultimate source of justification for all rational statements. As Husserl once expressed it, "he who seeks to ground seeing is a fool," i.e., seeing is the final court of appeal. This sounds very good, until one encounters conflict among dissenting "seers." Moreover, it is not possible to escape the need to confirm or to correct alleged "seeing" by means of more "seeing," including the testi-mony of other persons. This applies to Husserl's field of vision as well.

### 3. Empiricism as Skepticism

Husserl's position is finally formulated briefly, as follows: For "experience" *(Erfahrung)* the more general term "intuition" is substituted, whereby he rejects the identification of science in general and empirical science.

It is his belief that one who identifies the two and who will not admit the validity of "pure eidetic thinking" is led into a skepticism which proves to be absurd. His reference to the arguments of the first volume of the *Logical Investigations* notwithstanding, it would have to be shown anew that a critically and logically extended philosophy of experience would have to be "absurd" if it operates within the framework of nature. It is one thing to score critical victories against defective and limited naturalistic theories; and quite another matter, to consider a critical and logically oriented naturalistic philosophy.

Calling attention to "the principles of the modes of inference," Husserl asks whether they themselves are empirical generalizations, or whether such a conception involves the most radical absurdity. The reader must consider whether there are only *two* alternatives: (1) the narrow empirical view, and (2) Husserl's view. Is there a *third* view, which may avoid the eidetic entities and structures? The logic of inference, which is seen ultimately to rest on a *hypothetical* basis (and this in spite of Husserl's "logical absolutism"), goes along very well with a naturalistic point of view.

Husserl chides the empiricists with starting out from "unclarified, unfounded preconceptions," and with being guilty of bias. His failure to add new material to his former critique of empiricism suggests that a renewed discussion could offer little that was new.[3] In contradistinction to empiricism, Husserl proposes "to start out from that which lies *before* all standpoints: from the entire realm of the intuitively self-given which is prior to any

---

3. This impression is borne out by Husserl's arguments against naturalism in his *Logos* essay, "Philosophy as a Rigorous Science," which appeared about two years before his *Ideas* I, and about ten years after his *Logical Investigations*.

theorizing thinking." It is a fair question, to ask whether there *is* anything like the "intuitively self-given." How could he be sure that he has dispensed with all theory, that he is dealing with "primitive" data? In what sense does it "lie before" all standpoints; and is it correct to speak thus of "all" standpoints, when the correct standpoint would, if correct, allow for the basic evidence? Husserl does not clarify the meaning of the "priority" of his self-givenness to "theorizing thinking." But he is not antiscientific. On the contrary, he states his respect for natural science when it speaks. "But," he adds, "it is not always natural science that is speaking when the investigators of nature speak; and surely *not* so when they speak about 'natural philosophy' and 'natural scientific theory of knowledge.' " He believes he has scored a point against the positivists representing the latter when he objects to the interpretation of "general self-evidences" or axioms as expressions of empirical facts. He professes to know, "with complete insight," that such propositions "bring data of eidetic intuition to explicative expression." His examples are not happily chosen, as a group. They include "a $+ 1 = 1 + a$," which is a postulate rather than a "self-evidence," and "that a judgment cannot be colored," which follows from what we know about the nature of judgment, and the fact that color is a quality "strange" to the domain of judgment. We do not depend upon "eidetic intuition" for such propositions. The latter type of examples can be multiplied indefinitely. But their utility will be quite restricted, in any case.

### 4. Obscurity on the Idealistic Side

Not only is naturalistic empiricism regarded as eventuating in absurdity; Husserl maintains that obscurity prevails on the opposite (i.e., idealistic) side also. Although pure thought and an *"a priori"* are accepted by idealism, it is not recognized that there is such a thing as pure intuition, "a kind of givenness in which essences are originarily given as objects, just as individual realities are given in empirical intuition." To speak of essences as "given" is to reason assumptively. If one insists upon speaking of the meant objectivities as "given," when he reasons constructively, or when he abstracts meanings, or when he imaginatively conjures forth hitherto undreamed of forms, he should at least make it unmistakably clear that he is merely analyzing and describing activities of experience, along with what is meant by those activities.

## 5. Essence and Concept

Husserl concedes that essences are "concepts," if, as the ambiguous word allows, we regard "concepts" as meaning "essences." In that case, he adds, the talk about psychical products is nonsense, and also the talk about concept-formation. Thus, numbers are spoken of as essences by Husserl, who asks, "Are not the numbers what they are whether we 'form' them or not?" The number *two*, for example, as a unique term of the number series, "is a non-temporal being." To designate it as a psychical formation is declared to be an absurdity, "an offense against the completely clear meaning of arithmetical language, the validity of which is open to insight at all times, and which lies *before* all theories." In short, numbers can only be regarded as concepts if concepts are not taken to be psychical formations.

The critical reader will ask, however, whether it is legitimate to ask "what numbers are," and to speak of the number *two* as "a non-temporal being." Strictly speaking, a number is not anything in fact, it "is" not, the predicate of existence is foreign to it. Numbers belong to the order of meanings. If Husserl did not try so terribly hard to settle accounts with various "standpoints" (especially naturalism), in which he is not nearly so successful as he believes himself to be, he would be in a stronger position. Descriptively, alone, he could do justice to the nature of number as a meaning. As matters stand, Husserl courts difficulties because of his own idealistic leaning, and because of the use of some infelicitous terms, often misleading even to himself. It is nonsense to speak of a "being" which is non-temporal. "Being" and "existence" are coextensive terms; they may be used interchangeably. All existent things have a space-time locus. They are "somewhere and somewhen." It does not make sense to speak of a being that is "nowhere and nowhen."

## 6. The Principle of all Principles

The most general and basic principle of method, as Husserl views it, is called "the principle of all principles."[4] It states "that every originarily giving intuition is a source of rightness for knowledge, that whatever presents itself in 'intuition' in originary form (so to speak in its bodily reality), is simply to be taken as what it gives itself to be, but only within the limits in which it gives itself." In other words, if one presents something "in its bodily reality," under the conditions of "originarily giving intuition," he has an incontestable experience, an "absolute." As Husserl views it, every statement which does nothing more than give expression to such data through mere "explication" is thus really an "absolute" beginning. The natural scientist follows the "principle" by looking for the experiences upon which all assertions about the facts of nature are grounded. This principle is declared by Husserl

---

4. Cp. Chapter IV, D, 2, herein, for a later formulation of this principle, introducing the element of "clearness."

to be "obtained directly from general insight," and to be "not itself open to empirical insight," like all knowledge concerning essences.

Is Husserl right? That which is "bodily present" to me must be accepted at its face value, as what it is. But how do I know that it is really present, and how can I be sure that I have given a correct account of what is present to me? "Having the experience" may well be "absolute"— if the experience really comes off. Are we to resort to the position that having the experience is a finality, but is ineffable? As soon as one talks about his alleged experience, various sources of error and disagreement are opened up. If we restrict ourselves to essences, is the situation different? There may be differences in accounts of essential relationships. Husserl himself was well aware of that fact. One never escapes the limitation of probability that is attached to all experience, "inner" as well as "outer," even though there is admittedly a greater region of possible error in the case of "outer" experience.

One other question is raised by Husserl's rather fast way of attributing the methodological principle in question to "general insight," while denying that it is open to "empirical insight." A naturalist can (and does so conspicuously!) formulate and justify the principle on the basis of actual experience. In short, he can state that experience, and human welfare, require that all assertions be tested by reference to the experiences on which they are based. The naturalistic universe of discourse is large enough to make this principle quite comfortable; there need not be any complaint about lack of room.

## 7. On Positivism and the Use of Mathematics in Natural Science

As Husserl sees it, the positivist rejects knowledge of

essences when he reflects "philosophically," and is deceived by the sophisms of empiricist philosophers. As a natural scientist, however, he is guided to a very large extent by his essential insights. The evidence for this is provided by the prominent use of pure mathematics in the theoretical work of natural science; and geometry, arithmetic, and analysis do not proceed empirically, as Husserl insists upon construing the term "empiricism." His argument points out the necessity of using deductive disciplines, with the use of ideal meanings and abstractions. To acknowledge that necessity is not, however, to go along with a philosophy of ideal "being."

In order to know what a mathematical axiom "expresses," Husserl turns to consciousness (and not to the empiricists), for complete insight. Pure essence-connections are viewed as coming to expression in the axioms without any "positing" of empirical facts. He admonishes us to enter into the activities of geometrical thought and intuition, and to analyze their "immanent meaning." But it is precisely an "outside point of view," which Husserl would like to rule out, which will enable us to know how geometrical knowledge developed, and how it was originally stimulated, through practical problems of measurement. It would also require an "outside point of view," to show us what the "pure" geometrical system of knowledge is for, and how it may be applied physically. Furthermore, it appears that Husserl's "absolutism" becomes a serious hindrance, when the question of alternative mathematical systems arises. His "axioms" prove to be old-fashioned. As a person trained originally in mathematics (his Ph. D. in mathematics included courses in Berlin with Weierstrass), Husserl was in a good position to go along with recent developments in mathematics. Much as he admired them, his philosophy of absolutism, making use of frozen essences and immanent meanings, prevented him from recognizing the possibility of a larger point of view, which would encompass the truth of empiricism, along with the truth of deductive rationalism. Husserl nevertheless had something important to contribute, for a strict "phenomenology" of rational experience and of reflective thought, indeed, of all modes of experience, must be greeted as an important addition to knowledge. His procedure was warped again and again by the irresistible temptation to snipe at representatives, real or imaginary, of naturalism and empiricism, and to annihilate specially fabricated and well-nigh worn-out "straw men."

## 8. Sciences with the "Dogmatic" and Sciences with the "Philosophic" Point of View

It is simply too easy a victory to expect, to suppose that readers will be convinced by the argument, that "the natural scientists [which ones? all?] *speak skeptically* about mathematics and everything eidetic, but with their eidetic method they *proceed dogmatically*." If the issue hinges upon the natural scientists' use of mathematics, there is little room for dispute. The meaning to be attached to "skepticism" conditions the argument. It is likely that Husserl would have been embarrassed by a pointed challenge and a demand for concrete references. He speaks vaguely of "skeptical tendencies" which limit the possibilities of the work of the natural scientists. That would have to be shown, in detail, or the assertion must remain vague, if not empty. Husserl does indeed clearly state the fact that, instead of toiling over such problems as the question of the possibility of knowing "external" nature, or of trying to meet the difficulties discovered by the ancient skeptics, natural science concerned itself with the question of the *right method* for a science of nature. It can be said that man has been enabled to conquer nature thereby, that he is in effective control of his food supply and of his environment. The traditional sharpness of the conflict between empiricism and rationalism has tended to be superseded by a well-balanced methodology. In the course of the upsurge of the evolutionary movement, and the development of scientific psychology, there was an understandable reaction against reflective ("inner") description. It is also understandable that the prevailing spirit of scientific psychology should be unreceptive to any talk of "essences." The extent to which the exponents of "psychologism" affected the philosophy of logic is now a matter of history. The "relative" autonomy of formal logic, and with it, of all formal science, had to be safeguarded, and it was Husserl's most striking achievement, in his early period, that he took up the cudgels against "psychologism." That he went too far, in his talk of logical absolutism, in his sketch of "the idea of a pure logic," is shown by his subsequent development. It is easy to forget that essences, concepts, and idealities in general, are constituted for the sake of experience, and that they are bound up with the nature, functions, and needs of human beings. The alternative to Husserl's characteristic demeaning of the naturalistic view, and the subordination of the latter to a subjective, idealistic, and constitutive philosophy, is clearly indicated. It is the development of a more complete naturalistic philosophy, with an unlimited methodology, comprising "inner" and "outer" procedures,[5] and with complete freedom to extend conceptual devices to all fields. Such a broad naturalism need leave

---

5. As a matter of terminology, Husserl prefers the terms "transcendent" and "immanent" to "outer" and "inner."

nothing out, for the subjective-reflective procedure of phenomenology, applied strictly and solely for descriptive purposes, would be recognized as useful, and, at present at least, indispensable. It should be observed that Husserl disclaims any intention to depreciate natural science when he declares it to be "dogmatic." He forgets this rapidly, however, as shown by his frequent use of the term "dogmatic," which does not fail to carry with it a sense of disparagement.

## C. THE THESIS OF THE NATURAL POINT OF VIEW AND ITS SUSPENSION

### 1. The World of the Natural Point of View and the Ideal Worlds About Me

The phenomenological reduction is the most crucial step in Husserl's methodology. It is designed to delimit the sphere for descriptive analysis, and to provide the necessary conditions for the "pure" inquiry of experience and the objects of experience.

It is necessary, first of all, to "suspend" the "natural" point of view or "attitude" *(Einstellung)*. Before doing so, Husserl endeavors to acknowledge the degree of "right" he thinks it has. He begins with the natural point of view of human beings, who judge, feel, and will with the "natural attitude." In conscious life, a person finds himself at all times, and without ever being able to change it, in relation to the one world which, despite all changes, always remains the same. It is continually "present," and the experiencing person is a part of it.

It is reassuring to note that the world of the naturally oriented person is regarded as infinitely extended spatially and temporally. In the main, the account is a fair one, except that it would be still more reassuring to have it pointed out as an indisputable and overwhelmingly established *fact* that we as knowers are parts of an independently existing world.

Husserl's good behavior in giving an account of the natural point of view is carefully controlled up to a point. Weakness and uncertainty concerning his intentions come to mind soon enough. The reader can only agree with him, that "the arithmetical world is there for me only if I have studied arithmetic." It is "there for me" only so long as I am "here for it." That really says nothing; but it is an innocuous statement. The sequel is more interesting: the *natural world,* the world in the ordinary sense of the word, is (and was) *continually there for me,* so long as I carry on my natural life. This may be harmles, but it does raise the question as to why the natural world is not "there" (where else could it be?) by itself, *as a matter of fact,* whether I "carry on my natural life" or not.

In connection with § 28 of the *Ideas* ("The *Cogito:* My Natural World About Me and the Ideal Worlds About Me"), Husserl asked, in the year 1922 (Cf. Supplement VII, Biemel ed. of Husserl's *Ideen* I, pp. 390 f.): "Is what is said here correct?" In his remarks, he clarifies the distinction between the ideal worlds and the real world, and gives a more satisfactory account of the status of the real world of experience. The "world" of arithmetical forms, the infinite series of pure numbers, and the theoretical forms of pure arithmetic were not "there" for me, were not "constituted" for me in any way, so long as I had not studied arithmetic in school. Actually, this world is only seriously "present" for me, while I am occupied arithmetically. Only in "original arithmetizing," in the production of arithmetical forms, do I have them in view as arithmetical realities. I have an indirect consciousness of a wider arithmetical world, accessible to me, in which I have now stationed myself. But it is different with respect to the real world, which is actually present to me continually, in so far as I have anything "from it," any realities in my field of experience. I do not first have to station myself in it, even if this experience is not actually going on. That which is actually experienced is surrounded by that which is not experienced, in the manner of an infinite horizon, which is accessible to experience, and into which I can penetrate step by step.

The real world was therefore present for me directly and indirectly through real and possible experience, also at the time when I had not yet acquired an "ideal world," and it also remains present if I, for example in my arithmetical activity, entirely "lose" myself in the ideal world of the arithmetical.

In short, the two worlds are "out of connection," and the arithmetical does not order itself within the horizon of my experiential realities.

## 2. The "Radical Alteration" of the Natural Point of View

Husserl submits his characterization of what is "given" to us from the natural point of view as a piece of "pure description prior to all 'theory.' " Is it not claiming too much, to state that the present studies of Husserl are free from all theories? Sheer description is an ideal. In practice, it is not possible to dispense with "preliminary" thoughts, or with explanatory ideas. The important thing to do is to recognize them as preliminary, or as explanatory.

Husserl now proposes to alter the "natural point of view" radically. Descartes's procedure of systematic doubt comes to mind in this connection. This was often referred to by Husserl, who points out here that Descartes's attempt to doubt everything had an entirely different end in view. It was led by the purpose of setting up an absolutely indubitable sphere of being. Linking on to Descartes at this point, Husserl makes it emphatically clear that the attempt to doubt everything should serve only as a "methodological expedient." It should also be recognized that the "suspension" of judgment, of beliefs of all kind, which is instituted by Husserl, is also a *methodological expedient*. Accordingly, it should be ordered under the general heading of "Methods in General"; and as such it should at all times be subject to the canons of good behavior which apply to methods of inquiry.

### 3. The Phenomenological *Epoché*

The universal "phenomenological *epoché*" is presented by Husserl as a well-defined procedure, involving "suspension" or "bracketing" of all judgments and beliefs. It is his design "to discover a new scientific domain" with the aid of the method of bracketing, although only a limited form of bracketing is employed in his *Ideas*.

The "general thesis" which belongs to the natural point of view is "set out of action"; and everything that it encompasses "ontically" is placed in brackets. That means, of course, the entire natural world, which is continually "present for us" as a "reality," even if we decide to "place it in brackets." Placing the expression "reality" in quotation marks might tend to suggest that it is not so secure after all. Husserl's way of speaking about the bracketing of "reality" is disconcerting at this point. The reader begins to feel that an important step is about to be taken, and in truth he will not have long to wait.

The "suspension" of judgment does not mean a sophistical denial of the "world" (now the bracketed world), or any skeptical doubt as to its being there. The "suspension" of phenomenology is intended to bar me from using any judgment that concerns spatio-temporal existence. It is a question, as to whether it is really possible to carry that through, even as a device of method. It should be considered whether it is possible to suspend space and time, for knowing with any "point of view."

Husserl is careful to warn against confusion with the *epoché* demanded by positivism. That *epoché* concerns the removal of preconceptions, and the construction of a science free from theory and metaphysics. Husserl's procedure sets the whole world in brackets, along with all theories and sciences, including positivistic sciences relating to the world. All of these "suffer the same fate," as Husserl gravely states it.

### D. CONSCIOUSNESS AND NATURAL REALITY

### 1. Concerning "Pure" or "Transcendental" Consciousness as the Phenomenological Residuum

Disturbing to the reader is Husserl's way of formulating his goal, as "the gaining of a new region of being." It is disturbing because it clouds up the whole point of the *epoché,* which undertook to place in abeyance all judgments of existence. Nothing could be gained by using different terms, so long as there is any suggestion of assigning a metaphysical status to the "new realm" which is "opened up" by the method of phenomenological reduction. Husserl is convinced that consciousness is to be conceived as a closed sphere of being, with its own forms of "immanent" temporality, a sphere of being which is to be shown to be unaffected by the phenomenological suspension. It remains as a "phenomenological residuum," as a peculiar "sphere of being." This is the field of the new science of phenomenology.

Husserl has the deep feeling of a prophetic discoverer. With the natural point of view, the transcendental sphere of being "must have remained unknown, and at most suspected." He divorces the two points of view, or the two attitudes (the natural and the phenomenological) too violently. The reader will be led to ask whether excessive claims have been made for what is in principle a reflective procedure, now defined in detail for the first time. It does not help matters to make use of the term "transcendental" along with "pure," as applied to consciousness. But it does call attention to the fact that Husserl has a place in the tradition instituted by Kant. In fact, Husserl may be viewed as endeavoring to elaborate a truly consistent "transcendental" (i.e., purely reflective) philosophy.

Husserl's concluding remarks, written in 1929, in connection with § 33 of the *Ideas*, which deals with "pure" or "transcendental" consciousness as the phenomenological residuum, are of particular interest (Cf. Supplement IX, Biemel ed. of Husserl's *Ideen* I, p. 395). What remains is not the realm of pure psychological intuition, but its meaning-transformation, its total proper essence. What remains is the transcendental, absolutely autonomous region of being, which suspends psychology itself. Just how this transcendental region in its "unworldliness" carries the world in itself, in a certain sense, and, viewed essentially, all possible worlds, is to occupy Husserl in detail. The point now is, as he states it, to bring to a really insightful understanding what is indicated here.

But the really interesting question for the reader to bear in mind is, what is the "certain sense" in which the "unworldliness" causes the world in itself? That is the main obstacle. The talk of "all possible worlds" is less disturbing, especially since they are to be thrown in "essentially."

## 2. "Objectification" and Transcendence

In accordance with the phenomenological procedure, a "reduction" to pure consciousness and its correlates is performed. The "intentional" character of experience requires that one attend to what is meant in and by the experiences. The "intentional" nature of experience (perception is perception *of* something, etc.) becomes a theme for extensive descriptive analyses. Curiously, and perhaps fatefully, Husserl speaks of a process of "objectification" as being responsible for natural things facing us, in the natural setting, and also values, cities, dwellings, tools, etc. After the performance of the "reduction" to the realm of pure consciousness, all objectivities are regarded as merely "intended," or "intentional" objects; and one may speak of "objectification" as responsible for the natural things and cultural objects. There would be no objection, if only the phenomenologist could rivet in his mind certain basic facts, *viz.*, that the natural world not only antedated the formulation of the "reduction" by an infinite amount of time, but will survive the author of the reduction, and all future performers of the reduction; and that the transcendental researcher needs food, shelter, and human society, which do not have to wait for his "objectification." It is well to forestall the possibility of nonsense, which is sure to intrude itself again and again.

In the course of his later remarks bearing upon § 38, "Reflections on Acts: Immanent and Transcendent Perceptions" (Cf. Supplement XI, written in 1929, Biemel ed. of Husserl's *Ideen* I, p. 398), Husserl reverts to the troublesome theme of "transcendence." A thing-perception is an experience, in which I consciously have that which is perceived in the modus of bodily self-apprehension. In immanent syntheses with new perceptions I mean it more-

over in the modus of "the same," which each of these perceptions has apprehended as "bodily" itself. But the
bodily apprehended thing itself is transcendent. It is thus
for the entire real world, of which I am conscious "in me"
within my stream of experience, no matter in which
intentional forms. What holds for me, holds for everyone,
of whom I can have a presentation or knowledge in accordance with consciousness. Furthermore, the stream of
experience of any other person is transcendent to mine.
By "transcendence" is meant the peculiarity of intentional
objectivities, of "passing beyond" the singular proper
essence of pure experiences.

Thus the matter stands "descriptively."

### 3. The Immanent Nature of Perception and its Transcendent Object

It is now Husserl's concern to gain deeper insights into
the way in which the transcendent and the consciousness
that knows it are related, and to see how this mutual
connection, which has its "riddles," is to be understood.
Suppose that one begins with the *fact of the occurrence*
of "intentional" experience, i.e., experience that refers or
is directed toward an objectivity of some kind. Then there
is no "riddle." The "riddles" result from analysis under
special conditions, or from theory, which may enter in
even if all theory is supposedly eliminated. Husserl
"excludes" ("suspends") the whole of physics and the
whole of theoretical thought. That leaves him "within the
framework of plain intuition and the syntheses belonging
to it, including perception." The "exclusion" is a matter
of procedure. The "problem of transcendence" which
arises is therefore "methogenic," i.e., it arises because
of a method which has been instituted. It is not a problem
of natural experience, at least not in the present sense.

In order to maintain a universal field of description, Husserl is compelled to maintain the essential relatedness of perception and the thing perceived, "although they are not immanently and essentially one and united." In fact, "the perceived thing can be without being perceived . . . and it can be without itself changing." The perceived thing, and all its parts, sides or factors, are taken to be "necessarily transcendent" to the perception. This distinction applies also to the "perspective shadings" *(Abschattungen)* and that which is "shadowed forth" *(Abgeschattetes)*. "Perspective shadings," as experiences, cannot possibly be spatial, in Husserl's view. On the other hand, that which is "shadowed forth" is only possible as spatial, and is declared to be "spatial in its essence," while not being possible as experience. This dualism may be challenged. It is really the familiar Cartesian dualism that lives on in Husserl's analysis. Is it satisfactory to say with Husserl that "experience is possible only as experience, and not as something spatial"? Can anything be real without having a locus in space, in the physical universe? And is not experience real? But the reduction has been performed, we shall be reminded. "Reduced" experience is, however, still experience, and it represents a series of real events in the cosmos. The reduction-performing phenomenologist still breathes, eats, and *experiences*. And we shall not deprive him of a *place* in which to carry on his interesting work. He shall have space!

## 4. Being as Consciousness and Being as Reality

Naturalists will not deny Husserl's assertion that "a thing cannot be given as immanent in any possible perception or in any possible consciousness." They will agree with it as a plain matter of fact. Husserl, however, makes it to be a matter of "eidetic insight," holding in "absolutely unconditioned generality or necessity." There is thus "a basic essential difference" between "being as experience" and "being as thing": experience is essentially perceivable through immanent perception, whereas the essence of a spatial thing makes that impossible. But what is really the difference between this "eidetic insight" and the *factual* knowledge that says the same thing, in its own terms? A statement about an essential possibility, or impossibility, may be transformed into a universal proposition, of the form "All a are b" or "No a are b." Terms such as "necessity," "unconditioned generality," "eidetic insight," etc., add nothing to the force of universal propositions. The equation which describes the reaction of two chemical compounds holds "universally," assuming that new conditions do not intervene. There could be no gain in applying "eidetic insight" to validate what is already secure enough. It is factually true that a perception and the thing perceived must be distinguished, and that the thing is not immanent in the experience itself. That is a modest enough statement. If, however, one resorts to "determinations of essence," and separates "on principle" the realm of experience from the transcendent realm of things, he is setting the stage either for an untenable dualism which eventuates in agnosticism; or for an idealistic theory which "annuls" the world of things by a methodical device, in order to "constitute" it in the context of pure consciousness. It is a risky matter, to go along with Husserl in speaking of two fundamentally different "modes of being," *Consciousness* and *Reality*.

Spatial things, says Husserl, can "on principle" "be given in perceptions only by way of perspective shading," whereas there are no such "perspective shadings" in the case of experiences. This is stated as a matter of essence. Why not as a matter of fact? Wouldn't that say it adequately? Husserl writes: "Where there is no spatial being, the talk of seeing from different standpoints with a changing orientation is meaningless." But if an alleged "being" has no "being in space," then it has no being at all—and this in opposition to Husserl's easy-going "essential" dichotomy! It turns out that, for Husserl, "a spatial thing is nothing other than an intentional unity, which, on principle, can be given only as the unity of such modes of appearance." Husserl does not make it clear whether he means that a spatial thing is an intentional unity *really,* or as a matter of method.[6]

This conception of a thing as an intentional unity enables Husserl to conclude (in § 43 of the *Ideas, Ideen* I) that it is a fundamental error "to think that perception does not come into contact with the thing itself"; and the same applies to "every other kind of thing-intuition." The spatial thing is given "in its bodiliness," and no image or sign is given in its place. The consciousness of a sign or an image is not to be substituted for the perceiving. In perception, a "self" is presented and apprehended "in its bodily presence, . . . in accordance with the object's own meaning." Husserl moves here on descriptive ground, on which he is a master. His various discussions of perception and other types of experience rightly command admiration. It is advisable, however, even in the study of his descriptive work, to be ever alert to his peculiar usage

---

6. In the 1950 edition of the *Ideen* I, p. 98, the passage in question is amplified to read as follows: "A spatial thing, with respect to its meaning established through outer experience and its style, is nothing other than an intentional unity, which, on principle, can be given only as the unity of such modes of appearance—to begin with, for me, if I do not yet speak of others."

and all too frequent readiness to move beyond description, in the direction of a novel system of transcendental idealism.

### 5. "Phenomenal" Being of the Transcendent, and "Absolute" being of the Immanent

That perception is "inadequate" will readily be assented to. The "inadequacy" that belongs to the perception of things is called "an essential necessity" by Husserl. A thing can on principle be given only incompletely. That is factually true. What is gained by calling it "an essential necessity"? It may seem innocuous to state that "if the meaning of thing is determined through the data of thing-perception . . . it must require . . . incompleteness." But this way of putting it may suggest the thesis of idealism. It may be forgotten that we as knowers and inquirers stand in relationship to a world of things which are existentially independent of us.

In contradistinction to transcendent things, *experience* "does not present itself through perspective shading." The perception of experience "is plain seeing of something which in perception is given . . . as 'absolute' . . . An experience of a feeling does not 'shadow forth' one-sidedly. If I glance at it, I have before me an absolute . . . ." The term "absolute" is a questionable one to use, in any case, in view of its ambiguity, and its pretense. It may be questioned whether the perception of experience is free from error, which is what anything "absolute" should be. If the meaning is completeness or adequacy, with an absence of perspectives and aspects, a question may again be raised. Would one be likely to "have" the "same" experience twice? How could that be guaranteed? By an introspective report? The experiencing person is likely to change more rapidly than any "transcendent" subject matter. Moreover, as Husserl states, one can think truly or falsely about an experience; but "that which is there as the object of my vision is there absolutely with its qualities, its intensity, and so forth." This is in contrast to the tone of a violin, which is given with changing modes of appearance. There is a difference, it will be agreed. But the difference is not so complete as Husserl would have it be. It is saying too much, to assert that "it is essential to the immanently given to present an absolute which does not appear from different sides, or shadow forth *(sich abschatten)*."

The claim to absoluteness is qualified somewhat by Husserl, when he admits that even an experience *(Erlebnis)* is never perceived completely, and that it cannot be grasped adequately in its full unity. An experience is "something that flows," and one can "swim after it" reflectively. Retention is required, if one is to be conscious of what has flowed past him. In short, the experience is "absolute" until you try to experience it! Still, Husserl insists that the incompleteness or "imperfection" that he has indicated, "which belongs to the essence of our perception of experience," is essentially different from the incompleteness due to perspective shadings, etc., in the case of "transcendent" perception. In view of his own remarks, Husserl should have dropped the term "absolute."

In general, it is of no advantage to appeal to "essential insights." A different mode of statement is desirable, one which suggests that every statement is to be tested by logically acceptable methods. When Husserl states that it belongs to the essence of presentations that there be gradual differences of relative clearness or dimness, he would do better to make a simple factual declaration. In this case, it would be a general proposition about the nature of experience, which would have to be explained further and tested. Care should be taken to avoid the encouragement of self-styled seers who are ever alert and on the lookout for essences, which are simply allowed for by means of "eidetic insight." The support which Husserl derived from the consideration of mathematical reasoning would have little to do with the "eidetic" processes uncovered by fideists and mystics ostensibly participating in the phenomenological movement.

In a passage written in 1922 (Cf. Supplement XII, Biemel ed. of Husserl's *Ideen* I, pp. 398 f.), concerning § 44, on the "merely phenomenal being of the transcendent and the absolute being of the immanent," Husserl states that the absolute givenness and its correlate, the "Absolute," is falsely defined. Interesting though the self- criticism must be, the reader should not promise himself too much. It does not indicate any important deviation on the part of Husserl. The point to be noted, in his view, is just this, that thing-givenness is not only a givenness through perspective shadings, but continually presumptive givenness, with respect to every point in which the thing is given bodily as existing now. Whatever may be given of it, it is possible that it was a false pretension. That depends upon the continuation of the harmonious perception. For immanent being that does not apply. It does not matter if a presumption concerning future being does not work out. If it stops, in so far as it is experienced, it is also necessary; the experiential belief for the really experienced is not concerned through the course of further perception. But, Husserl observes, he has always viewed the thing only in possible *perception,* and not in the synthetic connection of separate experiences.

If this is intended to correct and to sharpen the concep-

tion of "absolute givenness" and its correlate, in contradistinction to ordinary perceptual givenness, it is still not
adequate. Many readers will be reluctant to accept the
portrayal of natural experience as being so precarious.
The danger of "false pretension" is overdrawn; the probability value of natural experience is really very high. The
"uncertain" realm of nature contains all the reality, and
all the interests, the joys and tears, which concern human
beings. It is reality itself. The "immanent being," which
is really a fiction and no being at all, does indeed enjoy a
kind of definitional absoluteness, and the thin certainty
of nothing in fact. But it is either an analytic type of
"certainty" which results, i.e., following from definitions
and premises, or it remains an unwarranted claim.

## 6. Indubitability of Immanent Perception, Dubitability of Transcendent Perception

Reminiscent of Descartes is the formulation concerning
the "indubitability" of immanent perception, and the
"dubitability" of transcendent perception. In Husserl's
view, "every immanent perception necessarily guarantees
the existence of its object." This can only be acceptable
in a very limited sense. The experience is there while
you reflect upon it. In that sense, it is "indubitable."
But a moment later it is no longer there, and only
remembrance could "guarantee" it. It is tempting to validate a particular experience as indubitable, and then to
proceed to the glorification of *"I am,* this my life is, I live:
*cogito,"* as Husserl expresses it. How much is to be com-
prehended under the professed title of "cogito"? The reply
is certain to be: enough for all eventual idealistic purposes. Rabbits can only be taken from a well-stocked
hat of rabbits.

To begin with, it is my own experience which is

indubitable. Husserl holds that it is not absurd to suppose "that all alien consciousness which I posit in the experience of empathy does not exist," but that "*my* empathy and my consciousness . . . is absolutely given, . . . not only essentially but existentially." It may be suggested that the existence of at least two "alien" persons—one's parents—must be as indubitable as one's own *cogito*. While one is at this point, of determining the sufficient conditions for one's own existence and store of ideas, language, etc., he could readily point out many more items which are similarly "indubitable," albeit "alien." The "distinctive state of affairs" which Husserl takes to hold for oneself is by no means unassailable. Indeed, it may be argued that there are "distinctive" matters of *transcendent* fact that are "prior" to the *cogito,* and to all subjectivity. Let us not forget the most rudimentary facts about existence and life.

Husserl's awareness of objections to his position is indicated by some later comments, incorporated in the text of the 1950 edition of his *Ideen* (Biemel edition, *Ideen* I, pp. 107 f.). Admitting that my experiences are a part of a real human being, and that the sensory data are naturally caused, is not, in his view, to admit that such things belong to the experiences themselves "in their own absolute essence." Husserl concedes that I may be presupposing the absoluteness of the constituents of remembrance if I am to speak of my stream of experiences "in its own essential purity." But he holds that an answer is possible here. It is his familiar thesis, that "a closed unified being" which cannot be "cancelled" is the presupposition for experiencing and knowing a mundane reality. Thus, he contends, there is a peculiar essential being prior to the being of the world. This attempt is disappointing, like all other attempts of the kind. But the fire of the opposition is not to be discouraged by the apparent recognition of the facts of natural experience and knowledge. Neither will dialectical arguments concerning "presuppositions" of knowledge and experience dispose of considerations of stubborn fact.

In contrast to the certainty of immanent perception, Husserl holds, it belongs to the essence of the thing-world "that no perception gives anything absolute." Every experience (of something transcendent) "leaves open the possibility that the given, despite the continual consciousness of its bodily self-presence, does *not* exist." The further course of experience may force us to abandon what has been "posited" empirically. There may be illusions, for example. But in the "absolute sphere," illusion has no place; there is only "absolute position." The world of things is "only a presumptive reality," whereas I myself, or my experience, am *"absolute* reality," given through an unconditioned positing that cannot be annulled. The "thesis of the world" is thus "accidental," in contrast to the necessity and indubitability of my pure ego and ego-life. The "essential law" reads: "all bodily given things can also not be, no bodily given experience can also not be."

Is this sound? Can one think of *all* bodily things as not being? That is fantastic, and is certainly self-contradictory. One's body is not to be dismissed as dubitable; and neither can the bodies of one's parents, and of their parents, etc. It is also fair to allow such bodies to have an atmosphere, *terra firma,* and clothes, if possible. Neither should they be permitted to go hungry. Hence we might as well throw in our industrial economy, into the hopper of the "indubitable."

How seriously—and literally—Husserl took the consequences of his position is shown by his statement that
no proofs obtained from the empirical view of the world
are conceivable [he is sure of that!] which could assure
us with absolute certainty of the world's existence. He
means that "a doubt is thinkable," because the possibility
of non-being is on principle never excluded.

With this, Husserl has reached the climax of his study;
he has "gained the knowledge he needed." He has considered "the detachability on principle of the whole
natural world from the domain of consciousness." This
is not stated as a general canon of empirical procedure,
or as a principle of inquiry in Dewey's sense. Husserl
is too close to Descartes and his evil demon, as indicated
by an exaggerated sensitivity to the danger of illusion
and hallucination.

Let us not fail to remind ourselves: (1) the natural
world *cannot* be dispensed with for "the domain of consciousness"; and (2) there *is* no such thing as a "domain
of consciousness." With this reminder, it is safe to follow
Husserl in the remaining "supplementary" discussions.

Husserl was not entirely satisfied with his original treatment of the indubitability of immanent, and the dubitability of transcendent, perception, in § 46 of his *Ideas*.
In some remarks written in 1929 (Cf. Supplement XIII,
Biemel ed. of Husserl's *Ideen* I, pp. 399 ff.) he states that,
although it is important and brings material not yet
attended to, it is by no means sufficient. He had always
contrasted the perception of experiences, in original self-
givenness, and that of real things, to begin with, material
things. But may we restrict ourselves to single thing-
perceptions, and to single things?

He now asks: Have we not continually presupposed,

that we have a stream of experience, an endlessly streaming procession of a pure life, that I, as the perceiver, not only perceive this and that experience, but have a *unified experience of my life,* of which I am certain? And have we not also presupposed that we may talk as "we," i.e., that other egos and lives are given, in addition to my own? He observes that the entire discussion in question occurred with the natural point of view.

Husserl then suggests that we place at the central point the proposition that the world exists, but that we consider what this statement involves. It is a legitimate statement, so far as I experience the world. If I had no world-experience, no original world-perception, in which the world were given to me as a "continuously" living present, then "the world" would not be an expression with sense for me, and no world-statement would have a meaning of being to be justified. But world-perception is essentially limited to the givenness of single things in a restricted field of things, as a perceptual field. Now the world is more than this streaming, changing field. There is the indicated horizon which widens it; and that it is a thing-horizon in its perceptually unfulfilled emptiness refers to my ability to "penetrate" into this horizon, in the further course of experience. Past and future realities are possible and only partially real givennesses of experiences of remembrance and anticipation.

Things and the world are continually valid for me, and not merely for a perception which is limited to single things and equipped with a horizon, but rather for a universal horizon-consciousness. In Husserl's view, this also requires a critique, in so far as I go in on questions concerning the validity of world-experience and the justification of my world-certainty, whether or not it has apodictic indubitability, which absolutely precludes non-being, and that in contrast with a pure ego and its experience. The latter, too, is a universe "out" of which only singularities are actually given, if also apodictically, and there too I must penetrate into the horizons of my life. The critique of immanent experience, as experience of my being and the being of my life, must be carried over to immanent remembrance, expectation, and in short to the entire immanent and concrete self-experience.

This indicates involved and difficult investigations, which have, in Husserl's view, only recently begun to be successfully handled. In the first draft of the *Ideas,* they were not yet carried out satisfactorily.

In the meantime, Husserl states, it is not to be foreseen, on the basis of what is already in view in the living present, that the existence of the world has being-validity for me only on the basis of the "subjectivity" of the experiences in which the world "appears," and that all further evidence always refers me again to the subjective, to phenomena of the various synthetically connected experiences, and to a certain *style* of evidence, which is itself a thoroughly subjective occurrence.

How much Husserl really meant here in this implied reservation concerning earlier idealistic arguments is not clear. Is it merely a wistful and passing note of caution; or is it the consideration that, if you cannot dispose of naturalism in this way, i.e., by speaking of a real world as dependent upon subjective processes—the desired result may be achieved by means of a "pure" procedure, for which a "world" is only significant as an end-term in a constitutive procedure. The idealistic principle would then be invoked at the appropriate time.

Is it not evident, Husserl continues in the indicated

direction, that this subjectivity can be apprehended purely in its peculiar essence, which does not posit anything of the world, and restricts itself to what is offered by the appearance and experience of the world? He asks further: Does not my being and consciousness essentially "precede" for me the being of the world, and also the mundane being called I the man-in-the-world, a real being among the realities of the world?

The term "preceding" is used in the sense of *a priori* founding, and not in the sense of logical-judgmental founding. To speak of my being in its immanent universality, and to argue that if I were not, then for me there would be no world, would sound like a tautology, Husserl observes at this point. But, looked at more closely, he continues, is not the most wonderful fact indicated therewith, that the world as it is for me is a unity, which is presented in my subjective experiences and the "representations" appearing in them, and is to be viewed only in this correlation?

It is noteworthy that Husserl considers the possibility that he has been toying with a tautology, and backs away from it. It is a spectacle to which we are now well accustomed. Husserl tries to give full standing to the natural view of the world, in its own reality. Then, as though crossing himself with the idealistic dogma, he divulges the "wonderful" truth that the world can only be in the context of experience. The outcome is always the same, whether it be a not-completely ripe Husserl, or a thoroughly purified and transcendentalized partisan of idealism.

Husserl concedes that the structure of the necessity and certainty of my being as the pure ego of my pure life, and this itself with respect to the immanent-temporal whole of this being, has its difficulties. Immanent remembrance, for example, can very well be deceptive, and hence conflict, illusion, and being otherwise, as intuitive remembrance shows, are very well possible outside the intuitive, immanent present. But if, despite such possibilities, the concrete being of my stream of consciousness were apodictic, and were to be made essentially insightful, the apodictic principle holds the first place: Being is basic to every appearance. It is not just any kind of being that is meant, but only an immanent being, exhibitable with an apodictic content, which makes the complete determinateness of this being accessible as an infinite "Idea."

But if all that can be carried through, Husserl continues, there still remains the palpable difficulty, that the evidence of the world is not a matter of my own experience, but is rather a matter of intersubjective, mutually supplementary, enriching "experience," and thus the world is first exhibitable there as that which is the existent for us. Furthermore, am I not the one, in whose life "others" must attain meaning and being-validity, and in which the being-with-others, experiencing-with-others, etc., receives its first and last firmly rooted power of evidence? In me, finally, the world also exhibits itself as intersubjective. How that occurs is declared by Husserl to be a great problem.

Husserl's question, as to whether I am the one in whose life "others" must attain meaning, etc., is not to be taken literally, as though he wished to have an answer. If it were a bona fide question, the answer would be simply, that *I* am not *really* the kind of fundamental being indicated here. Only for an artificial, pure-descriptive procedure is the answer in the affirmative. In that case, however, the question would not have been asked with such a tone of conviction.

Husserl has not really moved away from any of the ground of the first draft of his *Ideas*. His later comments show how much he was disturbed by the gravity of the problems of which he was aware. His failure to distinguish clearly between problems which arise in experience and problems which result from methods that have been adopted was a serious handicap in his prolonged discussions. The problems to which he alludes at the close of Supplement XIII are engendered by the phenomenological procedure itself. They are not *real* problems of experience, and it takes considerable schooling in philosophy and falsification in fact to make them emerge as methogenic problems.

## Chapter IV

# PURE CONSCIOUSNESS

## A. THE REGION OF PURE CONSCIOUSNESS

### 1. The Natural World as the Correlate of Consciousness

Not only could it be said, in Husserl's view, that the things of the natural world "could also not be." To suppose that the physical world itself might have been other than it is, with different systems of law, would be an empty conjecture, making use of the widest concept of possibility. But it is also conceivable, declares Husserl, "that our intuitable world should be the last, and 'beyond' it no physical world at all, . . . that the data of experience should exclude every type of physics similar to ours." Is this "possible" in any sense related to the evidence of real experience? If the things of the world were different than they now are, in their qualities or relationships, there would still be a physical world. The term "conceivable" as used by Husserl is an empty concept, because nothing speaks for the possibility that "our intuitable world should be the last," with no physical world beyond it. The test of conceivability in a logical sense is non-contradiction. Although there may not be any self-contradiction involved in the exclusion of the physical world, the supposition violates all our knowledge and experience, and is therefore "contradictory" ("inconceivable") in that sense. If there is any justification in speaking of "essential possibility," it may be declared to be "essentially impossible" that there be no physical world at all. Rather than have a duel with conflicting "eidetic insights" as weapons, it would be better to rest the case on the verdict of the facts.

From the eidetic point of view, "the real world," or "the correlate of our factual experience" is viewed as "a special case of manifold possible worlds and non-worlds, which, on their side, are no other than correlates of the essentially possible alterations of the idea 'experiencing consciousness'." Husserl cautions us not to be deceived by any talk of the transcendence of the thing in relation to consciousness. The genuine concept of thing-transcendence is to be derived, in his view, from the essential content of the perception, and is "the eidetic correlate of the pure idea of this evidential experience." The subject-object limitation of reality is required by phenomenology *as a matter of method*. It is necessary to guard against regarding it to be a matter of *existence* as well. The connecting link in the illicit extension of the argument would be the consideration that it is not "meaningful" to talk of transcendence otherwise than in the subject-object relationship. That this principle of limitation is a wheel horse for idealism is well known, and Husserl is not above exploiting it in that connection.

As for the "reduction" of phenomenology in general, the reader should reflect that any idea in "reduced" experience is not therefore a "reduced" idea, any more than the statement "Iron is heavy" is a heavy statement. One is not free from the restrictions of the "empirical" world. It should also be asked, when mind emerged in the cosmos. That was, cosmically speaking, only a few brief moments ago. To hold that everything is in an experiential relationship to me now, would not only be grossly anti-Copernican, but simply false in fact.

But if one goes along with the procedure of detaching the natural world from the domain of consciousness, he must be prepared to adopt a new set of concepts, or at least a new vocabulary. Thus, the term "motivation" replaces the term "causality." It is "motivation" that must do the work of causality, but without any of the factual commitments of the latter. It would have been more appropriate to choose a different term, with no naturalistic connotations. Husserl himself concedes that there are "ambiguities" to contend with in the use of this term. The use to which the concept of "motivation" is put is neither sufficiently clear nor effective for the purpose in hand.

In the course of his discussion of "the natural world as the correlate of consciousness," Husserl states what seems to be a realistic principle, only to quickly take it away. "It is a matter of essence, that whatever exists *realiter,* but is not yet actually experienced, can come to givenness, and that means then that it belongs to the undetermined but determinable horizon of my experience-actuality." This horizon, however, as "the correlate of the components of indeterminacy," is taken to depend essentially on the thing-experiences themselves. The principle of the subject-object limitation, the "correlative principle," is always operative.

## 2. The Logical Possibility and Real Absurdity of a World Outside Our Own

"If there are worlds or real things at all," Husserl states with well-feigned open-mindedness, "then the experience-motivations which constitute them must be able to reach into my experience, and that of every ego . . . ." He asserts that "there are things and thing-worlds which cannot be definitely exhibited in any *human* experience, but that has its purely factual grounds in the factual limits of this experience." This is certainly true, but how does Husserl know it on *his* premises? As the legend of Tannhäuser has it, he who has been in *Venusberg* will betray that fact in his speech. The natural world is the *Venusberg* of the transcendentalist. For the rest, Plotinus regretted the necessity of having a body. Husserl labored under both types of difficulty.

Husserl made some pertinent comments in 1922 on § 48, whose theme was the logical possibility and real absurdity of a world outside our own (Cf. Supplement XIV, Biemel ed. of Husserl's *Ideen* I, pp. 401 f.). The objection will be made, he wrote, that a frivolous conclusion has been drawn. It is possible that my experiences will make no demonstrations of a world of experience which is mine impossible. But for that reason it is possible that there be a world which is inaccessible to me and the world which is real, but that I am insane, and nothing further. Now if I want to recognize that, I must be able to have insight into the possibility of a world, and how would this insight itself look, which requires an intuition of such a world? Could an intuitive presentation have the form of a harmonious manifold of phantasies, in which a phantasy-world appeared? But what lies in such phantasies? They are perceptions as if, fictions of perceptions, of synthetically connected perspective variations, appearances of, and hence related to, a co-phantasied correlative stream of experience of a pure ego. The possible world is inseparably related to a possible ego and ego-experience, and if it is to be a really possible one, which is ever to be exhibited as a possible fact, then it must be able actually to exhibit itself in an actual ego and ego-life. That is to say, the actual life of this actual ego must form an actual connection of intentionality, in which the "insanity" in question is exhibited as a particular kind of appearance, which has its real being behind itself. Either I am the one, who in his pure proper essence can know this possibility, or it is another ego. This other one cannot be an empty possibility for me; it would itself have to be grounded, or it would have to be capable of being grounded, in my experience.

Husserl is right in concluding that an insane style of experience would prove nothing concerning the non-being of the world. Furthermore, a universal style which would have no real possibility of harmonious confirmation in itself is nugatory.

## 3. Absolute Consciousness as the Residuum after the Nullification of the World

But it must not be inferred that Husserl was willing to make non-phenomenological concessions unqualifiedly. He did not mean to imply "that there *must* be a world or thing of some sort." The reader will feel constrained to ask: Is it not enough to *know* that there *is* a world? From Husserl's point of view, "the existence of a world is the correlate of certain experience-patterns marked out by certain essential formations." That is to say, viewed phenomenologically, and subject to the conditions defined earlier. Husserl neglects to remind the reader of that fact, so that he seems to be speaking about matters as they *really* are.

Recalling the "results" already achieved, Husserl asks us "to think of the possibility of non-being which belongs essentially to every thing-like transcendence." He holds it to be evident that "the being of consciousness," although it could be modified by a "nullification of the thing-world, could not be affected thereby in its own proper existence." The term *"Vernichtung"* (destruction, annihilation, or nullification) is used to name what seemed to be the innocent procedure of "cancellation" of judgments of existence, in the performance of the *epoché*. Little did the reader realize what the cost in human *(natural)* lives and material fortunes would be. At any rate, the phenomenologist should not be led to exaggerate his actual powers by his linguistic usage. "Being of consciousness," and its "proper existence," are phrases which lend themselves to metaphysical abuse. The stream of experience is referred to as "endless in both ways," recalling Husserl's dictum that the stream of consciousness can no more end than it can begin—a dictum that is certainly and demonstrably false. It is Husserl's contention that no real thing is necessary for the being of consciousness itself. This recalls the absoluteness of "immanent being." On the other hand, Husserl continues with his use of the idealistic principle, "the world of the transcendent 'res' is related unreservedly to consciousness." How much is involved in that "relationship" to consciousness is not revealed at this point.

Insisting that both immanent or absolute being and transcendent being are indeed "being" and "object," he is led to the conclusion that pure consciousness is a self-contained system of absolute being, "into which nothing can penetrate." Therewith Husserl has progressed from Descartes to Leibniz, whose monads are strikingly suggested. Nothing can escape from this absolute system of being, "which has no spatio-temporal exterior, and can be in no spatio-temporal system; which cannot experience causality from anything nor exert causality upon anything," i.e., causality construed as a relation of dependence between natural realities.

That Husserl appears determined to forget the purely procedural character of his whole undertaking is suggested again and again. In the present context, he juxtaposes "the whole spatio-temporal world" with the "absolute" realm; and he regards it as being "mere intentional being, according to its own meaning." That is, moreover, the world "to which man and the human ego claim to belong (!) as subordinate singular realities." It will be noted that the spatio-temporal world, as mere intentional being (by its own showing!—"according to its own meaning"), "has the merely secondary, relative sense of a being *for* a consciousness . . . a being which consciousness . . . posits . . . ."; and "over and beyond this, it is just nothing at all." Once more the reader must ask: is this the case *really,* as a matter of fact; was not the world there *before* the "positing" (in any case, "positing" is one of the most mysterious and slippery terms derived from the speculative arsenal of post-Kantian idealism); and is not Husserl simply forgetting that he requested us to perform the *epoché* for philosophical purposes, for the extrusion of all dogmas? Are we to be led into the lion's den of pure ("reduced") consciousness, with all footprints pointing inwards? And is there anything reassuring about the "constitutive" realm which is to emerge, with the aid of phenomenological activities?

## 4. The Phenomenological Point of View and Pure Consciousness as the Field of Phenomenology

The frequently suggested "cloven hoof" of idealism appears unmistakably in Husserl's text (§ 50), in what may well have been an interpolated section. Having been led to perform the reduction, and having listened to conciliatory words about the "rights" of the natural point of view, the reader now learns that "the common meaning of 'being' is simply inverted." The being which is first for us is really second, i.e., "it is what it is only in 'relation' to the first" (Husserl appropriately places the loaded term "relation" in quotation-marks). "Reality," he informs us, "whether of things taken singly or of the whole world, essentially lacks independence." The term "essence" is to be understood in Husserl's own "rigorous" use of the term. Not only is reality not in itself something absolute; "it is, absolutely speaking, nothing at all, it has no 'absolute essence,' it has the essentiality of something which is on principle *only* intentional, *only* known. . . ." Husserl's system-directed dogma is therewith given expression. The claim that the world "essentially" lacks independence is not rendered more meaningful, by a reference to a "rigorous" use of the term "essence." It is a vapid argument at best. That reality is "only intentional" could never be made plausible to anyone not hurt and confused by epistemological pseudo-arguments. This nonsense was not necessary for Husserl's otherwise meritorious descriptive interests, for which the *epoché* was instituted in the first place.

Husserl does not, even here, present the alternatives fairly, the choice, namely, between the natural view, in which we live "naïvely" in experience and subject transcendent nature to theoretical inquiries, and the way of the phenomenological reduction. The term "naïve" does not do justice to the methodological rigor of the natural sciences. It is not necessary to demean the natural view when arguing for the use of a purely reflective procedure. The two types of approach may and should be used cooperatively. It is all the more discouraging to note that Husserl supposes that, for the natural view, nature is constituted by "consciousness with its transcendent theses."

Instead of carrying out such acts "naïvely," Husserl sets all these theses "out of action," and moves on to "pure consciousness in its own absolute being." The latter is the sought-for "phenomenological residuum." Elated by his success, Husserl is sure that "we have literally lost nothing, but have won the whole of absolute being, which, properly understood, conceals in itself all transcendences, constituting them within itself." This is to be accomplished in spite of dropping causality. The amazing "destruction" (nullification) of the world in phenomenology not only turns out to be no loss; in fact, it is a gain. Instead of asking whether it profits a man to gain the whole world, if he loses his own soul, Husserl was content to gain a soul (an appropriately prepared phenomenological soul), and to lose the world.

## 5. The Significance of the Transcendental Preliminary Reflections

It is denied by Husserl that the "field of pure consciousness" is a portion of nature itself. The reason given is that nature is possible only as an intentional unity. It has already been objected that there cannot *be* anything which is not a part of nature, with a locus in space and time. Husserl never proves that the field of pure consciousness cannot be a part of nature. If he means this to be really the case, then he is guilty of sophistical reasoning, even though he is unquestionably sincere in his objective. He could say that the subjective "realm" (a doubtful metaphor in any case) is not to be *treated* as a part of nature; that it is to be viewed *as though* it were independent of nature; and even that the field of nature is to be viewed as the correlate of intentional experience—for investigative purposes. Having maneuvered us into that position, it is downright confusion—or worse—to prate at frequent intervals about the dependence of nature on experience. As a matter of fact, one *cannot* "look on consciousness as an absolute region for itself alone." The "pure transcendental consciousness" is spoken of as though it were the "promised land" to be gained by a process in the course of which nature is a casualty. It should be called something like the "radically reflective point of view," with no casualties, and, it is hoped, with many gains.

The "realm of experiences as absolute essences" is "firmly closed within itself." This claim invites a pertinent question. Without the experience of independent realities, could you extract "essences," and your field of pure consciousness? If it is factually true that there are independent realities, and that they are needed for the process of experience (natural and cultural), how can one speak of a realm that is "closed" in itself? Only abstractly, of course, for the purposes of an ancillary philosophical discipline.

In a manner reminiscent of Spinoza, Husserl argues that this realm has no boundaries which might separate it from other regions. That is because anything serving as a boundary would have to have something essentially in common with it. Since "Absolute Being" as a whole is in question (analogous to Spinoza's substance), that is precluded. This absolute realm, Husserl is proud to relate, has no need of nature for its existence. He again confuses methodology with supposed facts when he argues that "the existence of what is natural *cannot* condition the existence of consciousness since it arises as the correlate of consciousness; it *is* only in so far as it constitutes itself within ordered organizations of consciousness." This is plainly a case of begging the question, with nature deprived of its well-known powers. Husserl's text should be rewritten, to make it clear that here, as elsewhere, he has no metaphysical designs, and that what he says is merely "from the phenomenological point of view." After his day's work of describing essences and tracing out constitutive activities, Husserl should be able to sit down and enjoy his pipe, along with his evening meal, without further thought about the "absolute."

In a cryptic "Note" appended to § 51, Husserl touches upon the question of a place for theology in phenomenology. Without being explicit, he admits that phenomenology may indirectly have important bearing on theology. Although he does not indicate how theology might enter into the consideration of the "realm of the absolute" of phenomenology, the door is not closed to such efforts. A world-God is "evidently impossible." On the other hand, "the immanence of God in the absolute consciousness cannot be grasped as immanence in the sense of being as inner experience." But, Husserl asserts, "there must be in the absolute stream of consciousness . . . other ways of manifesting the transcendent than the constituting of thing-like realities . . .; and there must be intuitive manifestations to which theorizing thought can adjust itself." He speaks of coming to understand "the undivided rule of the supposed theological principle." This rule could not be taken to be causal in a naturalistic sense, "which is lowered to the pitch suited to realities." Obviously, a new terminology is needed, which would serve to exclude all naturalistic terms such as "causality" (as connoting impersonal, objective truth), while retaining such homespun, patriarchal conceptions as are suggested by the revealing expression "rule."

This passage of Husserl's may prove to be very important in years to come, in view of the obvious advantages to theology held out by a philosophy of pure immanence.

No longer at the mercy of the facts, and with causality reduced to a lowly status, the stage is set for the use of a non-temporal, eternalistic philosophy of essences. The problem would be to connect with religious interests via a philosophy of values. Despite Husserl's seemingly permissive comments on the point, it would be an incredibly far cry from his rigorous and legitimate interests in the philosophy of formal thought and his painstaking studies of experience, to the type of mystical ecstasy or authoritarianism which might well be required to bridge the gap to theology.

## 6. The Physical Thing and the "Unknown Cause of Appearances"

It is simply quaint on Husserl's part, to chide ordinary realism with confusing sensory appearances with "the absolute experiences which constitute them." He speaks as though the absolute experiences really do that work. The tendency to regard "physical being" as resting on a "mythical absolute reality" is declared by Husserl to be due to the absurdity of turning physical nature into an absolute. It will be recalled that Husserl is convinced that physical nature is not independent; it is the "intentional correlate of logically determining thought." But one does not have to postulate an unknown or an unknowable reality, if one fails to accept the idealistic principle of the dependence of nature on absolute consciousness. Another alternative, not considered for a moment by Husserl, would be a critical naturalism or realism, which allows for all the complications of experience, including those discussed by phenomenology. Husserl, for his part, commits himself to the idealistic alternative: "the transcendence of the physical thing is, on principle, the transcendence of a being which constitutes itself within consciousness and remains fettered to consciousness."

All that has been said by Husserl about the facts of nature also applies to the axiological and practical objectivities, including aesthetic objects and cultural creations, which are grounded on them. But there are important differences to be considered, which will occur to the reader at once. The subject-object relatedness, which was so dangerous a restriction in the broad theoretical discussions of nature and experience, had to be justified as an artificial restriction. Here, in the field of values, a form of subject-object relatedness is *really* essential, as it is in all the fields of scholarship that concern human activities and human interests. And this does not support the philosophy of idealism in any way whatsoever.

### 7. Animalia and Psychological Consciousness

On the one hand, consciousness is the absolute within which all transcendence is constituted. But on the other hand consciousness is a subordinate real event within this world. The way in which both of these propositions are embraced in Husserl's philosophy is reminiscent of the idealistic tradition. His language is suggestive: How does consciousness, so to speak, "enter into" the real world; and how can that which is absolute in itself "abandon its immanence" and "put on" the character of transcendence? Through the empirical relation to the body, consciousness "becomes real in a human and animal sense," and it thereby wins a place in nature's space and time. Are we to suppose that consciousness was there first, or that it is "first in itself"? Undoubtedly. And with that premise assured, it is possible to be generous in allowing for animals and human beings as parts of nature—especially since that cannot be avoided anyway.[1]

## 8. Transcendent Psychological Experience Distinguished from Transcendental Experience

Curiously, Husserl supposes that the world could be "annulled," as set forth in the foregoing, without interfering with the absolute stream of experience. As he states it, "there would then be no more bodies, and therefore no men . . . and I should have no neighbors." How then could "my consciousness remain an absolute stream of experience with its own distinctive essence"? Why would not consciousness also stop, at the moment of the nullification of the world? The answer can only be in terms of a variation of Husserl's "correlative point of view," which pervades his whole philosophical development. Only now it goes all the way to linguistic playfulness. He *could* say, simply: by "nullification" we mean "suspension of judgment." Hence, nothing really comes off, and men do not disappear. But he prefers to say, dramatically, "there would be no men, and no neighbors."

Husserl insists (again!), but without justifying his position (once more!), that absolute experience is the assumption on which empirical experience depends for its very meaning. He is sensitive enough to declare that this is not a metaphysical construction, but can be indubitably exhibited in its absoluteness and given in direct intuition.

---

1. That the course of phenomenology is factually (if not essentially) circumscribed has been expressed in the spirit of a well-known passage in Goethe's *Faust:*

> *Der Geist der Phänomenologie ist leicht zu fassen:*
> *Ihr analysiert die subjektive Welt,*
> *Um es am Ende gehn zu lassen,*
> *Wie's der realen Wissenschaft gefällt.*

To be sure, that is not to deny the instrumental value of sciences concerned with essential relations and structures.

The case must rest with the appeal to our insight. "One must convince himself," says Husserl, now pleading for a point of view, *"that the psychical in general in the sense of psychology,* that psychical personalities and properties . . . are *empirical* unities, and are therefore . . . mere unities of an intentional 'constitution'." *In their own sense* they exist truly, and yet they are "merely intentional" and therefore merely "relative." Husserl concludes that to hold that they exist in an absolute sense is therefore absurd. The reader will ask: absurd in fact; or only if you *arbitrarily* or *voluntarily* adopt the phenomenological precedure? Husserl seems to forget this point "absolutely." You can only establish a formal contradiction if you state that the relative is absolute, assuming that the "relative" has been correctly designated as "relative." But that is precisely a point at issue.

### 9. All Reality as Existing through "Meaning-Bestowal": No "Subjective Idealism"

The very caption of this section, which concludes Husserl's discussion of "The Region of Pure Consciousness," illustrates the "duality of interpretation" which unhappily affects so much of the text. Is the reader to understand that all reality *really* exists through 'the bestowal of meaning,' or that it is to be viewed in that way? The "proper care in the use of words" which Husserl himself mentions leads him to state that "all real unities are 'unities of meaning.' " Now "unities of meaning" are held to "presuppose" a meaning-giving consciousness, which is absolute, and hence not dependent on any other meaning-giving source. Husserl reminds the reader emphatically that this is not a matter of deduction from any metaphysical postulates, and that "we can exhibit it in our completely doubt-free intuitive procedure."

But the term "presupposes" assigns priority to the "meaning-giving consciousness," which suggests the danger of using it in the form of a "metaphysical postulate." If "meaning" is construed as involving reference to consciousness, it is not yet said that the consciousness must be "meaning-giving" and, in effect, autonomous ("absolute"). That is to say, unless it is made clear that this is all a device of method, with no questioning of the *real priority* (in a causal and temporal sense) of the natural world. But of the natural world not even ashes remain, after the great nullification. There are only processes of pure consciousness, with their intended objectivities.

It is evident from his text that Husserl does not wish to deny that a naturalistic version of reality is possible. But he insists that it can only be incomplete, and that it cannot be said to comprise the totality of being, and thus be considered absolute. It would be "nonsense," in his view, to derive the "universe," or nature as a whole, from the unities of possible experience, and to take it to be the whole of being. But he does not inform the reader why that must be nonsense. The answer must be simple and direct, if one is straightforward about it. It is close at hand: the adoption of the phenomenological method leads us to "suspend" nature. But it does not allow us to extend the region of "being"— that is a dogmatic error on Husserl's part. The straitjacket of method ought to keep Husserl straight on this point, but it does so only at intervals. Thus, he states that "reality and world are just titles for certain valid *unities of meaning,* namely, unities of 'meaning' related to certain organizations of pure absolute consciousness which bestow meaning [he should state: which are regarded as bestowing meaning] and show its validity in *essentially* determinate ways."

The charge that he has led himself into subjective idealism, and that he has committed himself to an idealism like Berkeley's, is simply rejected by Husserl as a gross misunderstanding. This is reminiscent of Berkeley's own reply to critics. Husserl insists that the real sensory world is not "recast" or denied, but that an absurd interpretation of that world, "which contradicts its *own* mentally clarified meaning," is set aside. Now it turns out that the trouble with the naturalistic view is that "it absolutizes the world in a *philosophical* sense"; and this is held to be "foreign to the way in which we naturally view the world." The natural view is never absurd. The absurdity is incurred when one philosophizes, and seeking final information about the meaning of the world, "does not notice that the *being* of the world consists in a certain '*meaning*' which presupposes absolute consciousness as the field of meaning-bestowal." Furthermore, it is not recognized that "this being-sphere of absolute origins is open to intuitional research, and contains an infinite wealth of insightful knowledge of the highest scientific worth." The failure to notice this possibility for research is held to contribute to the "absurdity" of the naturalistic position.

All of this indicates how stubbornly Husserl resists, or forgets, the fact that he had initially adopted an artificial procedure, the justification for which could only be provided by valuable or interesting results. It is a safe way of putting it, to state that absurdity arises if one fails to notice that the whole being of the world consists in a certain "meaning" which presupposes absolute consciousness. The reader is asked therewith to accept the idealistic dogma, with the tenuous term "meaning," as a kind of "essential necessity." To be sure, Husserl declares that it would be absurd to ascribe reality to the absolute or pure transcendental consciousness which is left over as the residuum, following the phenomenological reduction. Husserl's declaration should be reassuring, however; and it helps to open the door to a defensible way of interpreting phenomenology. "Reality," however, remains a naïve and dogmatic affair. The ultimate "philosophical" domain, pure consciousness, is allowed to have "being." The "world-problem" of phenomenology is raised therewith: the *meaning* "world" has to be "constituted." The whole procedure is restricted to essences and essential formations, to the constitution of complex meanings out of simpler meanings. How can one then get to the order of facts? Evidently "essential necessities" are not to be violated by "matters of fact." Numerous questions would then arise. For example, if you have the essence of a duel, can you tell what will happen in a given case of a duel, or would one be limited to knowing that a duel is not a battleship or a prime number, that there must be at least two contending individuals or parties, etc.? Furthermore, does one get the knowledge of essences from the inspection of essences in pure consciousness, or from his fund of "natural" knowledge?

## B. THE PHENOMENOLOGICAL REDUCTIONS

### 1. The Question Concerning the Extension of the Phenomenological Reduction

Husserl states that it was the suspension of the thesis of the world, of nature, that was the methodological means making it at all possible to turn one's view upon the pure transcendental consciousness. If the term *"Ausschaltung"* is rendered as "disconnection" ("disconnection from nature" is the way this passage reads in the English edition of *Ideas* I), the impression is strengthened that one is somehow emancipated from the natural conditions of experience. It is therefore better to use the term "suspension," or some other English equivalent such as "exclusion" or "elimination," applied to the "thesis of nature." At this point, Husserl speaks of the peculiar and essential nature of phenomenology as a science of "origins." The "origins" are unheralded, so far as any clarification is concerned, although the frequent use of the term "originary" *(originär)* tends to make the reader receptive to this suggestive term. It can only appear odd to speak of "origins" in the context of a science which restricts itself to essences and essential connections, and for which actual temporal records are irrelevant.

## 2 The Question of the Suspension of the Pure Ego

Although not unheralded, the "pure ego" is equally unclarified and unjustified. It "remains self-identical"; and it "appears to be *necessary* on principle, and as that which remains absolutely self-identical in all real and possible changes of experience, it can *in no sense* be regarded *as an immanent part or factor* of the experiences themselves." The reader will still ask insistently, "What is the pure ego; and how does Husserl *know* that it remains 'absolutely self-identical' "? It is not enough to quote the words of Kant, that "the 'I think' *must be able* to accompany all my presentations." We can indeed supply that reflectively, even in wholesale fashion. But that is not what is in question. It turns out that there is a set of pure egos, "an essentially different one for each stream of experience." The ego is not suspended in the phenomenological procedure, "although for many investigations the questions about the pure ego can remain *in suspenso.*" It is a revealing way of putting it, and calls attention to the fact that the pure ego is indeed a "question." That

it can so safely "ride the rapids" of the phenomenological
reduction looks more like a special dispensation than a
"question." A truly "radical" procedure should not be
burdened with "non-constituted transcendences," or with
any such thing as a "transcendence in immanence."

## 3. The Transcendence of God Suspended

In contrast to the pure ego, which is "given" as
"immediately united to consciousness in its reduced state,"
there is the transcendence of God, which is known to us
"in a totally different manner." Husserl's language is
again misleading, when he speaks of "the reduction of
the natural world to absolute consciousness." That never
takes place, construed literally. But let us say: when the
"reduction" has been performed, "a morphologically
ordered world" is "constituted" within the reduced realm
of consciousness "as intentional correlate." This world,
"so far as its material basis is concerned" may be determined scientifically as the "appearance" of a physical
nature which is subject to exact laws. This is well known
anyway, and Husserl is merely stating an established fact.
He goes beyond the facts when he asserts that "the
rationality which the fact *(Faktum)* realizes is not such
as the essence demands," which leads him to conclude
that "there lies in all this a wonderful *teleology.*" The
reader can only exclaim: "Fast and fanciful!" But it is
well that the transcendence of a "divine" Being is suspended, in order to limit the inquiry to the field of pure
consciousness.

In the present section, there is evidence of Husserl's
fleeting attention to the naturalistic way of viewing the
world and man, which is quite an infrequent occurrence
for him. It is done with his own spectacles, as though the
world of nature must be rendered acceptable for the

purposes both of transcendentalism and, ultimately, fideism. Thus, such facts as "the factual evolution of the series of organisms up to man, and . . . the growth of culture with its treasures of the spirit, are not accounted for fully by the explanations of . . . the natural sciences." Husserl cannot resist calling this kind of inquiry "the systematic study of all *teleologies* which are to be found in the empirical world itself." He asks for "grounds," rather than for "substantive causes," which is consistent with the settled policy of breaking away from the conceptual apparatus of the natural sciences.

## 4. The Suspension of Pure Logic and the Material-Eidetic Disciplines

Phenomenology is defined as "a *pure descriptive* discipline which thoroughly examines the field of pure transcendental consciousness within the frame of *pure intuition*." Of course, this is to be established as an eidetic science, as the essence-theory of the transcendentally purified consciousness. Nothing may be presupposed, not even formal logic. Everything must be made "essentially insightful with respect to consciousness itself, in pure immanence." But what about such logical "axioms" as the principle of contradiction? Husserl passes this off lightly, when he states that the "universal and absolute validity" of this principle could be made "insightful with the help of examples provided by its own data." Is the use of examples sufficient to provide *knowledge* that this principle is universal and necessary? And how do you know when a principle is sufficiently "insightful"?[2]

It is important for Husserl's systematic purposes to emphasize "the explicit knowledge" he believes he has

---

2. The status of the principles of logic is considered in greater detail in the *Formale und Transzendentale Logik*, 1929.

attained. He maintains that a descriptive phenomenology is on principle independent of all other disciplines, including formal logic. The meaning of "independence" would have to be clarified, and also the meaning of "on principle." Husserl once remarked that, when he closes his eyes, all the sciences disappear. In a sense that may be true—the vanishing would be for him, that is to say. It could also be said, and with far more significance and truth, that if nature really disappeared, there would be no "phenomenologizing." The "independence" of phenomenology, while undeniable, is accordingly quite restricted.

Husserl argues that a science of facts must make use of the essential truths which relate to the individual objectivities *of its own* domain. Hence, we cannot dispense with the *a priori* consciousness, and it resists any process of "reduction." On the other hand, what would the "*a priori* consciousness" be like without a realm of facts? It would be as empty as it is ideal.

## 5. The "Dogmatic" and Phenomenological Points of View

We are "born dogmatists," says Husserl, and therefore we must take care to protect ourselves from deeply rooted confusions. It should be noted, however, that the natural scientists do not speak as "born dogmatists." The rigorous application of scientific methods, and acknowledgement of the principle that every scientific statement is subject to possible modification or rejection,[3] prevents scientists from

---

3. Cf. Felix Kaufmann, *Methodology of the Social Sciences,* New York, Oxford University Press, 1944, p. 53. Referring to this principle as "the principle of permanent control," Professor Kaufmann writes: "It is essential for empirical procedure that no proposition belonging to a science is exempt from the possibility of future elimination."

being dogmatists. Husserl, however, is perfectly willing to lump together all non-phenomenologists under the heading of "dogmatists"— or worse.

In Husserl's usage, all the sciences subject to the reduction are dogmatic. In his view, "it is clear from essential sources" [this is an empty appeal!] that the sciences which are "bracketed" are in need of "criticism." They are, he maintains, not able to supply the needed criticism themselves. But phenomenology is precisely the science "which has the unique function of criticizing all the others and itself at the same time." He does not justify his contention that the sciences cannot be self-critical. Neither does he make it clear as to how you can "criticize" phenomenology. Only the broad outline of an answer to these questions is indicated. Phenomenology comprises all eidetic forms of knowledge, or all unconditionally and universally valid forms of knowledge. What Husserl calls "the radical problems of 'possibility,' which relate to any of the sciences," are said to receive an answer. Phenomenology "supplies the ultimate criticism of every . . . distinct science, and . . . the final determination of the sense in which their objects can be said to 'be'." Not only that: "it also clarifies their methodology essentially." It is to be hoped that no phenomenologists will undertake to "criticize" any of the sciences without adequate study of them. Again, how can the nonscientist, *qua* phenomenologist, determine the sense in which the objects of a given science can be said to "be"? From what point of view? Is the *real* existence of the subject matter of a science to be illuminated? And if regions of "essential" possibility are defined, how can it be established that matters of fact will conform to such determinations? This will remain a mere programmatic formulation, reminiscent of early rationalism, until the phenomenologist succeeds in showing how his work can be useful to the special sciences. This applies also to the claim that the methodology of the sciences is "essentially" *(prinzipiell)* clarified by phenomenology. To date, this is an unfounded claim; and the nature of the "principles" involved remains to be indicated. The continued use of the term "clarification" also presents a problem, for it must itself be "clarified" (i.e., analyzed and defined) satisfactorily.

Husserl himself asks a most pertinent question after describing the function of phenomenology: "The only question that remains is the extent to which something further can be accomplished from here." Yes, what *can* be done from the alleged vantage point of phenomenology? The learned world will not be satisfied with general programmatic considerations. Concrete results are called for. Fortunately, Husserl was by no means empty-handed, when one considers the valuable descriptive materials in his huge output.

## C. PRELIMINARY CONSIDERATIONS OF METHOD

### 1. The Importance for Phenomenology of Considerations of Method

The performance of the reduction, with the suspending of transcendences and the restriction to essences, opens up an "endless" field of eidetic knowledge, "endless in every direction." It should not be forgotten that this admittedly immense field for inquiry depends upon the "mother ground" (to use a favorite expression of Husserl's) of the natural world and its natural experience (in which connection Husserl did not use the expression "mother ground," to be sure). Having attained to the realm of pure experience, Husserl calls attention to the initial difficulties to be faced, for one thing because we lack the advantage of the data of the natural point of view, "which through continual experience are so familiar to us." Phenomenology could not hope to dispense with such "familiar" data, which must be the real foundation for any attempt at a reflective philosophy. They are merely to be examined from another point of view, and with different objectives.

Contrasting phenomenology to the natural point of view, Husserl speaks of it as being in need of a method "prior" to all matter-determining method. He should have said instead that the methological needs of phenomenology are simply to be *distinguished from* all other types of method.

## 2. The Self-Suspension of the Phenomenologist

In a pause which is as refreshing as it is remarkable, Husserl asks the reader to consider a doubt as to method. *"Can* we as phenomenologists set *ourselves* out of action, we who still remain members of the natural world?" How reassuring to know that you still remain a member of the natural world! Whitehead's objection to the phenomenological procedure is also answered therewith. Whitehead once protested: "You cannot really get out of nature." Husserl expresses it very well: "As phenomenologists we should not cease to remain natural human beings." As a *"piece of method"* (this expression of Husserl's is also noteworthy), however, the rule of the phenomenological reduction is followed, "preventing us from bringing in any proposition which contains, implicitly or explicitly, such natural positings." The phenomenologist is like the geometer; like the geometer, he does not enter into the "eidetic content of the propositions themselves." If Husserl had always borne in mind the simple facts expressed in this section, much misunderstanding could have been avoided. But the clarity with which the nature of phenomenology was portrayed is quickly obscured by calling it a "theory of essential being *(Wesenslehre)*, developed within a medium of intuition," as is done in the English edition of the *Ideas*. The term "being" is a disturbing intrusion of potential metaphysics.

## 3. Concerning Clearness and Clarification

The concept of "clarifying" has been in need of clarification. Husserl is at his best in fixing concepts, and in making distinctions. The "procedure of making clear to oneself" is said to consist of two interconnected processes: "rendering intuitable," and "increasing the clearness of what is already intuitable."

"Perfectly clear apprehension," by its essential nature, permits us to carry out all "logical" acts with "insight," or with "absolute certainty (indubitability)." This is either a tautology, or it says too much. If being perfectly clear is taken to mean absolute certainty, we have a simple tautology. If it is not a case of equivalence, with certainty provided by definition, the burden of proof must be on the phenomenologist, to show that his insight is binding on all possible insights.

Is there any "perfectly clear apprehension," as a matter of fact? It might seem possible to establish it, on the ground that there must be clear seeing if unclearness occurs, i.e., there will at least be a clear apprehension of unclearness. But that is merely a dialectical argument which does not legislate for the facts. In practice, only more or less unclear, or more or less clear, experiences need occur. The upper conceptual limit, of absolute clearness, may never occur. One could not know if a given experience were infinitesimally distant from the upper limit. The phenomenologist, interested as he is exclusively in essences, does not concern himself with the factual problems.

In Husserl's view, "the general," like color in general, or sound in general, can be "fully given," whereas exemplifications of color and sound "should show a lower grade of clearness." It seems that we can be most sure of what we never have in fact, "the general."

## 4. Clearness, Free Phantasy, and Fiction

Husserl's contention (§ 70) that "clear perception, as it is needed, is always at our disposal," must be justified. It must be pointed out, how one can know perception to be clear. The meaning and tests of "clearness" in concrete situations must be determined. Although he fails to give examples, Husserl indicates the direction in which he looks for the solution to the problem of "clearness." It is important, in his view, "to make rich use of phantasy in the perfect clarification which is required here, to use it in the free transformation of the data of phantasy." The previous experience in "originary intuition" will serve to "fructify" it; and profit can be derived from history, art, and poetry, which represent fruits of the imagination. Husserl is led, finally, to assert, revealingly, "that the element which makes up the life of phenomenology as of all eidetic science is 'fiction,' that fiction is the source whence the knowledge of 'eternal truths' draws its sustenance." Ever sensitive to the hostility of his sworn enemies, he notes that this sentence might well bring "ridicule from the naturalistic side on the eidetic way of knowledge." Husserl's position is, however, really strengthened by calling attention to the use of phantasy and fiction, just as it is weakened by all talk of "being" and by a tendency toward an idealistic metaphysics. The whole phenomenological procedure has an element of artificiality in it.

Once one leaves the "point of view" of natural facts, he is indeed concerned with "fiction." And fictions, taken generally as comprising conceptual devices of all kinds, are enormously important for the understanding and control of facts.

## 5. Concerning "Mathematical" Sciences of Essential Being

As distinguished from formal disciplines, phenomenology takes its place with the "material eidetic sciences." Making use of a traditional distinction which has its dogma, Husserl compares phenomenology with "material mathematical disciplines such as geometry,"[4] and asks whether it can be built up as a "geometry" of experiences. It must be noted, however, that phenomenology as a descriptive science of essence "belongs to a totally different basic class of eidetic sciences than that to which the mathematical sciences belong." The expression "regional ontology" is questionable in the context of conceptual abstractions. If we were to allow "ideal entities," as a matter of usage, it would be unfortunate to assign ontological status, "being" of any kind, to the conceptual forms which are employed. How traditionally rooted Husserl is in his usage is shown further by his version of the axioms of geometry, as "primitive laws of essence."

### D. GENERAL STRUCTURES OF PURE CONSCIOUSNESS

#### 1. The Realm of Transcendental Consciousness

In "a certain definite sense," the realm of transcendental consciousness proves to be "a realm of 'absolute' being." Furthermore, it is the original region *(Urregion)* of being

---

4. Cf. also *Ideen* III, pp. 44 f. on the comparison of phenomenology and mathematics.

generally, as Husserl puts it, a region in which all other
regions of being have their root, to which they are
*essentially* related, and on which they are therefore all
dependent in an essential way. Now none of these theses
has been established. It has already been seen to be
merely willful usage to speak of transcendental "being."
To call it the "original region of being" is merely to extend the willfulness. The pictorial terms used so abundantly by Husserl serve to conceal his dogmatism, and help
to keep up the appearance of never-ending "description"
in his text. "Original," "root," "unreservedly," "realm,"
and "dependent in an essential way," are examples of
usage which tends to illustrate never-ending claims instead.
Revealing also is Husserl's statement that "the domain over
which phenomenology rules extends in a certain remarkable way over all the other sciences which it has suspended." The "rule" of phenomenology appears to have
taken place rather suddenly. It would be well to spread
the news. Only appropriately "reduced" spirits would
yield to the rule without a struggle.

## 2. Reflection upon Experience

Reflection has "a universal methodological function for
phenomenology," because its method "proceeds entirely
through acts of reflection."

Now reflection is a name for acts "in which the stream
of experience . . . can be grasped and analyzed with
evidence. It is . . . the name of the method employed by
consciousness for the knowledge of consciousness in general." A reflection is a "modification of consciousness,"
and every consciousness can, on principle, experience such
a modification. The concept of reflection comprises "all
modes of immanent essence-apprehension, and . . . all

modes of immanent experience." An "immanent perception" is in fact a reflection.

Husserl thinks one can see "with the most perfect clearness and with the consciousness of unconditional validity" that a "solipsism of the present moment" is ruled out. Following his discussion of the "absolute right of immanent perceiving reflection," the "absolute right of immanent retention," as well as the "relative right of immanent recollection," which we "grasp," Husserl is satisfied that a restriction to the "actual now of the present moment" has been rendered absurd. He admonishes the reader not to be confused by arguments which "miss all adjustment to the primal sources of validity, to those of pure intuition." The "principle of principles" is recalled; and it now reads: "Perfect clearness is the measure of all truth, and statements which give true expression to their data need fear nothing from the finest arguments." It appears that there is some degree of development, or of adaptation, in the "principle of all principles."

But has Husserl disposed of all the arguments? Has he not raised new problems, including the meaning of "clearness"? And is he not himself guilty of a *metabasis* from the order of "essences" to "pure intuitions"? Does he suppose that an experience of a pure structure is a pure experience; that an intuition of an essence is an essential intuition; and that an experience under "reduced" conditions is *really* a "reduced" experience? It is not enough to give a few general indications of an absolute point of view, and to refer ironically to "the finest arguments."

### 3. Phenomenology and the Difficulties of "Self-Observation"

It is a comparatively rare occurrence for Husserl to

pay attention to criticism. His attempt to reply to H. J. Watt and others shows how much concerned he was about the question of the relationship of phenomenology and psychology. In effect, the psychological critics were hostile to the point of total rejection of the worth of phenomenology. Protesting that his position was grossly misunderstood and misrepresented, Husserl attempts to dispose of his critics by proving their position to be "absurd." It would have been better to pause after showing that his position had been misunderstood, without going on to use his familiar and overworked argument concerning the "absurdity" of psychological arguments which deny phenomenology. The question of the relationship of phenomenology and psychology is not to be disposed of within the limits of a brief controversy, in any case. The second volume of the *Ideas* is referred to by Husserl, as concerned with the more detailed analysis of this relationship. But this question had also been discussed in his *Logos* article, "Philosophy as a Rigorous Science," in 1911.

In the present section, Watt's reservations concerning phenomenology are construed as "skepticism in relation to phenomenology."[5] Husserl emphasizes the difference between questions advanced by psychological method, which concern the *existential* determinations, bringing to expression the data of our inner experience; and the questions treated by phenomenology, concerning *essential* determinations, viewed on the basis of pure reflection, with no "natural apperception." That is not to suggest that the two approaches are unrelated. It turns out that the relationship is a very close one, and that no small

---

5. Henry J. Watt, "Sammelbericht (II.) über die neuere Forschung in der Gedächtnis-und Assoziationspsychologie aus dem Jahre 1905," *Archiv für die gesamte psychologie*, Vol. IX, 1907.

part of the significance and justification for phenomenology is to derive from its value for psychology. In short, it is Husserl's thesis that phenomenology is basic for empirical psychology, just as geometry and kinematics are basic for physics.

Insisting that Watt showed no real grasp of what was at issue, Husserl declares that the real meaning of an "absolute realm" had been missed by him. He sees the problem to be one of self-observation, which is retrospective. How then would a phenomenology of immediate experience be possible? Watt looks to experimental psychology, with its inductive method, to determine the validity of self-observation.[6]

Obviously indignant, Husserl speaks caustically about "this pious belief in the omnipotence of inductive method . . . a belief Watt could hardly maintain if he reflected upon the conditions of the possibility of his method." Husserl does not think that the essential science of phenomenology is called upon to deal with methods of assuring the *existence* of the experiences serving as a basis for its findings, any more than the geometer can be expected to consider how the existence of the figures on the board is to be rendered convincing. Geometry and phenomenology, as purely essential sciences, have no concern with real existence. As already pointed out, clear fictions serve even better than data of actual experience, as a foundation for these sciences.

Husserl is adroit in turning away from one type of existential question, which is emphasized by Watt. But

---

6. Watt states (*op. cit.*, p. 7) that a discussion of self-observation from the point of view of experimental psychology will perhaps shed new light on the question. Its answer will perhaps be more cautious, "since it lacks the zeal of the discoverer of phenomenology." In any case, he adds, it is more inclined to look to an inductive method.

he seems to forget the modest limitations of his own method, when he attacks the "omnipotence of inductive method." It is not necessary to depreciate inductive method when trying to secure a place for a method dealing with essences in "reflective intuition."

Watt argues that with self-observation the objective relation of the experiences to be described is altered; and that this alteration has perhaps a greater significance than one is inclined to believe. If Watt is right, Husserl replies, then we should be asserting too much if, in self-observation, we reported that we had just been attending here to his book and were continuing to do so. Although that held good prior to reflection, the attentive "experience to be described" has been changed due to reflection. But is this what Watt really said or implied? Did he say that there was a complete or necessarily a radical alteration due to reflection? Or was that meaning injected into his words?[7]

It is only one step further for Husserl to bring out his heaviest weapon of all, conspicuously directed against skepticism and naturalism in the past. It is characteristic of "every genuine skepticism" that it incurs the absurdity of presupposing implicitly in its arguments what it denies in its own theses. This is taken to apply to Watt's arguments. "He who merely says: I doubt the cognitive significance of reflection, maintains an absurdity. For as he asserts his doubt, he reflects," and this case of

---

7. Watt writes (p. 12) that differences of opinion are not lacking. "In general, it is recognized that self-observation is based upon immediate remembrance, in which the liveliness of the states to be observed and therewith the possibility of their observation rapidly decreases. Psychology must however make it clear to itself, that with self-observation the objective relation to the experiences to be described is altered. This alteration has perhaps a much greater significance than one was at first inclined to believe, perhaps not. That may be left undecided here."

reflection is thus presupposed as valid. In order to bring this logical weapon into use, the target must be specially prepared. That means, the position of Watt must be taken to be the universal denial of reflection. Without going that far, doubts and qualifications may well be raised about special conditions of reflection. That would not be "skeptical," and would not incur absurdity.

Husserl's further arguments are hardly more satisfactory. It is also not convincing to speak of the knowledge *that* there are unreflective experiences as being the same as to maintain or imply that one can have such knowledge unchanged. It seems to Husserl that skepticism (which is the opprobrious standpoint he has imposed upon Watt) "loses its force by turning back from verbal discussions to the essential intuition, the originary giving intuition."

In Husserl's view, the phenomena of reflection are a sphere of pure and perhaps of the clearest data. It is an *essential insight* always attainable because immediate, that, from the objectively given, as such, reflection upon the object-giving consciousness and its subject is possible; from the perceived to the perceiving act; from the remembered, as 'having been,' to the remembering. It is "evident" that essentially it is only through reflections of this kind that such a thing as consciousness or conscious content (in an immanent or intentional sense) can become known, and that God Himself could gain a knowledge of His consciousness and its content only through reflection.

So it is "an essential insight always attainable because immediate" to which Husserl appeals. Can such an "insight" be wrong? The answer would have to be: not if it is *essential* insight. But how do you *know* that it is? By another essential insight? Or does it *enforce* your acceptance of it, *as a matter of fact?* That would be a precarious answer. Unless Husserl can show us how to cross the bridge (or unless he can provide a bridge) from essence to existence, he is giving an empty answer to the "skeptical" objections in question.

All of Husserl's all too infrequent references to theology are of interest. In the present context, God is on the one hand made to be subject to "an absolute and insightful necessity." On the other hand, the idea of God is regarded as "a necessary limiting concept . . . or an indispensable index in the construction of certain limiting concepts, which even the philosophical atheist cannot dispense with." It is not clear why the alleged "necessary limiting concept" should be called God. Whether there is such a concept at all, would also have to be established. It is also difficult to see how it could be proved that even the philosophical atheist must acknowledge this idea. Would the line of thought, which is not given here, invoke the supreme weapon of "absurdity" once more, to show that the denial of the "necessary limiting concept" presupposes such a concept, with a final round of "essential insight" to finish off all the remaining opposition?

Special interest also attaches to Husserl's remarks in reply to Ziehen's criticisms.[8] Ziehen had spoken of "that suspicious so-called intuition or self-evidence which . . . changes from philosopher to philosopher, or from one school of philosophers to another school . . . ." He also characterized the "general objects" or essences of Husserl as "bluff." The "absolute exactness" that is claimed for them is regarded by Ziehen as "human presumption." It is noteworthy that Husserl here makes the rather extraordinary admission that "with the appeal to 'intuition'

---

8. Cf. Th. Ziehen, *Erkenntnistheorie auf Psychophysiologischer und Physikalischer Grundlage*, Jena, G. Fischer, 1913.

mischief has often resulted." In Husserl's view, "the question is only whether this mischief in the case of an *alleged* intuition could be discovered in any other way than through *real* intuition." He argues that there has also been much mischief in the appeal to natural experience, and that it would be hard if experience were regarded as "bluff," and if it required "the agreement of all individuals who think and feel in substantiating such 'experience.' "

In reply to Husserl, it might be maintained that one could only *know* the difference between the *real* and the *alleged* on the basis of the facts of "natural" knowledge, in the last analysis. Husserl has an interesting way of ignoring, if not reversing, the actual state of affairs. He suffers from the presence of idealistic "blinkers" *(Scheuklappen)*, to use a term he liked to apply to his foes, with reference to their naïveté and narrowness.

As for the analogy drawn between intuition and experience as "bluff," it must be noted that experience in general is not at issue. The two cases are not analogous. The validity of natural experience depends upon the objective evidence, which may be questioned or modified by any individuals. The agreement of all need not be expected. The "intuition" which Husserl is defending may be challenged without involving experience as a whole. The issue is obscured by the spectacle of a wholesale denunciation of phenomenology on the one hand, and a peculiar preference for rhetorical rebuttal, instead of a close consideration of the reaches of factual methods, on the other hand. If an abyss separates the contending parties, Husserl is not at all disposed to remove the obstacle.

Reverting to the heights of analysis reserved for phenomenology, Husserl maintains that every essential description which relates to types of experience provides an unconditionally valid norm for possible empirical existence. This has to be shown, of course. The expression "unconditional" is hardly likely to effect a closer *rapprochement* with scientific methodologists. Can anything—real or cognitive—be said to be "unconditional"?

It is Husserl's claim that phenomenology is the court of appeal for the fundamental questions of psychological methodology. The "general conclusions" of phenomenology must be adopted by the psychologist "as the condition for the possibility of all further developments of method in his field." Anything conflicting with such essential findings will be intrinsically absurd psychologically, just as, in physics, every conflict with geometrical truths will be intrinsically absurd scientifically. This analogy must be considered more closely, however. Is the question of alternative geometries to be dismissed, in the interest of the doctrine that "space *is* Euclidean"?

The hope that psychological induction, by way of experimental psychology, will overcome the skeptical doubts concerning the possibility of self-observation, is held to be "absurd on principle." But Husserl does not show why that is "absurd." His argument, by way of an analogy, suggests that it is as though one wanted to overcome the corresponding skepticism in the domain of the knowledge of physical nature, the view that every outer perception might finally be deceptive, by means of experimental physics, "which itself presupposes the rightness of outer perception." But it is by inductive and experimental procedures, aided by deduction, that particular observations and facts are established with probability.

The establishment of "the rightness of outer perception" is not in question. It is not the "presupposition" of outer perception that is involved, by this or any other type of argument. If each and every observation is tested, and if empirical judgments have a greater or lesser degree of probability, which changes in accordance with the evidence, there need be no talk of "the rightness of outer perception."

It is simply unwarranted to close the case for inductive method on "essential" grounds. In his general line of thought, Husserl shifts from the necessity of using concepts or essences, to the inadequacies of a narrowly conceived approach to psychology and the theory of knowledge. He holds "to the old ontological doctrine, that the knowledge of 'possibilities' must precede that of actualities," with the reservation that it be "rightly understood and correctly utilized." Does the idea that the "knowledge" of possibilities must precede the "knowledge" of actualities suggest a temporal and not merely a logical sense of precedence? But that could not be carried through, in fact. There must be first of all a knowledge of actualities, at least a beginning fund of factual knowledge. It may be helpful to call the temporal perspective the longitudinal view, and the perspective of essential insight the cross-sectional view. Each of them has its kind of "priority," each one "precedes" the other in a different sense. For natural experience, the funding of actualities is first, and the consideration of possibilities comes later. A long process of practical experience, and a protracted period of need, preceded the development of a science of geometry. On the requisite level of development, the construction of conceptual systems, and, as may be, the discernment of essential relations and structures, are powerful instruments of progress. Both types of approach, both types of method, are indispensable. The exaggerated spirit of conflict between them, while understandable historically, should no longer be a force in the minds of clear-thinking students of philosophy. It is neither illogical nor disloyal to be hospitable to both types of procedure, so long as they are correctly applied.

### 4. The Relation of Experiences to the Pure Ego.

Husserl emphasizes the "extraordinarily important two-sidedness in the essence of the sphere of experience." There is "a subjectively and an objectively oriented side." Corresponding to this two-sidedness is a division between two parts of the inquiry of phenomenology, "the one concerned with pure subjectivity, the other with that which belongs to the 'constitution' of objectivity *for* subjectivity." The "intentional reference" of experiences to objects, and the "intentional correlates" connected therewith, are prominent themes in the descriptive work of phenomenology.

It is evident that Husserl wishes to make it clear that subjectivity is prior to objectivity. The expression "constitution of objectivity for subjectivity" once more raises the question of what may be involved, beyond the sphere of description. In what sense is this to be understood? Under which conditions—real or artificial—is it operative? Is there a metaphysical principle involved? Is there any likelihood that it will be linked up with the "necessary limiting concept" (or the idea of God), of which Husserl spoke earlier? These questions are unavoidable under the circumstances.

### 5. Phenomenological Time and Time-Consciousness

Husserl's treatment of "phenomenological time," which is "a general peculiarity of all experiences," is only very briefly indicated in the *Ideas*. In general, his studies of time and time-consciousness are certainly one of his most successful undertakings in descriptive analysis. His distinctions are drawn clearly, and the functioning of essential analysis is indicated satisfactorily. But it will be questioned whether the relationship between cosmical time and phenomenological time is correctly portrayed. If cosmic time is our name for the way in which objective events succeed one another, it is not entirely helpful to link it to the "immanent essence of a sensory content" in an analogy. But, beyond that, there is the suggestion that phenomenological time is really (in a way being gradually prepared) at the basis of cosmic time, i.e., the conceptual, the "essential," is taken to be prior to the actual. Thus he writes: "Cosmical time stands to phenomenological time in a relation analogous in a certain manner to that in which the 'spreading' that belongs to the immanent *essence* of a concrete sensory content . . . stands to objective spatial 'extension,' to that, namely, of the appearing physical object 'shadowed forth' visually in this sensory datum."

The reader learns that the transcendental absolute "made known" through the reductions is not "ultimate." It "constitutes itself," with all due profundity; and "it has its primal source in what is ultimately and truly absolute." If Georg Cantor could provide for a series of powers of infinity, why could not Husserl have a series of "absolutes"? Being non-sensory and without passions, they could get along together very well. But Husserl is inclined to cut the series short, by proceeding at once to the "primal source." If that is "truly absolute," he should have edited his text about the earlier absolute, which enjoyed so brief a reign. The term "source" also stands in need of clarification, here as elsewhere.

"Temporality" is not only something belonging to every single experience; it is a "necessary form binding experiences with experiences." Every real experience endures— as Husserl puts it, it is "necessarily one that endures"— which, he submits, is "evident on the ground of the clear intuition of an experiential reality." The expressions "necessary form" and "necessarily one that endures" would have been complete enough without the term "necessary," which really adds nothing. As for the appeal to "evidence," in the sense of "self-givenness" or "self-evidence," the only objectionable feature is the use of such pretentious language. No one would be likely to object to the statement that "every real experience endures," if not for the far-reaching implications of the reference to "evidence" and "clear intuition." Furthermore, a real experience "belongs to *one* endless 'stream of experience.' " Now every single experience can begin and end, but that is held to be not true of the stream of experience, which cannot begin and end. The question may be raised, as to whether one is talking about the essence of the stream here. If so, it is irrelevant to say that it does not begin or end. But if it is a *real* stream, it has its history, its beginning and presumable end.

It is a matter of "evidence" to Husserl that "no enduring experience is possible unless it is constituted within a continuous flow of modes of givenness as the unitary factor in the process, or the duration; and further, that this mode of givenness *of* the temporal experience is itself in turn an experience, although of a new kind and dimension." Thus, I can observe the joy which begins and ends, "accompanying all its temporal phases." I can also pay attention "to its mode of givenness: to the modus of the actual 'now,' and to this feature also that with this very 'now', . . . a new and continuously new 'now' links up in necessary continuity. . . ."

But this is the merest indication of the analysis of time and time-consciousness. The reader will do well to study the already published 1905 lectures by Husserl, *Vorlesungen zur Phänomenologie des inneren Zeitbewusstseins;* and especially the as yet unpublished major work on Time, to which Husserl attached so much importance, and which is fortunately preserved in Louvain, along with the other manuscripts left by him.

In general, it is possible to go along with Husserl in his descriptive work, despite such disturbing but really superfluous terms as "necessity," "pure," "grounds of principle," "intrinsic essence," etc. When he states (§ 82) that "no experience can cease without a consciousness of the ceasing and the having ceased," he can only be referring to "conscious experiences." But even that raises questions, if one thinks of actual experiences, which may be cut off completely without any "consciousness of the ceasing." Even as a "rule of essence" it seems to be arbitrarily imposed on the stream of experience, in order to unite it under the sovereignty of a "pure ego." It is important to know how much is to be read into the "infinite," when Husserl declares the stream of experience to be "an infinite unity."

Especially interesting is Husserl's declaration, that "the further elaboration of these insights and the indication of their vast metaphysical consequences" are reserved for future publication. The reader is by now abundantly prepared for this statement. The metaphysical consequences would be quite innocent if they were at all represented by the "Law of Essence" of which Husserl speaks. The "now, before, and after," with the processes of "retention" and "protention," express features of experience which are found, discerned. There would be no talk of "vast consequences" unless an antinaturalistic and antirealistic development were in question. Of course, from Husserl's total output, one knows very well what he has in mind at this point.

### 6. Apprehension of the Unitary Stream of Experience as "Idea"

Husserl speaks of "eidetic possibilities," which are illustrated as follows: "to bring what is not seen into the pure view; to make that which is noted incidentally the object of primary observation; to raise the unemphatic into relief; and to make the obscure clear and ever clearer." But these are also *real* possibilities. Or should one say, they are *also* eidetic possibilities. The "real" is truly there "first," despite the idealistic dogma. This is not to be justified by "insight" or by rhetoric, but entirely by an appeal to the facts of natural experience and the sciences.

It is asserted by Husserl as an "eidetically valid and evident proposition," that no *concrete experience* can be held to be *independent* in the full sense of the term, and that each one is "in need of completion" with respect to some connected context. The term "evident" asserts a good deal, in its meaning of "self-givenness." Instead of stating that "no concrete experience can be held to be independent," it would be better to say that the essence of a concrete experience rules out independence. To regard this as "eidetically valid" is merely to maintain that the general truth in question can be "seen." No multiplication of instances would be of any avail, if universality is to be claimed. Finally, if the need for completion in some connected context is really inherent in the meaning (or the essence) of a concrete experience, this proposition could not be denied without "absurdity." That is the way of essences, and of the "eidetically valid." Thus far, the eidetic has been rather thin. The reader is enjoined to be open-minded, in the hope of greater "thickness," or of demonstrations of the value of the "thin."

**7. Intentionality as the Main Phenomenological Theme**

The general theme of "objectively" oriented phenomenology is "Intentionality." It is essential to experience in general "that it participate in intentionality somehow." By "intentionality" Husserl understands "the peculiarity of experiences to be the consciousness *of* something." It is to this "wonderful peculiarity" that "all riddles of the theoretical reason and of metaphysics lead back." To maintain that all "metaphysical riddles" are to be led back in any effective sense to "intentionality" is to suggest one of two things: either that they have no meaning if they are not reducible to terms of experience; or that all problems of being are problems of experience. In the latter case, the connecting link between experience and being is provided by the "constitutive" process. The former alternative, that the "riddles" have no meaning if not reducible to experience, is either a tautology, or it contains the unwarranted assumption that problems of being can substantively be construed as problems of experience. That would falsify the very meaning ("intentional") of experience as "experience of" something. Husserl's statement can only be treated with reservation until its complete use in phenomenology is made clear. Of course, it may well appear to be "obvious" that all metaphysical problems lead back to the relationship between experience and its objects. What could seem more plausible, on the face of it? Concerning "obvious" statements, it is refresh-

ing to recall a remark of Professor Whitehead's, when he
was asked to grant an apparently innocuous assumption.
"If you were to ask me to grant that $2 + 2 = 4$," he
exclaimed, "I would refuse to do so until you showed me
what you were going to do with it!"

## 8. Sensuous *Hyle,* Intentional *Morphe*

The very broad meaning of intentionality, as in the
last resort including all experiences within itself, even
those not characterized as intentional, would in itself
justify such caution. All the more is caution indicated
when Husserl speaks of "descending into the obscure
depths of the ultimate consciousness which constitutes all
experience-temporality." Such pictorial language could
only result in self-deception.

Also likely to mislead is the talk of an "animating,"
"meaning-giving stratum" of experience, "lying over the
sensuous factors of experience," which contain nothing
"intentional" in themselves. As Husserl formulates it, "intentional experiences are there as unities through the
giving of meaning." "Meaning-giving" is an inappropriate
expression if it is taken to name what actually takes place
generally, instead of what it is *viewed* as being, in accordance with the subjectivistic procedure of phenomenology.

Husserl's antinaturalism is manifested in his hostility
toward "a psychology without a soul," which has "disagree-
able" results. The "psychology without a soul," in his
view, confuses the exclusion of the soul-entity in the sense
of this or that nebulous metaphysics of the soul with the
elimination of the psychical reality given factually in experience, whose *states* are the inner experiences. Finding
the current use of the term "psychical" beset by ambiguities, Husserl holds to the word "noetic," and asserts that
the stream of phenomenological being has a material (or

hyletic) and a noetic stratum. The analyses on the noetic side are incomparably more important and fruitful, as Husserl envisages them.

## 9. The Functional Problems

Yet the greatest problems of all, says Husserl, are the "functional problems," or "the constitution of the objectivities of consciousness." Thus, "the way in which noeses, animating the material, and weaving themselves into unitary manifolds, into continuous syntheses, so bring into being the consciousness of something, that in and through it the objective unity of the objectivity may permit of being harmoniously 'manifested,' 'exhibited,' and 'rationally' determined"— this indicates the constructive phase of phenomenology. The aim is to study, in the most general way, "how objective unities of every region and category 'are consciously constituted.' " This "function" is "grounded in the pure *essence* of the noeses." It must be noted whether this location of an "essence" in the noeses sets up the analysis in favor of idealism. How pertinent this observation may be, is indicated by Husserl's further remarks about the nature of consciousness. It is used in the sense of "consciousness *of* something." It is essential to consciousness, "to conceal 'meaning' within itself . . . It is the source of all reason and unreason, all right and wrong, all reality and fiction, all value and disvalue, all deed and misdeed." It is evident that much of a metaphysical nature has been tucked away in this concept of consciousness — enough to justify Husserl's earlier remark, that all riddles of the theoretical reason and of metaphysics lead back to intentionality.

Recognizing that the procedure of phenomenology would be one-sided and merely negative, if it stopped with the "reduction," the reader will nevertheless be seriously concerned about the nature of the constitutive program. The point is, to constitute all things within the new framework, and among other things, "a" world, if not "the" world. Is it precisely *this* world that is to be constituted? Will the present alignment of economic and social classes be restored, i.e., "constituted," after the "reduction"? Will there be rich egos, poor egos, assassins' egos, etc.? With such enormous power concentrated in the hands (or rather, mind) of an egological phenomenologist, would it not be a good idea to miss certain essences, in the constitutive process? This is not too fantastic, in view of some of the claims made for the subjectivistic procedure. Might it not have been well to miss the constitution of the Nazi essence? But that would avail little, until the time when it is shown how matters of fact can be controlled through essences, by an "inner" process. Husserl's claims concerning "eidetic necessities" which "underlie" and condition actualities must be carefully reassessed in the light of the present questions, which will aid, it is to be hoped, in once more reminding subjectivistic methodologists that they are engaged in an ancillary mode of inquiry, which may well prove to be of real practical and theoretical value, but will never ("essentially," one is almost tempted to say, without presuming to invoke the appropriate "insight") displace the naturalistic methods as the gateway to the primary elements for all inquiry, empirical or "pure."

## E.  NOESIS AND NOEMA

### 1. Concerning the Study of Intentional Experience

It is easy to indicate what is meant by intentional experience in its general form, as "consciousness of something." More difficult is the understanding of the "phenomenological peculiarities of the corresponding essence."

Husserl speaks of a vast field of "toilsome determinations," and he is aware of the unsympathetic attitude toward "eidetic" results, on the part of the majority of philosophers and psychologists. For his part, Husserl enjoins the student not only to adopt the right standpoint with a complete absence of prejudice, but also to be "unconcerned about all current and acquired theories." They are to be disregarded in accordance with the ideal of "freedom from prejudgments." It is as though all non-phenomenologists were useless. But not only by definition, for Husserl once remarked, with deep conviction, that "all other philosophers of the world deserve to be deposited on a junk-heap." His feeling of aloneness, accented to an extreme degree by his severely rigorous standards, led him furthermore, to state, after the appearance of the sixth volume of his *Yearbook,* that nothing in them with the exception of his own initial contribution (the *Ideas,* Vol. I), was worth anything. It is of interest to recall contributions by Scheler in the early volumes, in this connection.

## 2. Immanent and Intentional Factors of Experience; the Noema

It is incumbent on the phenomenologist to provide an analysis of all the factors in intentional experience, as well as an account of the intended or meant objectivities— i.e., in his language, the "noetic" and the "noematic" sides of the experiences. Husserl speaks of the "immanent" (*"reelle"*) components of the experiences. *"Reelle"* is a convenient term. It really means "immanent." But it serves to preserve an ontological illusion.

"From the natural point of view," Husserl writes, "the apple-tree is something that exists in the transcendent reality of space." But this is also *really* the case; it is true in fact—assuming the confirming evidence. Husserl is concerned, however, about the fact that in certain cases, in such an experience-situation, it may be that the perception is a 'mere hallucination,' " so that the apple tree does not exist in "actual" reality. That seldom happens, and it is very easy to overestimate the importance of such "false" experiences. The "possibility" that it may happen is not enough to depreciate the "natural point of view."

### 3. Noematic Statements and Statements Concerning Reality

Husserl's distinction between "noematic statements" and "statements concerning reality" is clearly drawn. "The *tree simply,* the thing in nature, is anything but this *perceived tree* as such, which as a perceptual meaning belongs inseparably to the perception." It is reassuring to have Husserl observe that "the tree simply" can burn away, but not the meaning of *this* perception, which "belongs necessarily to its essence," for it has no chemical elements or real properties. That is what one can say of *fictions,* which is really what we are concerned with in our artificial phenomenological procedure.

Husserl asserts that "the phenomenological reduction can gain for the psychologist the useful methodical function of fixing the noematic meaning in sharp distinction from the object simply, and of recognizing it as belonging inseparably to the purely psychological essence (apprehended then as real) of the intentional experience." How this may really be useful for psychology must of course be shown in detail. In principle, every "eidetic" finding is translatable into real conditions, with the appropriate change of the "attitude," or the point of view.

## 4. The "Noematic Meaning" and the Distinction between "Immanent" and "Real" Objects

Every intentional experience has its "intentional object," or its "objective meaning." This is essential to experience, to the "noetic." Causal analysis is of course excluded. Otherwise one could ask for the conditions making "meaning-giving" possible. The goal is to give a "faithful description of that which is really present in phenomenological purity, and in keping off all interpretations that transcend the given." In the present context, the "given" is used in a narrow sense, in keeping with the positivistic character of the inquiry.

As repeatedly pointed out, the phenomenologist does not posit "real" things, or "transcendent" nature as a whole. But Husserl makes it clear that, if we do not place ourselves on the ground of natural things, we do not for that reason cast them away: "they are there to be sure; and they belong essentially to the phenomenon."

With the "reduction" performed, one sees that perception has its "noematic meaning," its "perceived as such," "this tree blossoming out there in space." That is to say, the *correlate* of the reduced perception. One can still say that "perception is the consciousness *of* a reality," if the thesis thereof is not allowed to be operative, just as one can describe this "perceptually appearing reality as such." The reader is warned, once more, not to put into the experience anything which is not included in the essence.

If the things are not there as "real," they are preserved in a special sense, as "reduced"— only it is no longer "they" about which one may speak. It takes Husserl a long time to state his case, too long a time. That suggests ulterior philosophical motives, and already present commitments, which are occasionally brought to light.

When he is not disturbed by such motives, and is concerned solely by descriptive studies, e.g., in his discussion of noesis and noema in connection with judgment, and in the spheres of sentiment and will, Husserl is at his best. Reminding himself of the fact that phenomenology is a science *in its beginnings,* he leaves it to the future to show how many of the results of the analyses undertaken by him are conclusive. Without divulging the source of his information, he declares that much of what he has described will surely be described differently, *sub specie aeterni.* In a spirit quite different from the claims to "necessity and universality" made earlier, Husserl concludes his brief declaration of humility with the admission that further research may call for new descriptions with manifold improvements, and that he proposes to preserve the habit of inner freedom also with respect to his own descriptions. Obviously, there is no unbridled claim—at this point at least—to the "certainty" and "perfection" of "inner" description. Also obvious by now is the fact that no one, unified version of Husserl's thought is possible.

## 5. "Doxic" (Belief) Modalities as Modifications

In the analysis of the noetic and noematic sides of experience, Husserl considers the various modifications of belief and their correlates. The "certainty of belief" plays the part of the unmodified, or the "unmodalized" root-form of belief. Corresponding to it, as its correlate, is the "being-character simply," which functions as "the root-form of all modalities of being." "All the being-characters which spring from it . . . have in their own meaning a backward reference to the root-form." Thus, the "possible" is a "being possible," the "probable" a "being probable," etc. In other words, "the intentionality of the noeses" is reflected in the noematic relations, which run "parallel" to the noetic side. Are these modalities really modifications of "being"? Is it sound usage to speak of them as "being," in any sense? It would be better to avoid such usage, recognizing that all the distinctions made are entirely peculiarities of experience, affairs of knowledge, and degrees of evidence.

Husserl points out that the term "certain" refers ambiguously to the noetic and the noematic side of "being certain." The question must be considered, however, whether there really is a difference of meaning on the noematic side, and whether we are being deceived by language. "Being certain," as the correlate of a judgmental certainty, may be no more than a linguistic expression, or a vacuous reference. Husserl's formulation of his view should be considered carefully in the light of this challenge: Every change of noetic characters constitutes new noematic characters, and "therewith *eo ipso new ontical objects (Seinsobjekte)* are constituted for consciousness." The expression "new ontical objects" must be viewed with misgivings. With sufficient usage, it seems to take on a reality of its own. "Ontical" is a slippery term, a presumptive epithet with an already unsavory past. There is the standing danger that when such terms roll off the tongues of philosophers, not only they, but their hearers, may think that something has been said about real being. It would be far better to speak of "quasi-being," an expression used by Husserl in his discussion of the "Neutrality-Modification of Being."

## 6. The Founded Noeses and Their Correlates

There are above all two things to be noted in connection with Husserl's noetic-noematic terminology, with its correlative gradations. (1) On the positive side, it is advantageous to consider the meaning-objects of all types of experience—for perception, phantasy, wishing, willing, etc. The universal field of experience is taken *in toto,* and "what is meant as such" is classified as the perceived as such, the phantasied as such, etc. (2) In the interest of a constitutive transcendental phenomenology, it is tempting to speak of "being" in connection with the "noematic correlates," and of "modifications of being." (1) is justifiable, in keeping with the descriptive function of phenomenology. (2) illustrates the illicit introduction of dogmas in the phenomenological precedure, and the very usage is to be viewed with caution.

Husserl carries the "universal double theme of noesis and noema" over to what he calls "the founded noeses and their noematic correlates." The affective, appetitive, and volitional noeses are based on presentations, perceptions, memories, symbols, etc. With new noetic phases, new noematic phases also appear. New meanings are constituted, and with them are constituted qualities of value, or concrete objectified values: beauty and ugliness, goodness and badness, works of art, books, etc. The "valuable," the "pleasing," etc. are similar in function to the "possible," "probable," etc. The "valuable" can be "doxically posited" as being valuable. The "being" belonging to the "valuable" as its characterization can furthermore be thought of as modalized, so that the consciousness may then be a consciousness of "possible value." Or we may be aware of it as "probably valuable," or as "not-valuable" (which is not the same as "valueless"— the cancellation of the "valuable" is simply expressed in the "not-valuable"). Such modifications inwardly affect the consciousness of value, the valuing noeses, and this also applies to the noematic correlates. The phenomenologist asks, how "formative syntheses of value" are related to those of fact, how the new noematic characterizations (good, beautiful, etc.) stand to the modalities of belief, how they group themselves systematically in series and divisions, etc.

A question to be raised here is, whether the problems of the phenomenologist really interest us in connection with value theory. It must be ascertained whether the undeniable usefulness of phenomonology for problems of the theory of knowledge can be carried over to the theory of value. What can be gained by the study of "founded noeses and their noematic correlates"? Description *per se* is not necessarily valuable, or even interesting. Not that any sort of description should be forbidden: it is an important principle, to be violated at our peril, that all conceivable types of inquiry be open to investigators. It would be unwise to insist on limiting inquiry exclusively to what has practical application. In fact, it could be argued, with reference to the cognitive enterprise as a whole, that the most practical course would be to set "practice" aside. It need not be possible to predict whether any specimen of pure, conceptual research (or, indeed, at times, of empirical inquiry) will ever have a rewarding practical application.

In view of these considerations, it would be remote from the present writer's thought to discourage any type of phenomonological description. But it does seem pertinent to observe that Husserl has, after all, a limited method, and that the tune which comes out for values is just like the subjective music, already droned out, with its essences, noetic syntheses, and noematic correlates. If pursued descriptively, such inquiry may help to provide an additional dimension of clarification to the naturalistic treatment of value and fact. On the other hand, the major value problems of our time may be stated, understood, and possibly solved, without waiting for the phenomenological clarifications. It will be sufficient at this time to mention such problems as capital and labor, war and peace, and the individual and society. It would be a sad thing, if agreement among philosophers on "timeless" fundamentals were prerequisite to the solution of the great problems of mankind. The world might well go to ruin before even an appreciable minority got to the second underpass in the "reduction."

The recognition of the merit of a descriptive phenomenological approach to value-experience does not, of course, commit us to a universal constitutive idealism. Husserl's approach is clearly narrow, as when he states that we become aware of value in valuing, of the pleasant in pleasure, and of the joyous in rejoicing. In his view, all acts generally, including the acts of feeling and will, are "objectifying" acts, "constituting" objects "originally." They are, moreover, "the necessary sources of different regions of being and of the ontologies that belong therewith." Thus, the valuing consciousness constitutes over against the "mere material world" the new kind of "axiological" objectivity, a "being" of a new region.

Clearly, the reflection concerning value which is made possible by Husserl's approach —"we become aware of value in valuing," etc.—is radically different from the objective type of reflection. One might well be "aware" of value, which could be just the opposite from the standpoint of objective reflection. To describe how one "lives in" his value experiences (and that essentially only) is not to determine the status of the "valuable" in the light of a system of values, individual or social. For the rest, it must be observed that no good is likely to result from the talk of "necessary sources of being," and of consciousness constituting a new "axiological" objectivity, a "being" of a new region. It is a misleading kind of jargon which could at best be a relatively harmless misfortune.

Husserl does not hesitate to inform the reader, and to remind him at intervals, that phenomenology is a very difficult field for inquiry, and that there is no royal road to it. As he once expressed it, the royal road to phenomenology is the "tedious" road. He has unfortunately done little to justify a denial of that judgment. Added to his plodding, extremely painstaking type of inquiry was the circumstance, of which he was aware, that his skill in literary expression suffered through the years. He seldom presented his ideas as effectively in his mature years as he had done in his early period. Without a doubt he could have done so. But he was more concerned with expressing his nascent ideas quickly, and with completing as much as possible of the "infinite" work unfolded to him by his peculiar mode of approach to philisophy. As a powerful and virtually autonomous professor of philosophy (a *Geheimrat,* a title conferred by the first *Reich,* which he prized) and department head, Husserl was able to confine himself largely to intellectual relations with his subordinates and students, with most of his time available for his own meditations and productive work. It is small wonder, then, that a highly specialized vocabulary and an ingrown development should result, leaving for posterity a perpetual problem of interpretation.

## F.  REASON AND REALITY

### 1. Object and Consciousness

Husserl asks pointedly a question which occurs repeatedly to all readers, whether the *object itself is real,* and whether it could not be unreal, even with "intuitionally fulfilled theses." The answer is, that he is not interested in the fact-world of consciousness; the interest of the phenomenologist is restricted to problems of essence. The conscious subject passes judgments about reality, and asks questions about it. The point is, then, to examine this process, "and, correlatively, the essence of 'reality,' within the essence-connections of transcendental consciousness." He asks, what "real" means for objects which are only given through meanings and "positings." He should have said: for objects which are *taken to be* "given" in that way, for a radically reflective inquiry. As Husserl expresses it, an object, "whether it is real or not," is "constituted" within certain connections of consciousness. He points out that questions concerning reality are also to be found in phenomenology, which relates to the possible constitution of objects. Husserl asks the question at issue clearly enough: When is the noematically "meant" identity of an object (of an "x") "real identity," instead of being "merely" meant; and what does this "merely meant" mean? This leads to the consideration of the problems of reality, and the correlative rational consciousness, to the "Phenomenology of Reason."

## 2. Phenomenology of Reason

It is possible to answer the question concerning reality within the frame of phenomenology by indicating what conditions must be present. There must be insight, and evidence in the sense of "self-evidence," or of the "bodily" presence of the meant objectivity. It is necessary to distinguish between adequate and inadequate evidence, because a real thing can only appear "inadequately," within the limits of a "closed" appearance. It follows, in the case of inadequate evidence, that one may not say simply that a thing is "real." It can only be said on the supposition that the further course of experience does not bring on the "cancellation" of the original positing.

It is not possible to say more in principle about "reality" in phenomenology. The factual question of determining reality in this or that case does not fall to an "essential" procedure. The various structures and relationships involved are to be outlined, of course. Thus, what it means to have complete evidence, or partial evidence, are relevant questions for phenomenology. The question of the *application* of essential structures and laws to empirical situations can be handled in two ways: by "naturalistic" procedures subject to future modification; or by way of a "pure" ontology, which, although it is restricted to essences, is supposed by Husserl to condition the occurrence of "possible" facts. This approach will be considered later, in connection with the argument set forth in the third volume of Husserl's *Ideas*.

Under the heading (§ 142) of "The Thesis of Reason and Being," Husserl formulates a principle of "equivalence" as follows: "To every object 'that truly is' there corresponds on principle (in the *a priori* of unconditioned essential generality) the *idea of a possible consciousness* in which the object itself can be grasped in an originary and *perfectly adequate* way. Conversely, when this possibility is guaranteed, the object is *eo ipso* something which 'truly is.'" The question is, however, how much is to be read into this "correspondence." The talk of the "correspondence on principle" of a "possible consciousness," along with the "*a priori*," is calculated to set the scene for an ontology with far-reaching significance. The "correlative" point of view is equipped to become in due course an effective subject-object limitation of all reality, in the sense of the actual reality of natural experience. That Husserl's interest and ultimate intention is the achievement of a universal philosophy is indicated clearly enough here, as well as elsewhere. Thus, he states that phenomenology really encompasses the whole natural world, and also all the ideal worlds it suspends; it encompasses them as "world-meaning" through the essential laws which connect objective meaning and noema with the closed system of the noeses, and especially through the rationally ordered essential connections, whose correlate is 'real object'. . . ." This accords with Husserl's statement that the concept which in its scope covers phenomenology in its entirety is "intentionality," which "expresses the fundamental property of consciousness." Its scope is as wide as all possible conscious experience.

### 3. Pure Logic and Phenomenology

Formal or "pure" logic, "dogmatically" treated, does not reach the level of phenomenological inquiry (§ 147). It "grasps through abstraction the apophantic forms" (proposition, categorical, hypothetical, etc.) and establishes axioms of formal truth for them. But it "knows nothing of analytic synthesis, of essential relations, noetic and noematic, of the ordering within the essence-complexes of pure consciousness of the essences . . . extracted and conceptually determined. . . . It is *phenomenology*, which, by going back to the sources of intuition in transcendentally purified consciousness, makes it clear to us what is really meant by the 'formal conditions of truth,' or knowledge. . . ." A distinction corresponding to the correlation between noesis and noema is made. In the syllogism, for example, judgments are viewed as noematic propositions, and their "formal truth" is of interest to us. In formal apophantic noetics we are concerned with correctness of the judging process, and standards of correctness are formulated. There is the principle, for example, that one cannot maintain that a contradiction is true; he who judges in accordance with the forms of premises of the valid inferential moods "must" draw the conclusions proper to the corresponding forms, and so forth. Husserl states that these parallels are at once intelligible when considered in the context of phenomenology. The term "must" is placed in quotation marks by Husserl, when he states that a conclusion proper to the corresponding forms "must" be drawn. Is it to straddle the obvious question that is at issue? Are we talking about psychical realities after all? The term "must" has no significance otherwise. Or is it that we are simply to determine the essence of the "must"? The answer is clear enough: compulsion in a naturalistic sense is as remote as the "certainty" which cannot be hoped for. But is it possible to legislate for the facts by means of essential (or analytic) determinations? *That must be shown.*

But it is not the task of phenomenology to develop mathematics, syllogistic exercises, etc. The axioms and their conceptual content are appropriate subject matter for its analyses. The repeated insistence on this point shows how much concerned Husserl was to distinguish phenomenology from formal logic and mathematics. But the reader will be sure to ask whether there are fixed "axioms."

### 4. Regional Ontologies and Phenomenological Constitution

Husserl states that every object-region consciously *(bewusstseinsmässig)* constitutes itself (§ 149). If he is not to cut himself off completely from all independently thinking readers, he must make it clear whether every object-region *really* "constitutes itself consciously." If he is talking about a deliberately instituted procedure, or way of looking at all things, his language should make that clear. But if he is presuming to talk about the *nature of things,* he must be prepared to justify what is so strikingly an unwarranted idealistic dogma. With such a commitment, there is added significance to the statement that "an object determined through the regional genus has, as such, so far as it is real, its modes of being perceptible, . . . conceivable, exhibitable, predelineated *a priori.*" The degree of "determination through the regional genus" may be sufficient to "predelineate" a great deal *"a priori."* But it may also be merely an outline of the *possible* modes that is listed, with all distinctions of type and degree credited to the "region."

Taking the region "material thing" as a "clue," Husserl states the problem of the general "constitution" of the objectivities of the region "thing" in the transcendental consciousness as the theme of a great phenomenological discipline. Expressed more briefly, it is the problem "of the phenomenological constitution of a thing in general." The term "constitution" requires careful handling. It may be taken literally, as referring to the structure of something, to the way in which it is "constituted" in the sense of being "made up." Or, it may refer to the activity involved in building something up, say a synthetic activity, with an identifying function. It would be better to restate Husserl's formulation of the problem of general "constitution," as it now speaks of the constitution "in" the transcendental consciousness. Strictly speaking, there is no such thing as being "in" consciousness of any kind. It should be said, rather, that, as viewed reflectively, one sees how a "thing" becomes an object of conscious experience, as a unity, etc.

Among the examples of "things" given by Husserl are winged steeds and golden mountains. "These would also be things," he states, and presentations of them serve just as well as presentations of things of real experience, for purposes of exemplification. But it may be misleading to call them *things*. They are "objects of thought." Furthermore, the "region" of "things" is not as useful as, say, the region of "physical events," or a region of "cultural objects." Of course, one could speak of a region of "perceptual objects," as a point of departure for further inquiry.

Husserl points out that the essence "thing" is "originarily given," but that this givenness cannot be adequate. As he stated it in another connection, perception is essentially incomplete; and an all-sided perception is simply unthinkable. But an "inadequate" insight into the essence is always obtainable. Husserl declares it to be a general essential insight "that every imperfect givenness contains within itself a rule for the ideal possibility of its perfecting." Thus, "it belongs to the essence of the centaur-appearance which I now have—an appearance which gives the essence of the centaur merely one-sidedly—that I follow out the different sides of the thing. . . ." The talk of *"ideal possibility"* takes away the force of an objection to it. But why speak of a "rule"? There is nothing in the nature of things that can be proved to be a "rule," to allow for more perfect "givenness." Empirically, one is likely to seek more information. But, also empirically, one might stop at any given stage of incompleteness, and no "rule" need impel him to go further, or to set his phantasy to work.

Husserl does indeed ask the right question: "But what does this talk about a rule or law mean phenomenologically?" His answer is: "To the essence of such a thing-noema there belong, and this is absolutely insightful, ideal possibilities of 'limitlessness in the continuation' of harmonious intuitions. . . ." But he does not tell us how we know that this is "absolutely insightful." That could only be assured analytically, as following from definitions and assumptions, which would require a different mode of statement. It is in Husserl's view "an essential insight that *every* perception . . . is capable of being extended," so that the process is endless. Accordingly no intuitive apprehension of the essence of a thing could be so complete as to prevent further perceptions from bringing something "noematically" new. The reader will be inclined to point out that this could be said as a matter of fact, and that all *known* cases are such that the incompleteness of the known permits of being supplemented by further experience. It would appear, then, that the formulation of this fact in terms of essences is merely a way of borrowing empirical facts and outfitting them as "essential necessities," expressing "rules."

The incompleteness of an experience is described by Husserl as "an 'and so forth' which is an absolutely indispensable factor in the thing-noema"; and this is held to be "insightful." Very much needed at this point is a satisfactory account of the meaning and criteria of "insight." It would also be pertinent to know just who the "we" are who have this "insight," and whether there may not be exceptions.

Husserl assures the reader that what he is developing here is not "theory" or "metaphysics." He is purportedly restricting himself to "essential necessities" of the thing-noema and the "thing-giving consciousness," with everything "to be apprehended insightfully." That is a good requirement, with only two difficulties: how can you know when it is realized; and how can you make it a general requirement for all knowers? Husserl would be forced to restate his entire position in terms of analytic knowledge, formal and non-formal. What he describes as "essential necessities indissolubly involved in the thing-noema" must, however, be shown to be "indissolubly involved" *as a matter of fact.* Otherwise, there could be no talk of "necessities," there could be no binding statements, no "certainty."

## 5. The Region "Thing" as a Transcendental Clue

As Husserl expresses it, the intuition of a thing as such (with respect to noesis and noema) "comprises infinities within itself." The English edition of the *Ideas* reads "conceals infinities." It would be better not to use the word "conceals," however, for that puts one in the position of "revealing" what is concealed, and that is bad for anyone, especially a philosopher.

The regional Idea of a thing is said by Husserl to prescribe rules for the manifolds of appearances, to prescribe series of appearances that are determinate, definitely ordered, and progressing *in infinitum,* and, taken as an ideal totality, firmly closed. It could not be said *factually* that rules are prescribed. All that can be said is that some kinds of series are to be observed.

But Husserl does not hesitate to place the exponent of natural experience on the defensive. The reader is asked to consider what the "phenomenologically naïve" take to be "mere facts." Thus, a spatial thing always appears to "us humans" in a certain "orientation," as right or left, near or far; and we see a thing only at a certain "distance." Such "alleged factualities" *(Faktizitäten),* "contingencies of spatial perception which are foreign to the 'true,' 'objective' space, show themselves . . . to be essential necessities." Even God, described by Husserl as the ideal representative of absolute knowledge, cannot alter the truth that whatever has the character of a spatial thing can only be intuited through appearances.

All that Husserl has done here is to take over what is seen "contingently," the "alleged facts." Now, in pure reflection, they are viewed as essential necessities. There is danger, however, that the language used will obscure the nature of the change from real facts to conceptual forms. This is well illustrated by the use of the term "origin." The problem of the "origin of the presentation of space," which has a "deepest phenomenological meaning," is described as "the phenomenological analysis of the *essential* nature of all the noematic (as well as noetic) phenomena, in which space presents itself intuitionally and that which is spatial is 'constituted' as the unity of appearances, and of the descriptive modes of such presentation." The term "origin" is misused in this way. There are borrowed peacock feathers connected with its use, to which the non-naturalistic phenomenologist is not entitled.[9]

---

9. The term "origin" is used in connection with the brief study of the "origin of geometry" by Husserl. Cf. E. Husserl, "Die Frage nach dem Ursprung der Geometrie als intentional-historisches Problem," in *Revue International de Philosophie*, Brussels, Vol. I, No. 2, Jan., 1939, with a preface by Eugen Fink; and the review of this article by Dorion Cairns in *Philosophy and Phenomenological Research*, Vol. I, No. 1, Sept., 1940. One can indeed carry through an analysis going from the simple to the complex without regard to the question of actual history. This is also illustrated in Husserl's studies of the basic logical ideas in his *Experience and Judgment* (*Erfahrung und Urteil*, pp. 94 ff.). The "original phenomenon of negation" is described by Husserl as a phenomenon of "suspension." It is illustrated by means of outer perception, but can also be shown in all cases of "positional" consciousness. Negation is not a matter of predicative judgment first of all;

( Footnote continued on next page.)

The very important term "constitution," like "origin" is affected by ambiguity. The problem of "constitution" is defined by Husserl as meaning that "the regulated series of appearances, *necessarily* belonging together within the unity of an appearing object, can be intuitionally surveyed and theoretically conceived." The point is to analyze and describe them "in their own eidetic peculiarity." The descriptive analysis will, in Husserl's view, remove all "riddles" (the English edition reads "and so disrobed of all its mysteries") from the correlation between the appearing object as unity, and the infinite multiplicities of appearances. Of course, there never were any "mysteries," and this term might well be added to "concealment," "revealment," and even "profundity," for a special linguistic *epoché,* so much needed by the phenomenological movement. There were, however, standpoint and "methogenic" difficulties, due either to a fixed point of view, with ontological commitments, or to the adoption

---

it already appears in its "primal" form in the pre-predicative sphere of receptive experience. It can be *seen* how belief conflicts with belief. The conflict consists in the peculiar "suspension" of an anticipatory intention, an expectation through a new impression, for which "disappointment" is another expression. Consider an example in which disappointment enters in, instead of the fulfillment of an intention. Suppose that an object appearing to be a uniformly red sphere is seen. For a time the course of perception is such that this apprehension is harmoniously fulfilled. Then, when one gets to the other side, he notes that it is *not* red, but green. There is a *conflict* between the still living intentions and the sense-contents now appearing. The new objective sense "green" in its impressional power of fulfillment has "certainty in primal force," which overcomes the certainty of the "pre-expectation" of being red. "Negation" is described as a modification of consciousness, as a partial "crossing out" on the ground of a certainty of belief, ultimately on the ground of the universal world-belief. "Doubt" as a mode of consciousness is regarded as a transitional "modus" to the negating suspension. The consciousness of possibility and other types of experience are similarly described.

of a particular procedure, with its own attendant difficulties.

The "constitution" of things as unities in "manifolds" on the level of the experiencing intuition is to be "completely illuminated." That is to lead, finally, to the "perfect insight into *what the Idea of a real thing represents in the phenomenologically pure consciousness,* how it is the absolutely necessary correlate of a structurally investigated and essentially described noetic-noematic connection." This is to tie down the Idea of the real thing to the context of consciousness. Even if one allows the Idea to be placed in that context, that is not to tie down the real thing. Even so, one should greet with caution the admission that the Idea is restricted to the context of consciousness. How much is admitted thereby? To an idealist, perhaps everything is granted thereby; but not to a naturalist, in any one of the varieties of the term "naturalism." For the rest, it may be gleaned how fixed the habit can become, to speak of connections as "absolutely necessary." That is especially likely if, as Royce remarked, the philosopher is like the rhinoceros, in that he walks by himself. The self-reflection required to meet such dangers is very difficult to achieve; and outside help is to be encouraged.

## 6. Constitution in Other Regions

It is not only things that are "constituted." The analysis carries over to "all object-regions." Since "thing" means "thing of experience" or "experienced thing," it is not something isolated from the experiencing subject. The experiencing subject itself is "constituted in experience as something real, as *man* or *animal,* just as the *intersubjective communities* are constituted as animal communities."

Although these communities are "essentially founded on psychical realities," which are themselves founded on the physical, they are seen to be "objectivities of a higher order." Husserl asserts that "it can be seen quite generally that there are many kinds of objectivities which defy all psychologistic and naturalistic interpretations *(Umdeutungen)*." Examples given include objects bearing a value, practical objects, and cultural organizations such as the State, the Church, and the law. These objectivities are to be described "in the way in which they come to be presented, . . . and in their proper order of formation, and the problems of phenomenological constitution set and solved for them."

Quite characteristic is the way in which Husserl rules out all naturalistic *interpretation.* It would have to be proved that a "naturalistic" account of the "consitution" of the "State," in *its* sense of "constitution," unavoidably leaves anything out, or falsifies in any way.

Husserl allows "material reality," as the lowest formation, to remain "finally the foundation of all other realities." But the "founded unities," if referred back phenomenologically to their "sources," are "new in kind"; and the new factors which are "constituted" can never be reduced "to the mere sum of other realities." How does Husserl know that? He reveals his source: this was learned from "essential intuition." The reference to the phenomenological "sources" as being in experience calls attention to another case of special usage, with its disturbing ambiguity. As for the apparently "solid earth" type of admission, that the phenomenology of material nature is in a sense fundamental, Husserl can well afford to make it. This stratum is to be "constituted" anyway, well within the secure frame of transcendental subjectivity.

**7. The Full Extension of the Transcendental Problem**

Husserl refers to the sequel to the present work for a discussion of the mutual relation of natural science, psychology, and cultural science, and of their relation to phenomenology. He regards the controversies about the cultural sciences as dealing with really serious problems. Along with Rickert and the others who were so strongly interested in the controversies, Husserl is opposed to the same enemy, naturalism. The aim was to "contain" the enemy, to delimit his sphere of activity, and above all to keep the fields of value-thinking and pure thought free of naturalistic concepts and methods. Although fighting a common foe, Husserl had little use for the half-baked type of idealism of the antinaturalistic group. In his way, he stood alone.

The program of phenomenology is to be carried through universally, without any exceptions. All types of syntheses "in correlation with the synthetic objectivities 'constituted' within them are to be subjected to an inquiry with the object of clarifying the different modes of givenness and their significance for the 'real being' of such objectivities, or for their veritable possible being or their *really* probable being. . . ." Once more, it must be observed that the exact function (i.e., the initially professed function) of phenomenology must be kept in mind. "Real being" as determined by scientific analysis is not to be touched by phenomenological analysis. It must also be shown how the latter can approach the question of "probable being," which is a "naturalistic" affair. Few people would prefer to exchange an infinity of "veritable possible being" for their own finite share of "probable being." The honorific usage is confusing; and it, too, should fall to the linguistic *epoché* which has been proposed.

In conclusion, Husserl states clearly that "the phenomenologist does not judge ontologically when he recognizes
an ontological concept or proposition as an index for
constitutive essence-connections. . . ." That should be
remembered. If it is not to be "founded" on the formal
and material ontologies, neither should it arrogate to
itself the power reserved only for theology: to make something out of nothing. It must always be borne in mind:
out of pure consciousness, only pure consciousness can
come, not an ontology, and above all not the natural
world.

*Chapter V*

# PHENOMENOLOGY
# AND
# NATURALISTIC PSYCHOLOGY

## A. ANTINATURALISM IN THE NAME OF RIGOROUS SCIENCE

### 1. The Motive of Antinaturalism

The antinaturalistic motivation of Husserl is clearly indicated in his *Logos* essay, "Philosophy as a Rigorous Science."[1] It takes the form of an attack on the philosophical potentialities of the sciences of nature. As Husserl states it, "To exercise radical criticism of the naturalistic philosophy is nowadays an important matter." The attempt by Husserl to expose the weakness and untenableness of "naturalistic philosophy" proves to be rather commonplace; and the attempt at a rapid dialectical refutation leaves everything to be desired.

Naturalism is portrayed as a consequence of the discovery of nature, of nature in the sense of a unity of spatial-temporal being, and as determined by exact natural laws. With the progressive realization of this idea, naturalism extends its range. The naturalist sees nothing except nature, and to begin with, physical nature. Everything

---

1. Logos, Vol. I, 1910-1911, #3, "Philosophie als strenge Wissenschaft." Referring to the critics of phenomenology, in the third volume of his *Ideen*, p. 45 (published in 1952 by Martinus Nijhoff, Haag), Husserl states that he has nothing else to say on the matter at issue, than what the *Logos* essay had said, perhaps too conditionally.

that exists is either itself physical, or it is psychical, but then only as a dependent variable, and at most a secondary "parallel concomitant fact." All forms of extreme and consistent naturalism, from the popular type of materialism to the most recent monism of sensation and energetism, in Husserl's view, are characterized by two consequences. On the one hand, they "naturalize" consciousness; and, on the other hand, they "naturalize" Ideas, and therewith all absolute ideals and norms.

Husserl argues that naturalism refutes itself, without being aware of it. Choosing formal logic as an example of all ideality, he recalls the interpretation of the formal-logical principles as laws of thought. At this point he is satisfied to refer to the criticism published a decade earlier in his *Logical Investigations*.[2] He believes that he had established the fact that absurdity follows from the naturalistic interpretation of the principles of logic, just as is the case for skepticism. Husserl asserts that naturalistic axiology, including ethics, can be subjected to a similar radical criticism, and similarly the naturalistic practice itself, with resultant absurdities. The naturalist is, Husserl finds it convenient to allow, in his attitude an idealist and an objectivist. He strives to determine scientifically what genuine truth, beauty, and goodness are essentially, regardless of the method by which individual cases are established. Through natural science and natural-scientific philosophy, he believes in the main to have achieved the goal, and with enthusiasm he defends the "natural-scientific" true, good, and beautiful as a teacher and practical reformer. But he is an idealist, who sets up and supposedly establishes theories, which negate that which he presupposes in his idealistic attitude, whether it be in construc-

2. Cf. M. Farber, *The Foundation of Phenomenology*, Cambridge, Harvard University Press, 1943.

ting theories, or in establishing and recommending values or practical norms. The naturalist teaches, preaches, moralizes, reforms. Haeckel and Ostwald are cited as eminent representatives, in this connection. But, Husserl argues, the naturalist denies what every sermon, every demand as such presupposes with respect to its meaning. Only he does not preach like ancient skepticism, in its denial of reason—theoretical, axiological, and practical. Indeed, he would reject the skepticism. It is Husserl's contention that the absurdity is concealed from the naturalist, because he naturalizes reason. Husserl believes the controversy to be decided really, even if positivism and pragmatism may gain still more in prominence. Prejudices cause one to be blind, he muses; and if one sees only facts of natural experience and recognizes only sciences of natural experience, he will not feel very much disturbed by absurd consequences, which cannot be shown in experience to be contradictions of facts of nature. He is likely to push them aside as "scholasticism."

In his criticism of naturalism, here and elsewhere, Husserl has firm confidence in the widely admired "Prolegomena" to his *Logical Investigations*. His critique of "psychologism" and his general style of disposing of "skepticism" have not been sufficiently challenged. The extreme form of skepticism was disposed of long ago; it did not have to wait for the *Logical Investigations*. It is doubtful, in any case, whether anyone ever took it seriously, and it was already an aged and much refuted position when Albertus Magnus pointed out the impossibility of denying all truth. Husserl's *ad hominem* attack on the naturalists really proves nothing, and is certainly not a proof of absurdity. There does not have to be a self-contradiction. One should not argue assumptively, with "idealized" scientific principles injected into the naturalistic position. Husserl introduces a rationalistic ideal of scientific laws, represented by the ideal principles of formal logic. But such *"a priori"* (universal and necessary) principles are not the only model which the natural scientist has in mind. With the conception of laws as "probable," he is in no danger of contradicting himself. He is not to be forced into the position of "exact" principles in the sense of ideal laws, in order to be a ready target for the charge of self-contradiction. Moreover, it is misleading to stigmatize as "skepticism" the position that all empirical knowledge is probable. "Probabilism" would be a less question-begging term, and would be consonant with the positive character of the position.

## 2. Circumscribing Naturalistic Psychology

The question of the status of scientific psychology was crucial at the time. Husserl was concerned with circumscribing its validity, as a naturalistic discipline, and with instating "pure" ("eidetic") psychology as a necessary foundation for empirical psychology.

Psychology is not suited, as a factual science, to provide the foundations for the philosophical disciplines concerned with providing norms, including pure logic, pure axiology, and "practics." In Husserl's view, such a position would lead to skeptical absurdities, which he has been endeavoring to expose and refute. Distinguishing theory of knowledge from pure logic in the sense of the pure *mathesis universalis,* he gives some indication of the nature of his objections against epistemological psychologism and physicalism.

All natural science is "naïve" in its point of departure, Husserl argues characteristically. The nature which it investigates is simply there for it. There are things in infinite space and time, which we perceive and describe. It is the goal of natural science to know them in an objectively valid and rigorously scientific manner. The same is true of nature in an extended psychophysical sense, and of the sciences investigating it, especially psychology. The psychical is not a world for itself. It is given as an ego or ego-experience, bound to certain physical things called bodies. That is taken to be a "self-evident givenness." To investigate scientifically the psychical, in a psychophysical context of nature, to discover the laws of its formation and transformation—that is the task of psychology. Even where psychology, the empirical science, is concerned with the determination of mere occurrences of consciousness and not with psychophysical dependencies, these occurrences are thought of as belonging to nature, i.e., to human or animal consciousnesses, regarded as having a self-evident connection with human or animal bodies. Accordingly, every psychological judgment includes in itself the existential positing of physical nature, whether that is explicit or not. The exclusion of the relation to nature would take away from the psychical the character of being an objective temporal fact of nature.

In Husserl's view, if there are decisive arguments which show that physical natural science cannot be philosophy in a specific sense, and can never serve as the basis of philosophy, then such arguments must also apply to psychology. He recalls the "naïveté" with which natural science takes over nature as "given," a naïveté which is "immortal" in it. Although natural science is admitted to be very critical in its way, it is Husserl's contention that quite a different kind of critique of experience is needed, in order to place in question all of experience and all empirical-scientific thinking.

This universal "placing in question" of all experience brings some of the central problems of the theory of knowledge before us. How experience, as consciousness, can give or meet with an object; how experiences can be corrected by experiences, and not be merely annulled or strengthened subjectively; how a play of empirical-logical consciousness can state something objectively valid for independently existing things; why the rules of the game (so to speak) of consciousness are not irrelevant for the things; how natural science is to become intelligible in everything, if it presumes to posit and to know an independently existing nature at every step—independently existing as opposed to the subjective stream of consciousness—all that becomes a riddle, in Husserl's view, as soon as reflection is immanently directed upon it. Despite all the efforts of the foremost investigators in the theory of knowledge, these questions were not answered in a clear and decisive manner.

Husserl speaks of the absurdity of a "natural-scientific theory of knowledge," as well as of every psychological theory of knowledge. If there are "riddles of natural science" which are "immanent on principle," it would not seem reasonable to Husserl, to expect natural science to contribute to their solution. He thinks it clear that every scientific as well as prescientific positing of nature in a theory of knowledge must be excluded on principle. That means the suspension of all statements positing the existence of things with relations of space, time, causality, etc. This is extended to apply to all judgments of existence which concern the inquiring man and his psychical powers.

Furthermore, Husserl maintains that if the theory of knowledge wants to investigate the problems of the relationship of consciousness and being, then it can only have being as a correlate of consciousness in view, as something "meant" in accordance with consciousness, as something perceived, remembered, expected, believed, etc. The inquiry then becomes directed toward a science of the essence of consciousness, toward that which consciousness "is" essentially, in all its formations; but also toward that which it "signifies," as well as the different ways in which the formations occur as clear or unclear, presentative or representative, signitive or pictorial, "simple" or mediated by thought, in this or that attentional modus, and in countless other forms.

### 3. Toward a Phenomenology of Consciousness

It is the study of consciousness as a whole that is needed. If consciousness is always "consciousness of" something, the essential study of consciousness includes the essential study of what consciousness signifies, and its mode of givenness. This brings Husserl to speak of a new science, of whose prodigious extent his contemporaries had no idea, a science which is to be sure a science of consciousness and is nevertheless not psychology. His goal is a *phenomenology of consciousness,* in contrast to a *natural science of consciousness.* As was to be expected, phenomenology and psychology are closely related, since both are concerned with consciousness, even though in a different way, with a different "point of view." Psychology is concerned with "empirical" consciousness, viewed as something existing in the context of nature; whereas phenomenology is concerned with "pure" consciousness, under conditions to be defined carefully. If this is correct, Husserl argues, it must follow that psychology cannot be philosophy any more than physical natural science can be philosophy, even though psychology is closer to philosophy and intimately connected with it, through the medium of phenomenology.

But Husserl is quick to qualify his assertion that psychology is in any sense close to philosophy. That holds to a very small extent in the case of modern exact psychology. Disputing the claim that experimental psychology is *the* psychological science, Husserl protests against the "pushing aside" of every direct and pure analysis of consciousness, and of immanent description; and he calls attention to the "raw" class-concepts used, such as perception, statement, counting and reckoning, estimates of magnitude, recognition, expectation, forgetting, etc. In his view, experimental psychology is related to "originary" psychology, analogously to the way in which social statistics is related to "originary" social science. Social statistics collects valuable facts and discovers valuable regularities in them, "but of a very indirect kind." Their understanding and real explanation are to be accomplished by an "originary" social science, i.e., a social science which brings the sociological phenomena to direct givenness and investigates them with respect to their essence. Unfortunately, Husserl fails to give any examples of such phenomena. Unlike Rickert's failure to give any scientific illustrations, about which Husserl once wrote, that they were also not missed, it must be admitted that Husserl's present programmatic aims are disturbingly empty, without concrete reference. Husserl admits that the method of experimental psychology is valuable for the determination of psychophysical facts. But, he maintains, without the help of a systematic science of consciousness which investigates the psychical immanently, it misses the possibility of deeper understanding and conclusive scientific realization.

The correction of the defects of the method of self-observation by experimental psychology is not in question here. It is Husserl's contention that only a pure phenomenology can show the meaning and method of the work to be contributed. The experimental method is admitted to be indispensable where one is concerned with the fixing of intersubjective connections of facts. But it presupposes something that no experiment is able to contribute, the analysis of consciousness itself. This thesis is central in Husserl's critical stand on naturalistic scientific psychology.

To the extent to which the criticism of naturalistic psychology is concerned with the avoidance of narrowness in method, Husserl's case has merit. That is not to say that he argued his case in a completely defensible way. Overstatement is understandable, but not defensible, in an acrimonious controversy. Narrowness is apt to result, on both sides; and that is precisely what happened in this case. The rarefied atmosphere of "pure immanence" is greatly in need of the "raw materials" of natural experiences, and of the concrete findings of the psychological sciences. On the other hand, pure conceptual analysis and description should not be disregarded, any more than pure mathematics is disregarded by physical scientists. If the phenomenological findings are for the most part still very elementary in character, that is no reason for discouraging the further development of that discipline. It will be suspected, with right, that the "originary" sociological phenomena referred to by Husserl would prove to be quite primitive, and far removed from the dominant interests of the social scientists. That would be no reason, however, for invalidating descriptive results, which, if correct, are valid on any level of inquiry. Any claims concerning the importance of such inquiry must of course be justified by their application to natural experience.

If a better spirit of cooperation is to take the place of the present spirit of conflict, the phenomenologist must also be careful not to insist on completely "founding" psychology, or on providing it with understanding for the first time. The pure mathematician is not likely to display such arrogance in his relationship with physical scientists. The vested position of philosophy in the great tradition has been radically altered by the development of the sciences. It is not to be expected that phenomenology will reverse that trend, and build up a new rationalism on the basis of a transcendental science of essence. Due regard for his scientific colleagues, including even some partially unenlightened, intolerant individual representatives, should lead the phenomenologist to approach his chosen work with appropriate modesty and a sound feeling of cooperation. It does not help matters, to speak of the "experimental fanatics," who ignored the work of the few psychologists (like Stumpf and Lipps) appreciating the "epoch-making" significance of Brentano.

## 4. The Concept of a Phenomenon

Turning to the "world" of the "psychical," and restricting himself to the "psychical phenomena," which the new psychology regards as its object-domain, Husserl asks whether the objectivity of "nature" is contained in every perception of the psychical. If that is contained in the meaning of every physical experience, and every perception of things, is it also true in the case of psychical experience? The answer is, that the relationships in this sphere are entirely different than in the physical sphere. The psychical is described by Husserl as distributed (and this, he adds, is only a simile, not to be construed metaphysically) among monads, which do not have any windows and only enter into commerce through empathy. Psychical being, or being as a "phenomenon," is not a unity which could be experienced in separate perceptions as an identical something. In the psychical sphere, there is no difference between appearance and being. It is clear to Husserl, at this time, that there is really only one nature, which appears in the thing-appearances. Everything that he calls a psychical phenomenon in the broadest sense of psychology is, viewed in and for itself, just a phenomenon and not nature.

A phenomenon is thus no "substantial" unity, it has no "real properties," no real parts, no real changes, and no causality, in the natural-scientific sense of these terms. To investigate phenomena with respect to real determinations or causal connections would be absurd, and would be no better than asking about the real properties and causal connections of numbers. That would be the absurdity of the "naturalizing" of something whose essence excludes being as nature. It is interesting to record Husserl as stating that "nature is eternal." To be sure, this "early language" would be suitably reinterpreted within the frame of the transcendental phenomenology, now in the process of being developed. The objective determinations of the natural sciences are capable of confirmation, or they undergo correction in new experiences. On the other hand, psychical events, or "phenomena," come and go, and do not have any lasting, identical being which would allow objective scientific determinations.

Nevertheless, Husserl persists in speaking of psychical "being," which is so misleading a term if one is seriously interested in description alone. It is not experienced as something which appears. It is an "experience," and, in reflection, an intuited experience, appearing as itself, in an absolute stream, as "now," and already receding into a past. The psychical events are ordered in a "monadic" unity of consciousness, a unity which has nothing to do with nature, with space and time, substantiality and causality, but rather has its own peculiar "forms." It is "a two-sided unlimited stream of phenomena, with a thoroughgoing intentional line" which Husserl envisages as the field of inquiry, in a way which describes the pattern of the *Ideas* of 1913. Rational inquiry in this field is possible, he thinks, if one is careful to avoid the confusion of nature and phenomena, in the sense here set forth. The phenomena are to be taken just as they give themselves, as this meaning, appearing, etc., or as something represented, phantasied, and the like. In other (later) works, the noetic and the noematic sides are to be included in the inquiry. The "objective something" involved may be a "fiction" or a "reality" from some point of view, and can be described as something "immanently objective," as "meant or presumed as such."

Husserl holds it to be absolutely evident that one can investigate and make statements here, with evidence. It is admittedly not easy to overcome the original habit of thinking with the natural point of view, thus "falsifying the psychical naturalistically." A "purely immanent" investigation of the psychical, in the broadest sense of the "phenomenal," is accordingly possible. That is to be distinguished from the psychophysical investigation of the same facts, which, Husserl states, naturally has its rights as well.

There is an advantage in recalling Husserl's earlier writings. He does not shake his fist at nature for all time, and he is aware of its stubborn independence at intervals. There are even admissions concerning the value of the naturalistic methods in psychology, beginning with the *Philosophy of Arithmetic* (1891), in which there is evidence of awareness of the importance of "naturalistic" (including technological) influences on experience. On the positive side, he is fully justified in undertaking to delimit a sphere of "pure experience," which is to be studied reflectively; just as he is justified in seeking to extend the field for "essential analysis" to conscious experience and knowledge as a whole. Whatever may be decided about the acceptability of the concept of "essence," the main point at issue is the extension of conceptual analysis to all phases of experience and knowledge. If phenomenology is to include among its functions the role of a kind of "pure geometry of experience," it can proceed descriptively, with no further justification. Whether it proves to have actual and potential usefulness for human welfare and understanding, is however still more important.

The early delimitation of the psychical and the physical, and the definition of a "phenomenon," are superseded by the ever-increasing subtleties and distinctions of transcendental phenomenology, as recorded in the *Ideas,* the *Cartesian Meditations,* and the later logical studies of Husserl.

### B.  PURE PSYCHOLOGY AND TRANSCENDENTAL REDUCTION

It was Husserl's habit to record his reflections stenographically, so that he was able to cover the desired ground as rapidly as he wished. Some things were done again and again, indicating the perplexity he must have felt. This was the case for the general theme of phenomenology and psychology, which was discussed repeatedly, and also repetitiously, in published and unpublished writings. Although not intended for publication, the more informal "meditations" are often revealing and sometimes valuable.

A "Self-Reflection" written during the period of summer session lectures in 1925 is just such a revealing writing.[3] It belongs to Husserl's fully mature period, in which his ideas on a "First Philosophy" are elaborately developed. Its theme is pure psychology, psychological reduction, the necessity of an intersubjective reduction for the purposes of a pure psychology, and psychological and transcendental reduction.

Of course, it is only a fragment, beginning with a rather Husserl-oriented psychologist (referred to as "the psychologist") who says to himself: The psychical process is immediate to me, given only in my self-experience in real originality—I myself and my own psychical life. Husserl recalls that the evidence of "inner perception" had often been emphasized, by Brentano, for example; and that Hume had already indicated, in the *Treatise,* that without the evidence of remembrance no knowledge would be at all possible, a thought which was again taken up by Meinong in our time.

As a positive investigator, the psychologist needs no critique of the reliableness and certainty of inner and outer experience, in the sense of a radical critique of reason. He no more needs such a radically founded psychology than the natural scientist needs a radically founded natural science. It is sufficient for him to show, with a certain naïveté, the advantages which come in question for him as an objective investigator.

For the psychologist, the question is, how he gains an objective experience with the greatest possible certainty. He therewith needs empathy from the outset, or the empirical reliability of mutual understanding—just like

3. Mss. of Husserl, BI9, X, Husserl Archives, directed by Prof. H. L. Van Breda, Louvain.

the natural scientist. Now self-perception does not reach far, and only through remembrance does identifiable experience arise. Husserl points out that there can also be illusions for self-experience *(-erfahrung)*, and that self-remembrance comes on much the same level as empathy, which is likewise a representation. The critical question of psychological knowledge is something other than that of knowledge of nature (or, natural knowledge). For something natural is only real, if it is also perceptually accessible for others. But, says Husserl, the psychological is real, without being perceptible for others, for it is only known through manifestation. Hence the psychologist must be more concerned here with the critical questions than the natural scientist.

The psychologist does not only need a critique of validity, in Husserl's view; he also needs a "critique of purity." The psychical life is a life of consciousness, especially as an "experiencing having" of experiences, appearances of something that is not immanently contained in the experience itself; whereas what is experienced, supposing that it is real, does not immanently belong to experience in its true being, as a part or factor of it. Hence the experienced as such, as something meant in the experiencing, belongs to the latter itself as an inseparable factor. The aim here is to see and to learn to describe the psychical process in its "peculiar being," and especially to eliminate confusions between that which belongs to what is simply believed, as opposed to its determinations, perhaps realized in successive acts of knowing.

A continual "critique of purity" is therefore needed, in Husserl's view, the determination of that which is in the psychical life itself, as opposed to what is meant in the psychical life. The psychologist knows many things from his side as self-evident, and then naturally interprets the phenomena of another person. The correct method of the critique of purity is a different matter, and it is only possible after an at first naïve study of the mental life, and the evident reflections connected therewith. It is essential for the psychologist, to proceed from the first objective experience, the prescientific experience, which is a psychophysical experience (experience of man), to a pure psychical experience, to the experience of the "pure" psyche, which before the analysis offers the wholeness of the inner (pure) self-perceptions as a field for inquiry. The mind purely in itself is to be the field of experience. Since the point of departure is the unified psychophysical experience, and the individual-psychical life is often given as physically indicated, the tendency can arise, to view the psychical life exclusively as unified through the relation to the human body. But in any case, it is an important task, to pose the problem of the inner unity of a mind, and to describe it in its concretion as a unified and inseparable whole. On the other hand, it is also a task, to describe the objective phenomenon "man," and the phenomenal unity of mind and body. This description should be the departure for every scientific objectivation which makes use of natural knowledge and seeks an objective theory of mind.

If one has in phenomenological-psychological reduction the concrete unity of the pure psyche (Husserl uses the term "monad" here), there arises the task of an *a priori* essence-theory of the psyche-monad as such. In the original form of my own psychical life, I, the phenomenological psychologist, find various phenomena. I lift them out, that is, I abstract from their interlacings, I leave them undetermined, I can have them perceptually, or in remembrance, etc. I take these phenomena as an example and form for myself pure monadic possibilities, in their eidetic variation, pure generalities of essence. I gain elementary types for the relative critique in the experience-context of the monad, and try to work out the primal forms and the essential types of modes of formation of new forms out of the primal forms (primal phenomena), which I have clarified in the essential description with respect to their construction out of dependent factors. I seek forms which must occur *a priori* in every monad, and on the other hand I soon encounter universal structural forms, which give unity to the monad as a whole. The order of the procedure has its difficulties here. Everything that I have treated with the transcendental point of view or attitude as a phenomenological theory of structures, as phenomenology, appears here on the natural ground as an *a priori* descriptive psychology of the monadic psyche.

All the constitutive problems naturally belong here too, and therewith every possible world as an index for single-monadic and inter-monadic contexts, for something purely psychical. All possible objectivity enters into psychology as the intentional correlate of purely monadic subjectivity. Psychology as a phenomenological monadology is spoken of by Husserl as the basis of the spiritual (or cultural) sciences. Phenomenological psychology appears here in connection with the positive sciences, as a science with the natural attitude or point of view.

Husserl looks to "pure psychology" to cause a "revolutionary reform" of all the sciences; and he looks for still more from a further "transcendental purification" of pure psychology. He gives an example of a "pure monad," as follows: Every one of us practices a "turning inwards," and in the reduction draws back to his *ego cogito*. In a purely eidetic modification of himself one finds a world of possibilities; and to begin with in this reduction one transforms the entire world, and therein contained his body, into a mere phenomenon of his ego. My "inwardness" may, as inwardness, as that which animates my body, belong to total nature, the total world. I can free the inwardness from this relation, I can view it "irrelatively," purely as itself, with respect to its peculiar essence, which I grasp. I apprehend each of my experiences, contexts of experiences, or contributions of consciousness, as itself, absolutely, without in the least apprehending something, or positing something as being.

From here on one step is indicated. I say to myself: the world is for me only there as an objectivity in my experience *(Erfahrung)* and as confirming itself in its synthetic harmoniousness as existent, and in the form of true reality, as being in itself thus and so only as the theme of my (or of our social) scientific efforts and in the best case as the substrate of successful insightful forms, which are called theories. Nothing stands in the way of my placing the whole world "out of play," of my refraining from existential beliefs. It cannot then be said that there is nothing as a remainder; what remains is rather "I as the one who refrains from belief." The previous world and the further world are no longer valid for me as being, but rather as a phenomenon. But that must be correctly understood. What I want, is to make my experiencing subjectivity to be the theme—the thinking and valuing subjectivity in its intentionality, and the world only as what it is given therein, exactly as it is meant, believed, and valued. We can be world-children, we stand "on the ground of the world," we are in the world—quite self-evidently, we live in the belief. And now we do not want to be world-children, we do not "live any longer simply in the world-belief," we "do not live in" all the passive motivations of belief and actual thought-activities of belief. (In a marginal note, Husserl states that the talk of being a world-child applies to the *"naïveté"* of the natural and positive scientific life, which does not yet know anything of the transcendental. He speaks of the transcendental subjectivity as being "awakened.")

This whole belief, this whole world is set out of validity by us in a certain manner, not as skeptics, who doubt, but rather as investigating subjects, who have a fundamentally different attitude, who open up a fundamentally new direction of inquiry.

One should not overlook the fact, that the *epoché* can be repeated on every stage of the I-think, and hence also for the transcendental I-think, but that a sharp cleavage remains between the *transcendental* life in general, in which a real world is constituted as believed, and the *natural* life, in which the ego has an environment, and fits into it as a human ego. The natural ego which is unfolded through "introspection" apperceives everything subjective as an animation of the body. The transcendental ego, on a higher stage, apprehends everything subjective in the universal unity of the constitutive context, to which one's own body as a subjective phenomenon also belongs.

Now it is not difficult to clarify the difference between the phenomenological-psychological reduction and the transcendental-phenomenological. The psychologist, or I as a psychologist, do not perform a universal *epoché*. I regard the world "as valid," and want to remain with that. As a positive investigator, I am a world-child, I want to investigate the world and the minds contained in it, including myself as a mental subject of my natural body.

The thought is remote from me, with this attitude, to free myself of this being a world-child, and to perform the transcendental reduction. Precisely as a psychologist, however, I must place the world out of validity, if I am to prepare my pure psyche and the total content of my psychical events in their purity for a purely psychological inquiry.

In order to gain my purely mental realm, I must carry through the reduction, the *epoché*. But if I perform the *universal* reduction and "inhibit" all my real and objective being-validities, then I have really given up the ground of the objective world, on which my psychological inquiry was to be pursued, at least so long as I am concerned with my pure psychical life. Then I gain in fact nothing other than my transcendental subjectivity.

That Husserl is keenly aware of objections to his whole procedure is amply shown. Thus he goes on: Still there is the question, whether we do not describe better, if we say that I can live as in ordinary life with a consistent natural point of view or attitude, without ever "inhibiting" my "world-validity." I may, as a psychologist, for a time, and as a method of *mundane science,* change the point of view, and after the reduction has rendered its service, be active again on natural ground as a judging being. The world may thus remain valid for me as a psychologist, while I temporarily immerse myself in pure subjectivity. But my natural stand is maintained "habitually." This promising line of thought yields, however, to the systematic interest in a thoroughgoing "constitutive" philosophy.

Husserl speaks of the task of an eidetic psychology "and then necessarily also the task of a purely 'introspective' phenomenology." The transcendental reduction has the peculiarity of placing every natural validity radically out of play, and of admitting no natural ground as given. The entire natural point of view and its structures are then only constitutive occurrences in the transcendental subjectivity. "Transcendental philosophy" or "transcendental idealism" is then the result of the inquiry with this point of view, with the knowledge, that whoever carries it through consistently and practices science on the sole ground of transcendental subjectivity, can never again find the ground, to give up this point of view. No reason is given for this interesting contention, except to state that the transition to the point of view of practical life can then never again have the old character—possession of a simply existing world, in which we humans exist and act, and in which all possible knowledge is positive. The world-all is regarded from the point of transcendental intersubjectivity, as "a unity of constructive validities of a motivated content," and all natural life has its explanation on the basis of its "absolute sources."

If I "bracket" the world that is valid for me, and confine myself to the eidetic view of the transcendental field, and hence to pure possibilities, it turns out that the quasi-validity of so-called possible worlds must be removed. To every possible world, which I freely contrive, there belongs a possible transcendental subject, from whose life of consciousness, as life in belief, it receives its possible "being-validity." As a transcendental investigator, I thus reduce every possible world through the *epoché* to the possible transcendental consciousness constituting it. All the disciplines of a universal world-ontology have therewith undergone the *epoché,* and hence the entire *a priori,* that I gain by proceeding from the factual world through free variation of its possibilities.

There is then only one eidetic transcendental science,

completely closed in its kind, the *one* ontology of "pure consciousness" and of possible transcendental subjectivity in general. Since, however, all possible constitutive formations are contained in it, Husserl adds, all real ontologies are also contained in it. Everything objective, instead of being something absolute which precedes the subjectivity, has being only in the context of the concrete subjectivity, as a rule of intentionality belonging to the essence of that subjectivity.

To suspend the world thus means to posit nothing which is not to be derived in the systematic course of the pure intuition of consciousness from the consciousness itself, as an immanent factor lying in it, or as something meant, confirming itself, etc. But, Husserl states characteristically, as a transcendental observer, I also "recognize, what the lower, naïve ego did not see," that the latter has no other world, and can have no other, than a transcendentally constituted world. How is that justified? Only because, "as a transcendental observer," I also recognize that what the lower ego exhibits as the true being of things receives its "legitimacy" in the constituting itself in certain fully understandable contexts, and that it is "inconceivable" that there be a different view of true being for the ego than the true being which it itself constitutes.

The ultimate test is, therefore, " conceivability," which is not clarified by Husserl. It can be construed broadly, with non-contradiction as the limiting condition; or still more broadly, in the "empty" sense of anything being "conceivable," even contradictions. On the other hand, conceivability, like possibility, may be tied down to the actual knowledge we have about the world, so that what is conceivable is definitely conditioned by the level of our scientific knowledge. The appeal to conceivability (or to

inconceivability) thus proves to be tenuous and unsatisfactory. If the formal criterion of non-contradiction is
used, Husserl has by no means established his case, for a
non-contradictory doctrine of "lower egos" as capable of
radically reflective inquiry can really be carried through.
All the less could he establish his case with a factually
restricted criterion of conceivability.

Now, how do we come from phenomenological psychology to transcendental phenomenology?

The world is there for me and remains for me "in
natural validity," and the positive sciences remain valid
for me. I now respond to epistemological motives, and
say to myself: All my world-knowing leads back to outer
experience. If it were abolished, I would have no idea of
a spatial world. If I phantasy myself as I will, so that
my experiences are destroyed to a certain extent, are
suspended in continual conflict, instead of maintaining
their force in harmony and consistently maintaining an
existent world for me, then I would have a flowing-into-
one-another of sensations, and thing-apperceptions dissolving themselves. But the conviction of my own being is
untouched, even with a possible non-being of the world
for me. The self-experience "precedes" the world-experience, with respect to its ground. The question of the right
of this "presumption," that a world in itself exists, can
be left aside, as undecided, while I note: I am, and the
course of my exeperience is, just as it is in itself. Looking
back into the previous experience, I can be just as certain;
I had world-experience, and a stream of experiences, no
matter what their objective validity may have been. From
there I become attentive to the whole concrete life of my
"consciousness," closed in itself, my pure ego life, the
*ego cogito.* This now is the "transcendental." It is not

human, bodily-psychical life, but rather that in which the world appears and in which my body appears, and with it my human psychical life appears, spatialized and "mundanized."

Thus I have begun with the world and world-sciences, given and naturally valid for me, and I end with me alone—not as a piece of the world, but rather with me as "transcendental." In the stream of my transcendental life, the entire knowing of a world is contained as a transcendental fact.

Going back once more to the natural point of view, to the positive science of psychology, there is for it a given world, with people, and myself with this body and conscious life. Now Husserl reiterates: Everything that is valid for me as reality, nature, spirit, science, law, religion, etc., occurs through my experiences, my valuations, my judgments and insights. Those are experiences of my psychical life. The same holds for every other person. If as a psychologist I want to preserve these experiences purely and describe them in their purity, as they occur at an actual time-point as subjective experiences, then I have to leave out of consideration the objectivity meant in them (perhaps legitimately) as an existent reality. I have only to describe something that is meant. The pure conception of the life of consciousness, as it really occurs, requires thus a kind of exclusion of the reality regarded in it as being real. The experiences can even be illusory, false judgments, or wrong valuations. Whether they are to be confirmed as correct or rejected as false, they are facts, just as they are.

For me as a psychologist, the world remains in unbroken validity, and with this general stand I "abstract," I do not bring the psychophysical validities into consideration. As a psychologist, I make no use of them where I am concerned with pure consciousness. It is sufficient for me that they are experiences of the subject in question.

Now Husserl makes an essential distinction which is crucial for his purposes. There is, first of all, the procedure, with the world universally valid, of leaving out of consideration all meanings and beliefs referring to a world, and making no use of them abstractively, or admitting any of them methodologically. On the other hand, there is the procedure of "suspending" (submitting to an *epoché)* the complete ("posited") universe, with everything that was hitherto valid for me.

In the latter case, I make it clear to myself that everything hitherto valid for me was valid through my positing-as-valid, and I leave in question everything that was ever valid for me as existent. But the leaving-in-question, and the being valid as existent, remain untouched. And if I place that in question, I have again presupposed something existent *(voraus Seiendes).* Its evidence necessarily goes first, and I can now leave out of question the objective universe, or that which is meant, and make my theme to be the universe of meanings. The latter has the double sense of meaning and what is meant as such.

I can now proceed from my ego, viewing eidetically the pure possibilities of the ego. I can find a way to the corresponding absolute positing of a transcendental intersubjectivity, as belonging to the possibilities of an ego in general. Such an "eidetics" of transcendental consciousness has its correlate in an analogous psychological "eidetics," congruent with it in all essential determinations. But the psychological "eidetics" indicates belonging to psyches and bodies. As such, it appears within the possibilities of the sciences.

If I, as a transcendental ego, construct the possibilities of transcendental subjectivity, I come upon all possible formations of consciousness and all possible ego-acts, apperceptions, and world-experiences. Finally I see that a real world for an ego in general can only have the significance of a correlate, confirmed in harmonious experience, and in correct anticipation continuing *in infinitum*. I see that with the transcedental point of view I have placed the validity of the world out of play. But I also see that, with the free establishment of the pure subjectivity and of the confirmable realities and possibilities, I again come to the positing of a world. In the evidence of the systems of harmonious experiences there lies "contained" as a correlate the evidence of an existent world of experience. I now effect the natural thesis (i.e., posit the world as existent), but not naïvely, in the "positivity" which knows nothing of the positing consciousness and its transcendental purity. Thus I come to the positing of the world along with the scientifically knowable system of the essentially related modes of consciousness. Husserl asserts that the world is not thinkable without the related modes of consciousness, and that it would be senseless apart from the relatedness to consciousness. That is to say, senseless, nonsense taken literally, since it is seen therewith, that the world itself, viewed absolutely and all-sidedly, is only a fulfilled sense, or rather the Idea of a fulfilled sense. It is, conceived as an Idea, the all-comprehensive system of constitutive self-givenness.

Nevertheless, Husserl insists, the transcendental inquiry is not a method of giving up the world or of depriving it of its natural meaning. It is rather a method, so to come to the world of natural life and the positive science established in that world, that it reveals its meaning. This meaning, as a positive meaning, is given without question in experience, and it reveals itself in continuing experience and in the theoretical world-science. But a positive meaning is still a one-sided meaning. Husserl reaffirms a basic principle of his thought: all objective meaning is meaning from a meaning-giving subjectivity. Only if it is obtained therefrom and seen in it, does it gain the transcendental determinations inseparably belonging to it—which, as inseparable, with the point of view of positivity, first produce the absolute, all-sided and decisive world-knowledge.

Universal world-knowledge requires universal essential knowledge, eidetic knowledge of a possible world in general, with respect to all that is contained in it "on principle." That yields the system of ontology, closed together in the inseparably unified universal ontology. Contained in it, like the ontology of nature, is the ontology of psychical subjectivity and intersubjectivity, referred to the ontology of bodiliness. This founding-on-one-another and interlacing of ontology corresponds to the pervasive and manifold relativism of all mundane being.

It may well be asked, whether Husserl's meditation on psychology and phenomenology of 1925 represents any real advance beyond his earlier writings, especially in the 1911-1913 period. The repeated evidence of vacillation on the independent validity of natural science knowledge is revealing, however. There is evidence sufficient to indicate that he would not question findings established by any type of scientific method. In the background is his own ulterior commitment to idealism at all times, expressed in his final appeal to the "unthinkable" unrelatedness of anything to consciousness. Unfortunately, Husserl in his withdrawn mode of life escaped the need to justify that dogma, which amounted to an article of faith. He should have given careful consideration to Ralph Perry's critique of the argument from the ego-centric predicament.[4] As a matter of fact, when the present writer brought Perry's criticism of idealism to Husserl's attention, the latter simply rejected the idea of a "predicament," insisting that there is an "essential relatedness" instead. By the 1920's Husserl's position was thoroughly insulated, and his manner predominantly pontifical. It is indeed meaningful to regard the world as though it were a "fulfilled meaning," for the purposes of a special inquiry. But it is an unwarranted departure from such an undertaking, to argue that "the world itself, viewed absolutely and all-sidedly," is only a "fulfilled meaning." Husserl's metaphysical leaning is also ill-concealed when he has the transcendental observer "recognize, what the lower, naïve ego did not see"— that the "naïve" or "natural" ego has no other world than a "transcendentally constituted" world.

## C. THE IDEA OF AN EIDETIC ANTHROPOLOGY

In another "meditation," stemming from the period about 1925,[5] Husserl speaks of the psyche as having the remarkable peculiarity, to allow itself to be reduced phenomenologically. What I am conscious of "in my psyche" as a world is reduced to the corresponding world-phenomena, in manifold modes of consciousness, or modes of appearance. I then come to the context of the subjective, which is purely closed in itself; it is mine, and is unified concretely in my soul, as the manifold of its life and what is

---

4. Cf. R. B. Perry, *Present Philosophical Tendencies*, New York, Longmans, Green, and Co., 1912, pp. 129 ff.: "No one can report on the nature of things without being on hand himself . . . This predicament . . . proves nothing at all."

5. Husserl mss., BI9, I.

given therein experientially or phenomenally, in this or that modus. On the other hand, if I take the experienced world, just as it displays itself as given harmoniously in objects of experience, then I have the unity of my life as a mundane existent, and that as existent in physical nature. The latter is itself a unity of experience *(Erfahrung),* and is closed in itself, disregarding all my psychical processes relating to it, as well as the psychical processes of others that are also posited. Describing, and asserting empirical judgments, I can consistently remain in nature and view my body therein consistently, but I can also view my "pure" subjectivity just as consistently. With a certain indirectness, of interpretation or "empathy," I experience other people, co-determined by my self-experience, as well as animals; and I can also view them bodily and organically, or with respect to their pure psyches. But I experience the psyche as the animation of their bodies, and the bodies as systematic unities of "organs" of the psyches, of the psychical ego-subjects.

Husserl then goes on to speak of "eidetic anthropology and biology." If we "vary" nature eidetically,[6] there corresponds to it *a priori* a "variation" of possible experiences, modes of appearance of nature. Thus we come to an *a priori* psychical structure, which contains in itself the conditions of the possibility of the experience of space objects. That leads to the constitutive psycho-phenomenology. Belonging thereto is "an *a priori* sensibility, an *a priori* of visuality and tactuality," as *form.* That is to say, in so far as such senses are, with respect to the form, the kind of contribution which makes possible the constitution of space-form and that which is spatially formed. But that

---

6. Cp. E. Husserl, *Erfahrung und Urteil,* on the "method of variation" for the determination of essences.

prescribes an *a priori* to bodiliness. The question is then, what is necessary with regard to the body-relatedness of the sensory fields, so that the body itself can be constituted for the experiencing being, as his "primal body" *(Urleib)?* Perhaps the possibility of the mutual functioning with respect to one another of part-organs of the body? What is necessary here, in order for me to apprehend a strange object as a body *(Leib)*, and that as experiencing the same things which I experience bodily?

How far does this go? I must have hands, etc., to feel, and eyes to see, sense-organs, in order to experience spatial things and my body itself with its sensuous properties. Otherwise I could not experience anyone as experiencing what I experience; and conversely, another person could not experience me in that way. Therefore I must have a physical organization, as that is necessary empirically for a human being. And how far do the essential necessities reach, if I am to be able to be a man?

Husserl states that only an eidetics of the pure psyche in general, an eidetic inner psychology, makes possible the production of purely psychological concepts of a rigorous logical nature. Only such an eidetics makes possible the consideration of the thinkable possibilities in a psyche, and also the possibilities of a psychophysics. An eidetic psychophysics requires the eidetic consideration of the possibilities of bodily and psychical unity. In Husserl's view, the point of departure here would have to be the eidetic structure of a man, hence an eidetic anthropology. The question is, how is it possible? How can an eidetic structure of a human psyche be formed, with the experienced and experienceable bodiliness belonging to it in a nature and a world?

It must be observed, at this point, that Husserl has been

merely using certain promising phrases, such as "eidetic anthropology," which is no more than a hope. His general style of question is reminiscent of the Kantian quest for the necessary presuppositions of an ordered world of experience, or of a social life. What conditions must be met, if an ordered society is to be possible? That is a mode of approach which may well be justifiable, if properly handled, with due regard for the *findings and priority* of empirical knowledge. In the present context, the style of questioning is obvious to the point of being commonplace, and disappointing.

Why should the whole matter be made so difficult? Husserl has to see what is there empirically, naturally, and causally. Then, he reasons, the structures and relationships are "necessary." All that he could say, to justify the "necessity," would be, in general terms, that in order to have certain sensory experiences, there must be suitable sense organs. Even so, there would still be some "play," for possibilities that might emerge, or that might exist, unknown to us. About all that Husserl could say is that, to have a certain effect, there must be an adequate cause. To be sure, "causality" is replaced by "motivation" on his level of discourse. "Necessities" are limited to analytic knowledge. The fullness of the details is to be supplied by the empirical investigators, in the various sciences dealing with man. In view of the factual variability of all material things, and especially organic and cultural beings, it is not to be expected that very much could be included under the heading of an "eidetic anthropology." Like the term "ontology," which so frequently says nothing at all, this phrase is little more than an empty programmatic proposal.

To resume Husserl's meditation: With regard to nature,

we first have to treat the experienced nature as such "transcendental-aesthetically," the "appearances" of nature and the perceptual judgments pertaining to them. Then (and again in accordance with the Kantian pattern) there is the doctrine of the objectively valid judgments of nature. In the psychological sphere, we must consider the objective appearances of every psyche in the manifold of the subjects experiencing them. We must also consider the "perceptual judgments," the judgments about human beings, and in particular about their psychical side, and their personality in "direct objective experience." What is a human being himself, his person, his psyche itself? In how far is there a goal of a truth in itself, analogous to the "exact" nature?

As he has stated elsewhere, Husserl asserts that the thing perceived does not have to exist, that no perceived property really needs to exist. But, he holds, it is entirely different for a person, or a psyche. In self-experience there is always an amount of "psychical life" which is absolute and cannot be cancelled, as something psychical, as it is experienced itself, and as it can be experienced. Only in so far as nature also plays a role here, in the psychophysical whole as a physical body, do similar problems come in question. But for the inner-psychical processes we have the entirely different problems of the disclosure of their intentionality, the making conscious of the unconscious, the reflective preparation and fixing, the describing of that which was and is non-reflective experience and streaming life, as that which recedes but cannot be unattainable and a nothing. The point is here to produce out of the occasional psychical experience (reflection) a systematic, a methodical experience. That is also needed in the realm of natural experience, but for the latter there is no uncancellable absolute self as the substrate of determinations. My I-am, my subjectivity, is apodictically uncancellable, and what I directly perceive of myself is given absolutely during my perceiving, and not presumptively.

Obviously, it required a mighty effort on Husserl's part to convince himself, first of all, of the now familiar fundamental tenets concerning the special prerogatives of the "pure," inner realm.

## Chapter VI

# THE FUNCTION OF A CONSTITUTIVE PHENOMENOLOGY

The attack on naturalism which Husserl undertook in 1911, in his *Logos* essay, "Philosophy as a Rigorous Science," was incorporated in its chief essentials in the *Ideas* of 1913. Although Husserl actually wrote a sequel to the *Ideas*, he did not publish it, and it is only recently that the second and third volumes have been published.[1] The second volume is devoted to studies toward a "constitutive" phenomenology; and the third volume, to phenomenology and the foundations of the sciences. As Husserl described his plans for the volumes to come in the introduction to the first volume, he was undertaking an inquiry into important problems which must be solved in order to clarify the relations of phenomenology to the physical sciences of nature, to psychology, and to the sciences of the mind, as well as to the *a priori* sciences as a whole. The leading themes of the second volume include the constitution of material nature; the constitution of animal nature, with extensive discussions of the pure ego, psychical reality, and the constitution of psychical reality through the body, and in empathy; the constitution of the spiritual world, with studies of the contrast between the naturalistic and the personalistic world, motiva-

---

1. Edmund Husserl, *Ideen zu einer reinen Phänomenologie*, Volumes II and III, edited by Marly Biemel, Haag, Martinus Nijhoff, 1952, in the series Husserliana, under the direction of H. L. Van Breda.

tion as the basic law of the spiritual world, and the ontological priority of the spiritual world as opposed to the naturalistic. The third volume brings discussions of the relations between psychology and phenomenology, the relationship of phenomenology and ontology, and the method of clarification. Husserl's failure to publish these volumes can only indicate his feeling of uncertainty and dissatisfaction.

It would be pertinent now to consider in detail the main contents of the second and third volumes of Husserl's *Ideas,* but that is not possible within the limits of the present work.[2] Interest will center on the treatment of naturalism, and with it, of psychology, and on the significance of phenomenology for ontology. As always, it is necessary to be alert to the danger of dogmatic and unwarranted assumptions.

## A. THE ONTOLOGICAL PRIORITY OF THE SPIRITUAL WORLD

In the last chapter of his "Phenomenological Studies of Constitution"[3] Husserl shows how all the detailed "constitutive" analyses converge once more toward his central thesis of idealism. In the course of his discussion, there are insufficiently clarified views on the status of nature and the natural world, in which he appears to make important concessions. They turn out to be merely apparent concessions, however, when he is confronted by the pointed question: Is the natural world really independent of experience, or not? His answer is an uncompromising denial of independence.

---

2. Cf. Alfred Schuetz's discussion of these volumes in *Philosophy and Phenomenological Research,* Vol. XIII, Numbers 3 and 4, March and June, 1953.

3. *Ideen,* Vol. II.

Let us see how Husserl again comes to his conclusion concerning the primacy of the spiritual.

In so far as the stream of experience is the source of spiritual acts, the spiritual ego is dependent upon the psyche, which in turn is dependent upon the body. Hence spirit is conditioned by nature, although, Husserl maintains, it is not causally related to nature. It has a "lower stratum" which is conditionally dependent. As spirit it has a psyche, a complex of natural dispositions, which as such are conditioned through physical nature and are dependent upon it.

The spirit, as connected with its body, "belongs" to nature. But despite this coordination and connection, it is not itself nature. It is "effective" in nature, but not in the sense of natural causality. The reality of spirit is not related to real conditions which lie within nature. It is related rather to real conditions which obtain in the "environment" and in other spirits, and that is not nature. This can be seen by way of physical things, which have their real conditions in one another, and also in bodies and psyches, but not in spirits.

The relationship between spirit and physical nature as portrayed by Husserl is thus a peculiar one. It is a relationship of being conditioned, between two kinds of realities, which is not causality in a genuine sense. That is also the case with the relationship between spirit and psyche, as well as between spirit and body (as an "aesthesiological" unity and not as a physical thing). Husserl speaks of the body as a two-sided reality. The following are constituted: (1) the aesthesiological body, which, as experiencing sensation, is dependent upon the material body; (2) the volitional body, freely moving. The aesthesiological "layer" is the basis for the "layer" which "moves freely." An immovable body is a limiting case, as one that merely senses.

Similarly, the psyche is a reality with a double aspect. As bodily conditioned, it is physically conditioned, dependent upon the physical body. On the other hand, as conditioned spiritually, it is in a reality-connection with the spirit. Hence there are two "poles," physical nature and spirit; and between them, body and psyche. It turns out that body and psyche are really only "nature in a second sense," with respect to the side turned to physical nature. Husserl speaks of two "aspects," two reality-sides for body and psyche. Body as a thing in the environment is the experienced, intuitive body, and that is the appearance of the physical body.

Husserl's examination of "psychophysical parallelism and interaction" leads him to the "radical refutation" of parallelism; and in his renewed discussion of the "relativity of nature and absoluteness of spirit," he returns to themes already prominent in the first volume of the *Ideas*.

Husserl supposes that his examination of psychophysical parallelism and interaction indicated the limit of possible "naturalization." That is to say, the spirit can be conceived as dependent on nature and even naturalized, but only up to a certain degree. Husserl declares that a unique spiritual determination through merely naturalistic dependencies, a reduction to such a thing as physical nature, is unthinkable (Why not say simply, "a reduction to physical nature"?—the distaste for it would not be lessened if it were named outright). He reasons that subjects cannot be construed as nature, for then that which gives meaning to nature would be lacking. Nature can be a field of "thoroughgoing relativities" because the latter are relative to an absolute which carries all relativities, namely, spirit.

This shabby argument is in the well-worn tradition of idealism. It is reminiscent of the old stock-in-trade item of the idealist, to the effect that on the basis of matter, one *cannot* explain mind, whereas on the basis of mind, one *can* "explain" matter. To be effective, such an argument is to be pronounced with clenched fists, and expressed with the conviction of a revivalist preacher. But above all, there should be no chance for the voice of the opposition. In the present context, the opposition would be sure to flounder in the mire of "misunderstanding."

Although spirit, as Husserl views it, shows dependencies of many kinds in its relationship to the nature "constituted" in relation to the personal world, it is nevertheless absolute, non-relative. Husserl pictures it in this way: if we "erase" all spirits from the world, then there is no longer any nature (why that should be, however, Husserl does not show). But if we "erase" nature, the "true," objective-intersubjective existence, then something still remains. It is the spirit as an individual spirit. Although the possibility of sociality is lost, and despite all the enormous impoverishment of the "personal" life, we still have an ego with its conscious life, with its individuality, manner of judging, valuing, and motivating itself in its points of view.

The unity and individuality of the spirit is "manifested" in the stream of consciousness of the spirit. If I want to understand it, I must "reconstruct" this process. The "understanding" in question is intuitive. The objectivity "individual" is said to come to givenness in its own peculiar "being." Husserl speaks of "reliving" an alien spiritual life, and therewith an alien spiritual world or spiritual objectivity, and of understanding it in its individual significance, for example, the political situation, the spiritual epoch, the contemporary literature.

The term "reconstruct" is a much better term than "constitute," with its confusing ambiguity. It names precisely what one may undertake to do in this "constructive" phase of the phenomenological procedure. Surely the aim is not to render in a trite manner what everyone knows to be the case anyway; or to foist metaphysical additions upon the basis of physical reality.

When Husserl speaks about "reliving" spiritual objectivities, his entire discussion, and the examples cited, seem to have an exclusively honorific sense. If mention is made of the political situation, and of the contemporary literature, should one not also think of the notorious publication of the Nazi racist, Julius Streicher? Did it, too, have "spiritual" significance? And were his "spiritual" activities to be accounted for, "understood," by way of "intuitive," "non-natural understanding," or, rather, by means of causal analysis and other empirical methods on the physical, biological, and social levels?

But Husserl is firmly committed to his direction of inquiry. In his view, "individuality in a spiritual sense" is entirely different from "natural individuality." As distinguished from the "individual essence" of a thing, which is here and now, the "what" is something general. Every thing is thus an example of a generality; it is to be thought of as repeated any number of times. A real thing is dependent upon real conditions. It is the real causal context which distinguishes two things, and it presupposes the "here and now." Husserl argues that we are necessarily referred back therewith to an individual subjectivity, whether single or intersubjective, in relation to which alone the "determinateness of the positing" of space and time is constituted. It is his contention that no thing has its individuality in itself. The spirit, on the other hand, experiences, takes a point of view, and is motivated; and, unlike a thing, it has its motivation in itself. It does not have to be at a determinate place in the world in order to have individuality. The pure ego already possesses "absolute individuality" in any one of its experiences.

Spirits are not unities of appearances; they are unities of "absolute connections of consciousness," or, more exactly, "ego-unities." Appearances are "correlates of connections of consciousness," which have "absolute being." Now if appearances are "constituted" intersubjectively, we are led back to a plurality of persons, who can understand one another. The "absolute being" of persons and their experiences "precedes" the "relative being" of the appearances. All individuation of the appearances is connected with the "absolute individuation" of persons and their experiences. That is to say, all natural existence is held by Husserl to be connected with the existence of absolute spirits.

What can be said about the psyche, and man as nature? Is that also merely an example of something general? The answer Husserl gives is that in so far as a psyche is a "naturalized" spirit, that cannot be, for specific individuality belongs to spirit. On the other hand, he asserts that everything which determines the psyche as a natural reality is "exemplary" and general. The individuality does not lie in that which is nature here. Not much can be done with the nature depicted by Husserl. "Nature is the X, and on principle nothing other than X, which is determined through general determinations." Spirit, however, is not an "X"; it is "that which is given itself in spirit-experience."

Husserl's version of nature is as poverty-stricken an account as could be imagined. It is hard to believe that he could convince himself that he was really talking about nature. Forgotten is the whole idea of the "reduction," with its artificiality and, indeed, its programmatic falsification. It took some years of writing about "constitution" to rivet the belief in his mind, that reality is essentially "constituted reality."

### B. THE RELATIONS BETWEEN PSYCHOLOGY AND PHENOMENOLOGY

### 1. The Relationship of Phenomenology to the Sciences

In his "Phenomenology and the Foundations of the Sciences"[4] Husserl undertakes to deal with the basic problems of method and being which must be clarified if the potentialities of phenomenology are to be understood. The relationships to psychology are of crucial importance in the discussion.

Husserl seems to think that it is possible to analyze experience and the objects concerned, and to "prescribe" everything essential for the methods used, on that basis. Let us not forget one of the most suggestive of the fragments of Heraclitus: "Nature loves to hide." Only an antecedent idealist bias would lead one to suppose that methodological lines and norms can be derived from essential analyses. Husserl fails to take account of two pertinent considerations: (1) the free play of the scientific imagination, with even arbitrary explanations and wild guesses playing a role at times, and the method of "multiple hypothesis" as a most useful pattern for inquiry; and (2) the endless complexity, the variability of the facts of nature, which should be a standing warning against fixity of essence, or against freezing inquiry within certain "insightful" molds. Husserl's view goes along with the

---

4. *Ideen,* Vol. III.

idea of the fixity of species, as illustrated in his treatment of man, with the "ego," the "person," and the "spiritual" level. It is reminiscent of Plato's metaphysical (or "eidetic") heaven. Far better for scientists is the conception of method as something which has been forced upon them: methods as devised to solve problems. The methods may be group methods, using statistical devices; they may be imperfect causal procedures. It would amount to willful verbal twisting, to claim that the investigations of such scientists as Pasteur and Koch were guided by the "essential" nature of the facts. In short, Husserl has simply overstepped the proper limits of his procedure, in his regal manner of viewing the sciences.

Here is Husserl's argument: It is not what is called "modern science," and not those calling themselves "experts" who make a method, but rather the essence of the objects; and the essence of the possible experience of objects of the category in question (that is the *a priori* of phenomenological constitution) prescribes all matters of principle to the method. It is characteristic of a gifted expert, to grasp this intuitively, if not to formulate rigorous concepts and norms. All discoveries and inventions of the experts move within the frame of an *a priori* beyond which it is impossible to pass. This *a priori* can only be obtained from phenomenological intuition, and not from the doctrines of the scientific experts. To grasp it scientifically is, however, a task of philosophy, and not of the dogmatic sciences themselves. What determines method in general normatively is the theme of "general noetics," reaching out beyond all categories of objectivities and constitutive intuitions. This discipline does not exist as yet, and it will first be possible after the establishment of an extensive phenomenological essence-theory of knowledge on the side of intuition as well as on the side of "specific thinking." But it is already clear, in Husserl's view, that the method of all science must be determined through the kind of immediate ("originarily giving") intuition which belongs essentially to the object-category to which it is related. That all scientific grounding is finally based on acts of experience is held by Husserl to be a truism. By "act of experience" he means an "act originarily 'giving' the nature-objectivity" (a "truism" to an idealist, but hardly to a naturalist!). Husserl reasons that if we assume it to be valid, as we must, then methodical norms which experience sets forth and which are grounded in its essence, must determine the methods of the natural sciences. This is also taken to hold for all sciences in general. In all of them, the process of proof (or "grounding") leads beyond thinking to intuition, and finally to immediate ("originarily giving") intuition.

In reply to Husserl's empty programmatic claims, it should be pointed out that it is indeed the experts who ordinarily make, amend, or improve methods. It is above all the experts who learn to know about the nature of the facts in question. To put it in this way sounds so much better than to use the stilted and potentially deceptive language of "essence," "category," "originarily giving intuition," etc. The *"a priori* of phenomenological constitution,"* not having been fully incubated as yet, as Husserl himself allows, is in no position to "prescribe all matters of principle to the method." The vision of a new generation of phenomenologists, schooled in essential intuition (or at least in the use of the words), practicing "general noetics," and, as might well be the case, with hardly a modicum of scientific training, is not an encouraging prospect for the scientists. One can only wonder what the future specialists in "general noetics," with a thorough schooling in the methods of transcendental phenomenology, will have to say to entomologists, chemists, physiologists, and social scientists. Since Fichte and Schelling, it is no longer incredible that a principle as simple as $A = A$ be used to spawn worlds, and reality in general. Husserl is careful to preserve a basic patent on the "phenomenological intuition" that he holds to be so necessary for the determination of method. It is not to fall to the "dogmatic sciences." And all of this in the name of a discipline that has hardly begun to exist!

What Husserl is trying to say has its sound core, if one tones down the enormous pretensions of the system-builder, and the vested interests of the basic patent-holder. Only it is so commonplace, as Husserl revealingly states it himself. We must refer to the nature of the objects; we must depend upon experience; and we must discern all that can be established about the nature of the objects and the process of experience, in general and in particular. The final appeal is to actual, immediate experience. But that has been known for quite some time. There is no room in this acceptable precipitate of the discussion for anything like an "act originarily 'giving' the nature-objectivity."

Husserl's use of the term "constitutive" in referring to "constitutive intuitions" is noteworthy. Elsewhere, as already pointed out, the term "constitutive" may also be taken to mean, literally, the way in which a thing or objectivity is "constituted," in the sense of being "made up," out of elements and relations.

## 2. The Ontological Foundation of the Empirical Sciences

In his discussion of the "ontological foundation of the empirical sciences," Husserl sheds some further light on his conception of method. He regards method in all sciences as also determined through the *general* essence of the objectivity. The general essence allows itself to unfold in thought processes, and its unfolding "leads necessarily to an ontology." A complete or perfect method presupposes the systematic elaboration of the ontology. By that Husserl means the essence-theory which belongs to the object-category in question. The knowledge which it provides is an "unconditional norm" for everything which possible empirical knowledge of the factual sciences related to the categories can ever offer. Husserl asserts that it also enters into the knowledge of facts. He maintains that every advance in ontology must redound to the advantage of empirical science. For this reason, one is supposed to recognize the "unconditional necessity of a rational psychology." Husserl had long before, in his *Logical Investigations,* indicated the need for such a discipline. It was not to be something constructed "from above down" with empty concepts or vague word-meanings, like the old metaphysical psychology, but was rather "an essence-theory obtained from pure intuition." What is in question here is a psychological essence-theory.

Husserl's usage is to be noted carefully. "Ontology" means "theory of essence." This usage may be questioned seriously, if ontology is taken to mean theory of being, and "essence" is an affair of knowledge. It must be *proved* that it is also an affair of being, in each case. Possible being is not yet being. Furthermore, it is the event, and not the generality, that is real, that has "being." If the conceptual-logical treatment of events is in question, we may be able to interpret and test Husserl's assertion that every advance in ontological knowledge must be of advantage to empirical science. A universal mathematics would be a powerful instrument for theory and practice. Would a universal "material eidetics" also be so desirable?

That would not be the same thing as conceptual fictions or abstractions. The pretension is greater: the real is supposedly conditioned by the ideal; and the ideal belongs to the context of a constitutive consciousness.

Husserl also takes the opportunity to repudiate once more the ill-fated definition of phenomenology as descriptive psychology (in his *Logical Investigations*), or, in terms of the present context, his failure to distinguish rational psychology from phenomenology. Thus, he writes[5]: "Phenomenology is anything but mere descriptive psychology, and it is not even empirical-descriptive essence-theory, i.e., investigation of the essence of experience in the context, not of experience-actualities given to experience, but rather investigation of ideal experience-possibilities." A rational psychology, as an "ontology of a real that is constituted in the context of experience" cannot be identified with "the essence of the context of experience itself." In addition to that, Husserl repudiates the "old distrust of psyche-reality and ego-reality" of his earlier period.

The title "Ontology of the Spirit" provides the place for phenomenological idealism. It was really incumbent on Husserl to show why that was not "dogmatic metaphysics." The terms "ego-reality," "spirit," and "ontology," while plausible as a matter of simple usage, cannot be viewed without misgivings. The question, what *is* an experience in the sense of an "inner experience," must receive a physical answer. It is either a physical event with a space-time locus, or it is a fiction. If it is the latter, then "being" or "existence" are inapplicable terms. Other language should be used, and there should be no talk of "ontology."

5. *Ideen,* Vol. III, p. 69.

### 3. Regional Concepts, Psychology, and Phenomenology

In Husserl's view, every "radical classification" of the sciences, beginning with the experiential sciences, must be dependent upon the conception of a "region." Accordingly, there must be as many basically different empirical sciences, or groups of disciplines, as there are ontologies. Why should this not be stated in just the opposite way, that there are as many ontologies as there are different empirical sciences? As a matter of fact, the empirical sciences are there first, and their diverse findings make it possible for the "essentialist" (or phenomenological ontologist) to delimit "regions." There would surely be no objection to helping the empirical sciences with any pure ontological patterns, or even suggestions, which might be offered. In that case the "pure" analysis would be admittedly instrumental and ancillary. But Husserl endeavors to rule out empirical objections as "misunderstandings."

This rationalistic principle of the priority of ontology is carried over to the psychological sphere. Husserl holds it to be evident that there *must* be a rational psychology, whether we have it or not. In his view, the rational existence of the science as an Idea "precedes" its possession. If one can adjust himself to that language, which is suited to shift from a nontemporal to a temporal meaning if the occasion so warrants, he is prepared for a backward glance at geometry. The necessity of a geometry, Husserl asserts, could be seen just as well before its elaboration as we can now see the necessity of rational psychology, which we do not possess. However, that is not entirely true, Husserl observes, because phenomenology provides a significant portion of a rational psychology, even though the development of the Idea of psyche-reality is still lacking.

Husserl charges the naturalism prevailing in the ranks

of psychologists as well as other natural scientists with leading to a widespread misunderstanding of the nature of phenomenology and its possible value for the psychological science of experience. Thus, there is the already noted incorrect belief that phenomenology signifies a restoration of the method of inner observation, or of direct inner experience. This misunderstanding helped to prevent scholars from seeing that phenomenology had undertaken to prepare the way for a fundamental reform of psychology, as well as of philosophy.

In accordance with the phenomenological reduction, the essential analysis is restricted to the experiences as they are in themselves, disregarding all questions of reality. But everything that is investigated in that manner also belongs within the frame of inquiry of rational psychology. For it is evident, in Husserl's view, that the essence of an experience (as Idea and not as fact) does not and may not change through the change of point of view (the "realizing apperception").

Husserl undertakes once more to distinguish the naturalistic from the phenomenological approach, and this attempt is more successful as a piece of exposition. Suppose that perceptions of things are given in factual experience. In inner experience (in "reflection in the sense of Locke") they are "originarily given." They are given (it would be better to say: they occur) as the experiences of people or animals, with their real environment, and as parts of the one space-time world. The investigation of perceptions as psychical conditions of actual individuals is the concern of psychology as an inductive science. But we can also carry through an "eidetic reduction" and eliminate all questions of real existence. We are then concerned with that which belongs to "perception as such." This applies to thing-perception, perception of sensory appearances, which are not known as things, perception of conscious experiences, and the like. The "possible" perceptions are distinguished according to basic kinds, and the aim is to determine what belongs essentially to each kind, and to ascertain the changes, transformations, and connections made possible through its essence, whether it be with phenomena of the same kind or with those of another kind. The same problems occur for remembrances, phantasies, expectations, obscure presentations, thought-experiences of all kinds, and for affective and volitional experiences.

The experiences are taken with the entire content with which they are presented in eidetic intuition, and as eidetic it is based upon psychological intuition, whether it be natural psychological experience or psychological fiction. In the view of reflective inner experience which is concerned with essences, the relationship to the existent facts of nature is lost. The individual event is replaced by something "general." The reader is reminded that it is essential to experience to be "intentional," to have "reference to something." The important themes of noesis and noema are of particular significance for psychology, and all phenomenological findings are capable of "translation" into the actual psychological terms of real experiences.

When one adopts the "eidetic" point of view, and confines himself to "essential seeing," he gives up the thesis of the reality of nature. But there is an "essence-thesis," and the reader will do well to ask what is involved in that thesis. It can be rendered innocuous; there must not be a "concealed" realm of assumptions to take the place of the world of nature (often mistakenly described as an "assumed" world). If the comparison with the procedure in geometry is carried through carefully, and kept in mind, there will be far less likelihood of speculative excesses. Husserl refers to the case of geometry for elucidation. The geometer is interested in "pure" spatial form. In so far as form is an essential factor of a material thing, the geometer, as the essence-investigator of possible thing-forms, is a rational physicist at the same time. This is also seen in psychology, and in fact wherever the separation into the two kinds of sciences—the experiential and the eidetic—occurs. Here, as elsewhere, Husserl maintains that eidetic science "precedes" experiential science everywhere. The science of experience "cannot be without" that which is "prescribed" by the region and the "truths of essence" apprehended in intuition. These truths are regarded by Husserl as holding in unconditional generality and necessity, for everything possible, and for everything real in actual experience.

Still led by his guiding analogy, Husserl reflects that just as there was surveying before geometry, and an astronomy before mathematical mechanics, so there was also a developed psychology before eidetic psychology. It is modern experimental psychology to which he refers. He reasons that when there are enough eidetic truths, belonging to a region of reality, to make a science possible, the constitution of this science must also signify a great advance of the corresponding science of experience. By a science Husserl means an infinity of connected truths which can be investigated in systematic unity, truths which are only discovered by painstaking inquiry.

It will not be doubted that the successful construction of a formal science is potentially of practical value. The construction of "alternative" systems can only be considered desirable, for there is always the possibility of a future practical application. The significance of this conceptual device for physical science is well known. What can be shown in the present context, to bear out the practical promise of the essence-study of experience, remains to be seen. It is not to be ruled out as having no prospects. On principle, all experience and all reality may be approached with the help of conceptual systems. But a "universal science of essence" faces difficulties not encountered in formal science, for there is no escape from the dependence upon factual experience.

It also appears that the conception of science advanced by Husserl is too narrow to cover the whole field of scientific thought. Foremost in his mind is the ideal of the mathematician, which amounts to a bias in effect. The definition must do justice to the incomplete sciences in different stages of development, inductive as well as deductive. It would be better to define science as logically organized knowledge, as a starting point, with the term "logic" used in the very broad sense of "methodology," to include inductive and explanatory as well as deductive procedures.

The use of analogy is helpful and suggestive, but it must not be overdrawn. Husserl himself recognizes that danger, when comparing rational psychology and geometry. As he points out, rational psychology is not mathematics, and the phenomenology of experiences is no mathematics of experiences. They are both essence-theories, connected with a "regional *a priori*." But not every essence-theory is mathematical in type. The mathematical sciences which provide the "*a priori*" of their "sphere of being" to natural science are developed deductively from a few axioms. It is entirely different in "rational phenomenology." For the latter, the field of immediate insights is endless, and indirect derivation only plays a role by way of other sciences and their psychological significance.

What becomes of the analogy with geometry? Not only must caution be observed in pressing the analogy too closely. One must consider whether the propositions of geometry are "true." What does the sum of the interior angles of a triangle "really" equal? The term "really" is out of place here, for the answer depends upon the nature of the axioms in a given system. By analogy, one would have to ask whether the hoped-for "material-eidetic" type of discipline would yield "really true" propositions, or only propositions which follow "analytically" from a set of assumptions and conceptual forms.

There is no doubt in Husserl's mind as to the fruitfulness of a "rational" psychology. He is convinced that phenomenology, or the essence-theory of experiences involved in the idea of a rational psychology, opens up an infinite field of truths. Since they refer *a priori* to psychical states, they "enrich psychological knowledge infinitely," similar to the way in which mechanical (or mathematical) knowledge enriches empirical natural science. To suppose that psychology could accomplish what phenomenology offers would be, in Husserl's view, as unreasonable as to suppose that physical observation and experiment could accomplish what geometry offers to the physicist.

The beginner's failure to distinguish between descriptive psychology and phenomenology is fully understandable, especially since it took Husserl many years to develop a clear and thoroughgoing conception of the new science. But even if one did not distinguish between the essence-theory of states of consciousness and transcendental phenomenology, and Husserl did not distinguish them in the *Logical Investigations,* there would be important consequences. Husserl supposes that phenomenology would be recognized at once as an essentially new discipline if

it made use of formulas, drawings, and experimental instruments. Since it draws its findings purely from intuition, it is natural for critics to ask how it can contribute
something new, or be scientific. It is also natural to reason
that if intuition *(Anschauung)* is not something mystical,
then it must be natural experience, and that is nothing
new to the psychologists. The conclusion indicated is that
phenomenology may perform useful preparatory work,
which is to be ordered under psychology. In commenting
upon this attitude, Husserl refers to the famous Chwolson
"eleventh commandment,"[6] which he formulates in keeping with the present context as: Never write a critique
before you have understood that which is criticized in
its plain meaning.

It should be noted that Husserl rejects a "simple" type
of subjectivism and insists on the "essential" separation
of phantasy and perception. The view that phantasy-intuition is just as good for the psychologist as actual experience
since the "phantasy-image" has essentially the same kind
of mental existence, psychologically, if not the same "objective meaning," is a "pre-phenomenological" error. It
was only possible before phenomenology had shown that

---

6. It will be recalled that Chwolson invoked this "commandment" against
the naturalist Ernst Haeckel, whose *Riddle of the Universe* of 1899 was
so distasteful to the idealists and fideists of his generation. The admonition was simply: Do not write about anything which you do not understand (Cf. O. D. Chwolson, *Hegel, Haeckel, Kossuth und das zwölfte
Gebot,* Braunschweig, F. Vieweg und Sohn, 1906). Haeckel's "crime"
was a source of serious embarrassment to some philosophers, one of
them stating that he could not read Haeckel's book without burning
shame (Paulsen). Haeckel undertook to synthesize our knowledge of
nature at a time when the problem of transcendence was a serious
concern to immanentists and idealists. Although his work was clearly
imperfect and "dated," it possessed virtues rarely seen in the literature
of philosophy.

phantasy and perception are radically different kinds of experience.

Psychology as a science of experience describes such things as types of character, dispositions, etc., as facts of human reality. There is no description in this sense in eidetic phenomenology. As already amply indicated, all real existence is excluded from its domain. Its findings concern essences, not realities, and its truths express what is valid for such essences, as well as for all that falls under such essences, "in unconditioned necessity and universality." These truths refer to experiences just as the truths of geometry refer to bodies, the truths of arithmetic refer to numbers, and the truths of phoronomy refer to motions. Phenomenology does not deal with psychical states in the sphere of real existence, any more than geometry, arithmetic, and phoronomy speak of the earth or the factual world, and of bodies, motions, and numbers occurring in it. But what does the phenomenologist mean when he says that *there are* experiences, *there are* mental states such as perceptions, remembrances, and the like? The expression "there are" says no more than the mathematical "there is," for example, a series of numbers. Husserl holds that the "there are" (or "there is") is in both cases grounded in "essential seeing," not in natural experience. There does not have to be anything corresponding to the essences that are "seen." If there is anything corresponding to the essences, only actual experience could exhibit or prove it.

On this Husserl is unquestionably right; the "essential seeing" does not do the work of ordinary experience. But is he right in his interpretation of the existential expression "there are"? One thinks of the general point of view of "constructionalism," according to which existence in mathematics is construed in terms of constructibility. In every case, it must be shown or proved that "there is" a specified value or relationship. One cannot go very far with the "seeing of essences." A discussion which the mathematician and logician Ernst Zermelo[7] had with Husserl in his Freiburg period may be recalled, concerning the possibility of "intuiting" an infinite. The "and so forth" could be intuited, according to Husserl. "No, you must show me 'and how forth,' you must give me the rule of procedure," protested Zermelo. No form of intuitionism, including phenomenology, has succeeded in bringing formal determinations within the straitjacket of intuitive insight. Nothing that Husserl has set forth in his logical writings, including the *Formal and Transcendental Logic* and the *Experience and Judgment,* gives even a clue to a successful intuitionism in this respect.

To resume Husserl's argument: Truths of essence are portrayed as absolutely binding; they are "insurmountable," and are not to be confirmed or refuted by any natural experience. The truths of experience, which "posit" existence, are "accidental" truths; they may be modified or suspended in the course of experience. Husserl is well aware of the nature of empirical truth. It is, however, assigned a lowly status. The term "accidental" reveals the disparaging attitude that is so characteristic of Husserl, with very few exceptions. The empirical truths are not so loosely put together as Husserl indicates. Statistical generalizations "work" remarkably well; and it can be said that the statistical methods provide an invaluable source of knowledge, rivalling pure mathematical knowl-

---

7. Professor Zermelo had been one of Husserl's earliest students when he was a *Privatdozent* in Halle. In his later years he was an interested "hearer" of the mature lectures of Husserl, while maintaining an attitude of critical independence.

edge in practical importance. There is no need to make a choice between different types of logically acceptable method. One should think of a principle of *cooperation* among such methods, and not of warfare; and he can do so if he is not a "standpoint" fighter, or a partisan of a limited point of view, fitting into a vested tradition.

What Hussserl has in mind by way of an *a priori* science is certainly desirable, with two conditions to be met: it must be achieved; and it must be able to work. It would indeed be a "mighty extension of knowledge," to show that factual knowledge is "essentially necessary." It is not only with respect to physical nature, but, Husserl maintains, to a much greater extent with respect to psychical nature, that factual knowledge and laws have a background of "*a priori* and absolutely necessary laws of essence." The case rests, then, with the value of phenomenological inquiry for the sciences; that is to say, it is to be decided in the future. But there is no doubt in Husserl's mind as to the outcome. Although he admits that it is not easy to find one's way into the "unusual" kind of "eidetic seeing," he is aware also of the resistance of those who are completely satisfied with the method of the current experimental psychology. Their hostility to the eidetic view recalls to his mind the refusal of the Abbé Galiani to look through a telescope: he too was completely certain about his astronomy and completely satisfied with it. Husserl looks to the future to show that one cannot get rid of "evident data" by not looking. Furthermore, he expects the psychologists eventually to hold the "instrument" of the phenomenological essence-theory to be not less important, and indeed even much more important to begin with, than mechanical instruments. The amazing comparison with a refusal to look through a telescope

thus reaches its climax, with Husserl's indignation out-
doing itself. If the psychologists in question had had no
conceptual apparatus at all, his words would have some
force. Husserl himself sees that the comparison with an
instrument should not be overdrawn. He is careful to
add that the phenomenological method does not compete
with the method of experimental psychology, any more
than the mathematical methods in physics can be said to
compete with the methods of experimental physics. He
makes clear his view that experimental psychology should
not be given up, while maintaining that it can gain
greatly through a phenomenological foundation, and
through being formed thereby into an exact, rationally
explanatory science. The tendency to overvalue the possible contributions of an experiment would be avoided. It
would also be seen, in Husserl's view, that there is an
incomparably greater significance of the intuitive knowledge of essences in the case of psychology, than can be
illustrated in physical natural science. This is intended to
apply especially to psychology as a spiritual science.

Husserl tries to make it clear that he never intended to
attack experimental psychology. No doubt with his *Logos*
essay on "Philosophy as a Rigorous Science" in mind, he
denies that he ever said anything to depreciate experimental psychology. On the contrary, he holds that it is
as much entitled to respect as any other science, in view
of its serious and, within limits, its very fruitful work.
Husserl introduces another analogy to make sure that
phenomenology is elevated to the proper height: were
great surgeons such as Volkmann or Billroth less great
as surgeons, because surgery and medical therapeutics
were only to a small extent founded through the requisite
natural-scientific theory? But a conciliatory attempt toward

better relations with scientific psychology is certainly called for. Husserl can reason that he must have respect for experimental psychology, since he aligns it with other experimental sciences, like physics. It would be helpful if this reinterpretation of his former utterances could be made retroactive.

The nice words in tribute to experimental psychology are, however, only a momentary pause in the case against naturalism as a philosophy. Husserl asserts that the fusion of natural-scientific psychology and philosophy has promoted a false and shallow philosophy, which does not see a single genuinely philosophical problem. It is pertinent to ask, how one is to define philosophy, and how the nature and genuineness of its problems are to be decided. For one thing, the function of providing a synthesis of the scientific knowledge of the time is not to be denied. There are innumerable problems falling to a naturalistic philosophy, i.e., philosophy conceived as the generalization of the sciences, with some scientific inquiries of its own (thus, logic and value-theory).

Not wishing to stand alone on this issue, Husserl speaks of "every real philosopher" as knowing the situation, and as being in agreement in evaluating a broad stream of philosophical literature which goes under the banner of psychological and natural-scientific philosophy. All writers on philosophy are therewith divided into two camps, those that are "real philosophers" (meaning the German university hierarchy of vested "philosophers"), and the naturalists, of all types. He finds unanimity among the former in their denunciation of the latter. It would not be so easy, however, to establish further points of unity, as Husserl so well knew. His softness of tone toward the professorial hierarchy is truly "occasional." It was not a habitual attitude.

The severe judgment of the naturalistic movement is not intended to apply to psychology or the psychologists as such. The psychologists concerned are those who have "taken philosophy too lightly," especially those who completely "missed" the meaning of phenomenology.

The erroneous interpretation of phenomenology as an empirical analysis of one's own mental states or experiences had led to the view that one could obtain phenomenological results from the natural science of experimental psychology. In refuting this misunderstanding, Husserl does not mean to imply that experiments could not gain a phenomenological function "in a good sense." The investigator of essences does not need natural experience, for the latter would not establish the truths of essence in which he is interested. What he needs is intuition, clear apprehensions of single factors of the essence to be intuited. In principle, intuitive phantasy could serve him just as well as perception, although it also has its disadvantages, in quickly losing its fullness, or receding into the less clear and the obscure. Hence the phenomenologist will, whenever possible, draw from the primary source of clearness, the living "impression," even though he has so little interest in existence. This is where phenomenology and experimentation meet, for instrumental aids and experimental arrangements may help in gaining valuable intuitive material. That is especially possible in the field of sensory intuitions, valuations, and volitions. In this sense, a phenomenologist is always experimenting, "naturally, without a useless protocol," as Husserl interposes significantly.

The real kinship with experimental science has thus appeared. The phenomenologist is also an experimenter. It can now be said to the naturalist: Grant the phenomenologist his self-chosen standing, as supplying the "mother-ground" of the sciences, and as having an indispensable purifying apparatus in its transcendental frame, and the war is over. But why should a "protocol" be useless? Even though the "reduction" is performed, there may still be serious dangers in the way of the "experimental" phenomenologist. He might be no more reliable in some of his reports of essences than a golfer may be about his score, or a fisherman about his catch, if there are no objective records. "Revelation" could hardly be kept out of the realm of essences. "Holiness" is already there, with the help of Max Scheler. The "experiment," for phenomenology, is an "exemplary intuition," as a basis for the seeing of an essence. In Husserl's view, "the excellent instrumental means" of a psychological experiment can also be useful here, although with a completely different method, in accordance with the different aim. He notes that there are already small beginnings, due not to psychology itself, but to the stimulation of phenomenology; and he is sure that there will be further progress.

Husserl makes it clear that this is no retreat (it is characteristic of him, not to retreat), and that it strengthens what was said in his *Logos* essay and here. The possibility of using artificial means for "exemplary intuitions" had often been pointed out by him in the course of academic work. The first studies of the Würzburg School on the psychology of thinking were discussed in his seminar in connection with a study of the differences between psychological and phenomenological experiments. Geometry once more provides a convenient illustration. A collection of models, or drawings on the board, do not contribute anything more in principle than geometrical phantasy. But if phantasy will not provide the necessary clear intuitions, perception must be used, and any suitable means to "compel the intuition" and make possible the desired "liveliness of phantasy."

## 4. Phenomenological Descriptions and the Domain of Experience

As has been amply pointed out, the phenomenological study of consciousness, and the sphere of experiences with their essence-correlates, operates on a different level from empirical inquiry. Husserl thinks it is fundamentally wrong, to expect to obtain phenomenologically relevant findings through the questioning of experimental subjects and by the study of their protocols. That the "well-meant" descriptions of psychology hardly touch the surface, is "seen at once" by anyone who is practiced phenomenologically. In keeping with the times, Husserl refers to the way in which people operate with "catchwords" such as act, content, and object, and how things are mixed up under those names; and he points to the inability of ordinary descriptions to do justice to cardinal distinctions, such as the difference between presentation and the various modes of representation, for example, between material perception, the corresponding phantasy, remembrance, and expectation.

Husserl emphasizes particularly the importance of phantasy-intuition for phenomenological purposes. The "freedom of its movement" is necessary, if one is to follow out the connections and structures of consciousness, noematically and noetically. Husserl speaks of the large amount of knowledge which free phantasy, in the service of a phenomenological study of essences, would be able to offer to a scientific psychology. Recalling the traditional rationalists, he finds that they were right in holding that an infinity of possibilities "precedes" reality; and he speaks of the "infinity" of possible formations of consciousness and of noematic formations of psychological reality, ordered with "essential necessity." Although the present claims are largely directed to the future, that does not prevent Husserl from stating that it does not help matters to close one's eyes here. He refers to rational psychology as a great science, comprising the "apodictic lawful possibilities, to whose absolutely firm frame the psychological realities are bound." It can only be observed once more that, with these enormous claims made, and the basic patent duly filed, the final verdict will depend upon actual work performed.

## 5. Ontological Description in Relation to Physics and Psychology

The acceptance of the model of physics as a guide for psychology is, in Husserl's view, not the least of the circumstances causing the psychologist to err in his thinking. He has already made it abundantly clear where he thinks any "model" is to be sought. The rational disciplines on which physics is based are radically different from phenomenology. Phenomenology is concerned with descriptive analyses of essences, and is not a deductive science. Rational natural science, on the other hand—for example, pure geometry or phoronomy—is a field for deduction, but not for essential analysis and description.

The ideal of science which Husserl has in mind is always "rigorous science," with mathematics as the best example at hand. Most rigorous of all is the type of science which proceeds intuitively, with adequate evidence. Looking at the existing sciences, he finds much description in the empirical natural sciences. If one "comes from phenomenology," he reflects, one looks about for the essence-domains from which the descriptive concepts would have to obtain their normative essence through intuition. There must then be a rational discipline, to provide the field for essence-descriptions, and to serve as the basis of the natural science. But there Husserl notes the "astonishing" condition, that natural description does not fully claim objective validity, and that it claims anything but the conceptual rigor which is so necessary for psychology if it is to be a rigorous science. Thus, description plays a different role in external from what it does in psychical nature.

Husserl's being "astonished" is an indication of his narrow conception of science. It cannot be maintained that all scientific knowledge must be "rigorous" in his sense of the term. In the explanatory phase of science, one sees the extensive and indispensable use of hypotheses, which may be described as "intellectual pseudopodia," or explanations projected in the hope that they will be borne out in experience. "Probable laws" are also indispensable, and, properly construed, they are "rigorous" in an entirely acceptable logical sense. The notion that the sciences involving empirical descriptions must be "based" upon a "more fundamental" discipline conforms to a kind of geometrical pattern which in turn suggests the authoritarian order of the Middle Ages. Such pictorial terms tend to become fixed in one's mind, and to promote a rationalistic bias, obscuring the instrumental character of all concepts, including the frightfully "necessary" essences.

In any case, Husserl has made it abundantly clear that phenomenology is anything but mere descriptive psychology, and that it is not an empirical-descriptive theory of essences. Its object of inquiry is the field of "ideal experience-possibilities." The aim is to elaborate systematically the whole domain of the "phenomenological *a priori*," the "whole manifold of essences and essence-laws," in the interest of empirical psychology itself. As in geometry, where the study of the figures of factual bodies is the application of geometrical knowledge, Husserl proposes to proceed from a pure science of phenomenology. That is in his view "the only correct method."

## 6. Rational Psychology Distinguished from Pure Phenomenology

With so many new disciplines emerging, boundaries must be securely determined, and border disputes averted. As has been seen so often, philosophers can wage acrimonious warfare over the nonexistent, as well as the not-yet-existent. Not the least of the difficulties is due to the changes in Husserl's own development. Some further precision in definition is required, if the hoped for "rational psychology" is not to be a source of embarrassment to the program of phenomenology. Where is it to be located? If phenomenology includes rational psychology, as Husserl surmises the reader has surely thought, then it would appear that the part in a remarkable manner swallows up the whole. But, Husserl reminds the reader, pure consciousness has "absolute priority." The realm of being is accordingly the *a posteriori,* and this relationship between the *a priori* and the *a posteriori* is already to be found in the sphere of essence. Hence, Husserl emphasizes, it is of cardinal importance for philosophy to recognize that the "eidetics" of states of consciousness, which is a piece of the rational ontology of the psyche, must be distinguished from the "eidetics" of *transcendentally purified* consciousness. The latter, or pure phenomenology, is no more rational psychology than rational theory of nature. But is there any justification for calling the eidetics of psychical *states* of consciousness phenomenology, as

Husserl has done? He justifies it solely by the circumstance that the pure experience with its essence enters into the psychical state and undergoes a peculiar "apperception," which does not change the essence of the experience itself. It makes an *a posteriori* out of the *a priori,* and again presupposes the *a priori.* The pure experience belongs to a "pure ego," and it is an essential possibility that it be "apperceived" empirically. But, Husserl observes, once understood, this is not wonderful. The "wonder of all wonders" is the pure ego and pure consciousness, but even this wonder disappears when it is subjected to an essence-analysis. Husserl goes on, in his verbal play, to speak of incomprehensibles, which are needed as little as wonders that are no longer wonders, when he gets through with them.

## C. THE RELATIONSHIP OF PHENOMENOLOGY AND ONTOLOGY

Husserl has often been charged with inability to cope with the "ontological problem," because of his subjectivistic procedure. The existentialists purported to supply that lack, with their talk about existence and being. Most recently, Eugen Fink, one of Husserl's former research assistants, has stated that Husserl avoided the problem of "how the pure being of an existent *(das reine Sein eines Seienden)* is related to the being-an-object of this existent *(Gegenstand-sein dieses Seienden).*" As he states it, this question was rejected as a falsely put problem. In Fink's view, this is the most fundamental problem which phenomenology omits, because of its shrinking from speculative thought.[8] It may be observed that if Husserl missed

---

8. Cf. E. Fink, "L'analyse intentionelle et le problème de la pensée speculative," in *Problèmes actuels de la phénoménologie,* ed. by H. L. Van Breda, Brussels, Desclée de Brouwer, 1952, p. 68.

this problem, then so did the existentialists. Only Husserl had a right—and in fact an obligation—to "miss" it, and they did not.

It should be asked whether the so-called ontological problem is a *real* or artificially devised philosophical problem; or whether it is exclusively a scientific problem, and not the concern of philosophy. The "real" problem of ontology falls to the sciences, once the period of vague beginnings of speculation has been completed. If synthesis is a primary function of philosophy, the "higher level" problems which result have a distinctive character. They turn out to be mostly "cosmological" problems, however. "Ontological" questions may be summarized briefly, as very little is said under the heading of ontology. The reverence with which this term is often expressed would lead one to expect much from a treatment of ontology. But it is never a symphony that comes off, or even an overture. If it were not for bad philosophies of being, there would not be much left for philosophers to discuss under that heading. It is primarily a process of "debunking," with only a few positive points, distinguished above all by their sterility. For the purposes of illustration, N. Hartmann and M. Heidegger will serve very well.

## 1. The Question of the Inclusion of the Ontologies in Phenomenology

When he turns to the question of the relationship of phenomenology and ontology, Husserl is careful to place himself on the ground of transcendental phenomenology. From that point of view, all ontologies are subject to the reduction. This leads to an interesting and far-reaching question. The "roots" of all ontologies are their basic concepts and axioms. They appear to belong in phenomenology, because they permit of being interpreted in terms of essence-connections of pure experiences. If that is the case, however, then that must also be true of all the deductions, and hence for the ontologies as a whole. Recognizing this as a difficulty, Husserl draws a distinction between the *science* of transcendental consciousness *in general,* and the *intuitive essence-theory* of this consciousness. The scope of the former is very wide. It applies to experiences in general and comprises the whole of "transcendentally pure" essential knowledge, including indirect knowledge not derived from direct intuitions. The transcendental interpretation of all ontologies would also belong there. On the other hand, every empirical proposition becomes an index for transcendental connections, as a result of the theory of the constitution of all realities in the context of consciousness. Hence, Husserl reasons, a mode of inquiry must be possible which is concerned scientifically with the total realm of factual consciousness, or the totality of "absolute monads" with their factual content of experience. This may be under taken to begin with through the retrospective interpretation of the factual sciences in the constitutive connections of consciousness of the "monads." The rational and the empirical sciences are called "sciences of the onta" by Husserl, or "ontologies" in an extended sense, meaning that they are concerned with "unities of constitution"; and that presupposes a transcendental phenomenology. In Husserl's opinion, nothing which is to be contributed in the ontological sciences, for example in any of the natural sciences, can be compared in significance for human knowledge with the constitutive absolute consciousness. Phenomenology, as the science of trancendental consciousness on the basis of the immediate intuition of essences, is the great "organon" of transcendental knowledge, and of all knowledge which can be interpreted in terms of the factual and essential orderings of transcendental consciousness.

## 2. The Significance of Ontological Determinations for Phenomenology

It should be borne in mind that, as Husserl construes the term, "ontologies," in an extended sense, are concerned with "unities of constitution." Essences and essence-connections are "posited" in the ontologies by means of the basic concepts. These basic "ontic" concepts appear to belong to phenomenology from the outset. As a matter of fact, Husserl has regarded it as an important task of phenomenology, to investigate the reality "material thing" according to its modes of givenness, and to make it clear how this kind of reality is "constituted" as a unity. This applies also to the idea of geometrical bodies, the idea of psychical unity, the idea of animal essence, and in short for all regional categories of possible realities. It also applies to ontologies such as formal logic, or the science of thought-meanings in formal generality, and of the corresponding meant objects. All such concepts name whole domains of phenomenological inquiry.

One asks, for example, what is essential for an extended thing. It has extension and position in space, in which it moves freely; it has material properties, which have extension in their way; etc. This is brought to full intuition, and the essence-connections are followed out. The same propositions which function as axioms in ontology, and which "explicate" the essence of a regional concept, are ordered under phenomenology, with all their basic concepts, as well as all their essences which can be apprehended intuitively.

Husserl describes phenomenology as the science of "origins," of the "mothers" of all knowledge, and as the "mother-ground" *(Mutterboden)* of all philosophical method, since all of them lead back to phenomenology and to work in it. This is another sidelight on the nature of the desired realm. "Origins" is a seductive term. It is a subtle way of playing parent, as a foster parent, dealing with "origins" that are not really origins in a readily controlled, temporal sense. Real digging is required to arrive at genetic, naturalistic origins, in contrast to the inner inquiry for the phenomenological type of "origins," which are "genetic" in a non-natural sense, with no concern about the actual past history.

A clarification of basic geometrical concepts would only be phenomenological if it occurred subject to the conditions of the phenomenological procedure. That would distinguish it from a process within geometry as a "dogmatic" science. Since phenomenology is an essence-theory of transcendentally "purified" consciousness, its objects of inquiry, the "purified" experiences and all events essentially belonging to them are also called phenomenological. Despite the limitation to the sphere of mere intuition and eidetic insight, phenomenology is held to be a systematic science.

In Husserl's view, we pursue "dogmatic" science in the "eidetics" of space, of material nature, of spirit, etc. We judge about space-forms as such, psyches and psychical properties as such, and about human beings as such. How then can phenomenology have to do with "the same" essences and essence-relations, as in the case of the axioms of an ontology, for example geometry? Its domain is not the space-forms, the things, the psyches, etc., in eidetic generality. It is rather the domain of transcendental consciousness, with all its transcendental events to be investigated in immediate intuition and in eidetic generality.

The intuition and thinking of space-forms, the experiencing of things, scientific experience, and the like, are also included in its domain. Consequently, "space-form," "thing," and other ontological concepts and essences occur in phenomenology, although in an entirely different manner. In the case of thing-consciousness, the question is not "what *are* things in general like?" or "what is to be ascribed to things in truth?" It is, rather, "what must the consciousness of things be like?", "which kinds of consciousness are to be distinguished?" There is the characteristic question as to how consciousness can "from out of itself" be knowledge of existence and non-being, of the possibility and impossibility of a thing. As already well known, two things always come into consideration: consciousness itself, and the correlate of consciousness, or noesis and noema. To determine what is to be ascribed "eidetically" to things as meant, is not to investigate things as such. A "thing" as a correlate is not a thing, of course, and hence the quotation-marks. The theme is thus totally different from the investigation of things, even though there are essence-relations common to both types of inquiry.

### 3. Noema and Essence

The concepts of *noema* (correlate) and *essence* should be clearly distinguished. The noema of an intuitive experience of a thing is not the essence of the thing, and it does not contain the essence. However, a change of point of view and of direction of apprehension is "essentially" possible, by which the apprehension of the noema may lead over to the apprehension of the corresponding ontic essence. In that case, there are two different kinds of intuition.

The "positings" of the phenomenologist are exclusively concerned with experiences and their correlates. In ontology the "positings" are concerned with the objects simply. The distinction in question is expressed in the following way: to posit things actually is not to posit something-meant-as-a-thing, is not to posit something-posited-as-a-thing as such. Similarly, to posit essences actually is not to posit something-meant-as-an-essence as such. At the basis of these distinctions is the simple difference between positing meanings and positing objects.

## 4. Significance of the Ontological Concepts for Psychology

What has been said about phenomenology and ontology can be applied to the relationship of psychology and ontology. It is always possible to proceed from phenomenology to psychology, and conversely. Through "psychological apperception" every phenomenological description may be transformed into a psychological description with respect to the experiences of a psychological subject. Conversely, every description of psychical experiences may be transformed into a purely phenomenological description by the "reduction." Psychology is not concerned with the essence of "things," "space," etc., so that its interest is not ontological. It is interested in the perception of things, rather than in things. To the extent that a perception means something "thingish," the noema belongs in its descriptive sphere. The question is, then, whether Husserl's view that ontological axioms could serve as criteria for the correctness of noematic descriptions may be applied to psychology. Husserl asks the reader to consider simple intuitions of transcendent objectivities. They "necessarily" contain empty intentions which are capable of fulfillment; and it is always "essentially possible" that the empty intentions be fulfilled, and that the "intuited as such" persist harmoniously. Disharmonies occur when conflicting concepts are applied, or through synthetic actions, as when something apprehended as red is taken to be green at the same time. If such things are excluded, only simple intuitions remain, and an essence may be obtained from that which is intuited, just as it is meant there. Now every intuition, and every essence, is a representative of a "categorial type." There is the possibility, guaranteed for every intuition, of coming so far harmoniously that the categorial essence "thing" is apprehended perfectly, with all the axioms determining it realized in evidence. Accordingly, Husserl asserts the *"a priori* valid proposition," that a simple intuition "conceals in itself" the essence of the region corresponding to it, and of the regional categories belonging to it, which receive their "eidetic positing" in the corresponding ontology, and also "conceals in itself" all the axioms of the ontology in question. It is also "evident" that the concept of a region, and every concept which determines a region, can be applied phenomenologically as descriptive concepts for the intuition in question. It follows that descriptive concepts are to be rejected if they are excluded by the regional concepts and axioms. In this way ontological truths can serve as norms for descriptive concepts. That a natural-scientific description can only be valid if it agrees with the ontological concepts of nature, is regarded as self-evident by Husserl. Hence "incorrect" geometrical concepts cannot function as descriptive concepts.

This is all quite obvious, and it turns out that Husserl is saying much less than he seems to be implying. The application of regional and ontological concepts is a matter of *analytic* knowledge. Otherwise, the appeal to "self-evidence" would be too precarious and unsatisfactory.

If something is called a "thing," it must conform to what
we take a thing to be essentially. Otherwise, what we say
would violate the essence, and could not be applied. On
the other hand, if we mistakenly describe ideal mathematical meanings and relationships, we cannot correctly
say that we are dealing with material things. Husserl is on
safe enough ground. He asserts that a *psychological* description of intuitions of some kind of reality can only
be valid, if the descriptive concepts have the appropriate
relation to the ontology of the region of reality which is
in question. As he himself puts it, "that is apparently also
a triviality." Still, he insists, it is one of the trivialities
which offer such great difficulties to the "inner understanding." But the "triviality" is not the point of the
difficulty which Husserl feels. The real difficulty is not
one of "inner understanding." It is to show how anything
significant can be achieved by naturalistic description, with
the aid of ontological concepts and axioms. As matters
stand, one sees nothing more exciting than the dead-sure
proposition for the truth of which one could easily risk
going to the gallows—that if intuitions are described
psychologically, then the "intuited as such," the noema, is
described along with them, and no more. The descriptive
concepts, as transformations of the ontological concepts,
have an entirely different function than in ontology.
Husserl regards the rules of their validity as being an
important methodological problem for psychology, and
he states his belief that its solution has been provided by
his discussions. That is an indication of the modest nature
of Husserl's present undertaking.

One thing more is added. Ontological statements are
often faulty, and do not conform, as a matter of fact,
to the exacting requirement of "adequate intuition."

Nevertheless, Husserl states, ontology is not to be rejected entirely. It is only the intuitions themselves which will decide matters, and so it appears that it is phenomenology which has to make the final contribution. It turns out that ontology itself, with all its "ontic positings," is really something irrelevant, even though its "positings" may serve as indexes for noematic connections, with which they are essentially connected.

Since Husserl did not pass beyond the admitted level of "triviality," it can only be concluded that the really important methodological discussion begins at this point. That would include the whole question of the use of conceptual forms and systems for the purposes of empirical inquiry. It would necessitate the complete restatement of the "essence" theory and the nature and validation of phenomenological "evidence." A mode of presentation modelled after the procedures of symbolic logic as much as possible would help to relieve phenomenology of its aura of mystery and untold profundity, and of the misleading ambiguities of some of its language. The much more modest results that are sure to remain may still be important, and worth the effort. At any rate, that should be ascertained, once and for all.

## D.  THE METHOD OF CLARIFICATION

The reader is reminded again and again of the great value of phenomenology. Now Husserl speaks of "the unique contributions which it makes for our total knowledge." It is portrayed as a science continually referring back to itself reflectively, with no science "back of it" to which it could assign work. It has already been made amply clear that ontology cannot carry any part of the burden of phenomenological inquiry. Above all, phenomenology is a "radical" science, and that requires the most perfect "illumination" in the method of *clarification*. In connection with the theory of the "reductions," Husserl had referred to "the reduction to the greatest possible clarity," as a particular case of a general method of clarification, which has general scientific importance.

## 1. On the Need for Clarification of the "Dogmatic" Sciences

Husserl speaks of a "remarkable teleology" in the development of human culture, including science, as shown by the fact that valuable results can be achieved "without insight," or through a mixture of insight and instinct. That they are valuable, he thinks, is shown by a later grounding by means of perfect insight, which gives evidence for the "pretensions to validity." In referring to the "remarkable teleology," which surely goes far beyond anything Husserl could exhibit as evidence, Husserl shows that he felt compelled to recognize an obvious fact. That so much has been achieved scientifically without phenomenological clarification could not be ignored. The aid must come from another source, leaving it to later phenomenologists to justify it with "insight." It would have to be shown how "pure" insight may lead to empirical discoveries. In any case, the great results of empirical inquiry were not gained via "insight" in the sense of pure phenomenology. There are other types of "insight" which are very effective, even though they occur under naturalistic conditions. Thus, there is the use of alternative hypotheses as a pattern of inquiry. If one were not so overly enthusiastic in his criticism of the "dogmatic" sciences, he might be able to recognize the way in which limited suspensions of judgment are illustrated in the special sciences. "Clarification" can be seen in all the "dogmatic" sciences, even though there is no pretension to "final clarity." "Insight" is always present, and it does not detract from its value to show that it is "mixed." It is surely a fortunate circumstance that scientific progress did not have to wait for the emergence of phenomenology, or we might be restricted tree-dwellers, endeavoring to stimulate scientific activities with the aid of a transcendental eidetic discipline. Encounters with hyenas and cave bears, and the problem of controlling the food supply, would not be likely to be influenced by "perfect" insight; and it would seem to be pointless, if not perverse, to refer man's success in surviving to a "remarkable teleology." The fact that there has been so much suffering, and that entire cultures have disappeared, would require us to attach a new meaning to the term "remarkable," in "remarkable teleology." For the rest, it is quite unsatisfactory to see Husserl fall out of character and resort to speculation. Having combated speculation for so long a time, he is not able to handle it at all well.

Husserl points out that the more highly developed a science is, the richer is its methodology, and the more prominent its use of symbols. The tendency is to develop new symbolic modes of procedure, without making them insightful. In time, the sciences become "factories of very valuable and useful propositions," but without "inner understanding." But this is simply to use a phrase. If one has pure reflection in mind, then one can speak of its absence outside the field of phenomenology. But is that necessary in most cases; and how would it really help? It would hardly be enough to mention, to say that we can then know if we are mixing up "regions." Such things are quite well known without the help of a special procedure. It is also noteworthy that scientific progress on occasion *destroys* regions, for example, the region of the "soul," or the traditional ontological region of the mind. Curiously, it is the "radical" phenomenologist who wishes to keep that region going, with the aid of appropriately defined "insight" and a variety of assumptive terms and principles.

Despite the presence of a teleological principle, Husserl is led to observe that the progress of science has not enriched us in treasures of insight. The world is not in the least more comprehensible through scientific progress, he asserts; it has only become more useful for us. It is apparent that such statements could easily influence eager young students of philosophy to adopt an attitude of arrogant superiority toward the sciences; and they are not likely to protect themselves, as Husserl does, by special definitions of terms such as "comprehensible" and "insight." According to Husserl, we do not really have the "cognitive treasures" contained in the sciences; we must first gain them. For, in his sense, knowledge is insight and is drawn from intuition, thereby becoming fully understood truths. It is only by means of clarification and insight that we can obtain the "self-values" which are "concealed" in the sciences.

This shows how Husserl's carefully contrived language places him in an at least linguistically secure position. It is "self-values" then, and not "values," which require insight in the sense of intuition. In fact, the "insights" are self-values, according to Husserl. His whole case against the "dogmatic" sciences amounts to the demand that they consult phenomenology. It would be a caricature, but not without a point, to imagine that, instead of being equipped with a couch or a steam-room, there be a kind of transcendental room into which scientists are to go periodically, to check on their insights. When one considers some amazing developments following from Freud's sphere of influence, it is not too remote a possibility, to suppose that equally fantastic results may follow from the denial that scientific progress has made the world more comprehensible, and from the suggestion that we must first gain the "cognitive treasures" of the sciences— "we" as philosophers, as "immanentists" and "essentialists," with our transcendentally purified experiences.

According to Husserl, true statements, and methods for instating them, are only "self-values" indirectly. Only as means of insight do they have value, inasmuch as insights are self-values. But "insight" names more than a fleeting act of cognition. Only truths which are "primally instituted" with insight, and capable of being restored at all times to actual insight, have truth-value, or "genuine personal value."

Although he holds that "intuitionism" is right in its reaction against the development of the sciences as thought-techniques, Husserl warns against its leading over into mysticism. The point is, to be devoted to the descriptive tasks involved. The sciences are to be "led back" to their "origin," and the aim is to "transform" them into systems of insightful knowledge through clear and "finally-founding" work, to lead back the concepts and propositions to conceptual essences which are to be apprehended in intuition. It must then be decided, to what extent the sciences are one-sided, and how the goal of an all-sided and perfect knowledge, which solves all reasonable problems, can be gained from the "primal ground" of intuitive givenness. The term "reasonable" *(vernünftig zu stellenden)* may be the self-stabilizer in this formulation, which prevents it from foundering. The so-called problem of induction, in the naturalistic sense, would not be likely to qualify as a "reasonable" problem, because it could not be handled within the essentialistic realm. Indeed, it was with respect to this problem that Husserl said, "One should only ask questions that can be answered." How could phenomenology do "all-sidedly" what the sciences are able to do only "one-sidedly," with the whole armies of workers through the centuries? The "primal ground" of intuitive givenness would have to be provided with a rear aperture, to smuggle in all the "one-sided" items of the sciences, if it is not to disappoint us by its sheer emptiness. No doubt the answer would have to be: the scientists would have to become phenomenologists, and the phenomenologists, scientists.

## 2. Clarification of the Conceptual Material

The first work to be undertaken is concerned with the conceptual apparatus of a science, the primitive concepts to begin with. For a science which deals with individual being, there are three classes of concepts: (a) those common to all sciences, such as object, property, fact, relation, number, concept, and proposition; (b) regional concepts, such as "thing," "thing-property," and "thing-relation"—in the concepts of the natural sciences, there are formal components of "thingness," and in the concepts of psychology, those of psychical reality, etc.; (c) material particularizations of the regional concepts, the modes of number in arithmetic, the modes of the idea of meaning in the logic of meanings, and modes of spatiality in geometry. These are all formal modes, in contradistinction to the case of concepts like color, tone, kinds of sensory feelings, and drives.

Now every concept has its essence, which comes under an essence-genus, and this could function as the domain for an essence-theory. All essences would be included in the totality of ontologies, formal and non-formal. But only a very few ontologies are constituted, because of the perfection of intuition which is required. A geometry and a part of formal logic and mathematics developed very early; but still lacking are an ontology of material nature and a rational psychology. The psychological phenomenology now arising, of course, is to meet this need. Husserl has only a general program in mind for the remaining ontologies, all of which are to be aided by phenomenology in securing the requisite supply of adequate and "unconfused" intuitions. The program of clarification of the concepts of the sciences leads to the idea of an all-comprehensive system of ontologies, to be established by means of purely intuitive sources.

### 3. Explication and Clarification

In connection with complex concepts, Husserl distinguishes explication *(Verdeutlichung)* and clarification *(Klärung)*. "Explication" is a procedure which occurs within the sphere of thought. The explication of a concept is concerned with the meaning of the word—for example, "decahedron." But "clarification" goes beyond the sphere of word-meanings and the thinking of meanings. It involves bringing the meanings to congruence with the noematic side of the intuition. The noematic object of the former must be congruent with that of the latter. The congruences must be so perfect that to every partial concept referred to in explication, there corresponds an explicit factor of the intuitive noema. It may happen that the "matching" with a corresponding intuition leads to a conflict. Clarification also has the function of giving a newly constituted meaning to old words.

But the main work of clarification lies beyond the relations between word, word-meaning, and intuition. The

verbal meaning-analysis or explication has only a pro-
paedeutic function for the intuitive explication to be
accomplished. It is the goal of clarification to "produce
anew" the given concept, and to "nourish" it from the
primal source of conceptual validity, from intuition. The
goal is always perfect clarity. The process of clarification
must follow out the stages of the constitution of the
"exemplary" intuitive object in question. But a thing
is not given, and a thing-concept is not brought to "real
clarity," if a thing is simply seen. A phantom is also seen.
In order to make clear a "thing" or a "thing-property"
with its essential relations to real circumstances, the
"clarifying intuition" must follow out the manifolds of
sensory schemata; and it must bring to fulfillment the
intuitive components which give to the sensory schemata
the "value" of thing-intuitions.

As Husserl views it, the process of clarification means
two things: (1) making a concept "clear" by recourse to
"fulfilling" intuition; and (2) there is "clarification" in
the sphere of intuition itself, in the sense that the meant
object must be brought to ever greater clarity, must be
brought "closer," must be brought to more perfect self-
givenness. But one must ask here, as it was necessary to
ask in connection with the first volume of the *Ideas:*
what *is* clarity; and how do you *know* when it is "perfect"?
Husserl never really answers that because he cannot do
so in fact, and, fortunately, it is not incumbent upon
him to do so as a phenomenologist. He is talking conceptually, which makes it unnecessary to decide about
questions of fact. Yet, to speak of "ever greater clarity"
is to force upon us what turns out to be an irrelevant
question; and if that is so, what in the point in speaking
of bringing something "closer"? The answer would have

to be in some such terms as the following: "nearer" and "closer," "greater" and "perfect" clarity, can be designated conceptually, without deciding upon the factual degree of nearness or clarity. "Perfect" clarity would be an ideal limit, about which one could speak without necessarily achieving it in fact. That Husserl means more than that, however, is amply evident from his text, here and elsewhere. It might be replied that the phenomenologist, as a transcendental observer, can describe differences of degree of clearness, and that his own descriptions are adequate and clear. They would be adequate if correct, of course. But how could one know that they are "clear"? The distinctions "discerned" are really analytic in a broad sense; and they might be formulated by a sick person in a condition far removed from "clarity."

It turns out that "clarity" is really to be construed in terms of "constitution." One can speak of an "intuitive nearness" and an "intuitive distance" for all objects. There is "a coming up into the bright light" and "a sinking back into darkness," in which everything becomes indistinct. There is also the process of bringing the one-sided and incompletely presented object to a progressive "self-givenness." Husserl states that one can see from here "in perfect clarity" the general task and the ideal, although it lies in the infinite. The ideal is to view the world of possible essential kinds of possible objectivities with complete intuitive clarity, with systematic completeness; and, on the basis of the noemata lying in intuition, to obtain all the possible conceptual essences, and to coordinate with them the expressive word-meanings and the words themselves, which would make up a totality of perfectly clarified concepts, as well as terms. There is also the "infinite" ideal of a system of all ontologies and eidetic disciplines

in general. All such inquiry has a close relation to phenomenology, which is itself "eidetic." Hence an all-comprehensive system of eidetic disciplines also comprises it. The
"clarifying" ontological insight which is not directly phenomenological, becomes phenomenological by a mere
change of view. Similarly, the insights of phenomenology
must include those which become ontological by a mere
change of view.

"Clarification" belongs to phenomenology by definition. If the ordinary connotations of the term are removed,
that is merely to say that the phenomenological processes
belong to phenomenology. An example used by Husserl is
noteworthy. If I clarify a concept such as "psyche," then
I make the word-meaning clear to myself, and seek the
"genuine" or "real" meaning. That is to say, I seek the
"fulfilling" meaning, the noema, which belongs to the
fulfilling intuition. The point of view here is not ontic;
I do not want to transform the noematic object into the
object itself. Since noemata belong in phenomenology,
Husserl concludes, all clarification is phenomenological.

Through the "mere change of view," all the eidetic
axioms may be found in the context of phenomenology.
Not only is phenomenology "the mother-ground" from
which all ontological insights are derived. It also "is not
and cannot be" indebted to the other ontologies for
anything, just as it cannot be indebted to all the other
"dogmatic" sciences. Quite oblivious of the actual indebtedness of phenomenology to the sciences, "empirical" or
"ontological"—it owes *everything* to them and to natural
experience, as a matter of fact—Husserl goes on, in a grand
finale, to make sure that the leadership of phenomenology
is unmistakable. It is first through the systematic reflective
work of phenomenology, which determines all motives

which lie in the phenomena, that ontological inquiry can "unfold its full power," and "receive its full certainty." "Only the phenomenologist," he concludes, "will be able to perform the deepest clarifications with respect to the essences building themselves up in systematically constitutive layers, and thus prepare the grounding of the ontologies." The reader must reconcile himself as well as he can to the paradox of the "certainty" which is supposedly conferred by phenomenology, without any guarantee as to its achievement. He must also be sure to look twice at the language, in order to break the charm of such illusion-giving expressions as "unfolding full power" and "deepest clarification." Obviously, Husserl had lived alone too much. It was not for the best interests of himself as well as the cause of philosophy that he was free to remove himself so largely from the impact of hostile ideas. The "misunderstandings" of those critics he happened to expose were by no means an excuse for retreating from the really important thought-movements of the twentieth century. The enormous progress of the sciences had virtually no impact on his thought, as he painstakingly dug ever "deeper" into a non-natural "dimension of inquiry," always motivated by his early antinaturalism. It is almost incredible that he could bring himself to say that his "pure" procedure owed nothing to the sciences, and still hope to "reform" the sciences.

If it is true in any sense that Descartes had discovered a "new world" without knowing it—and Husserl means by that the world of "pure subjectivity"—it also turns out that Husserl himself mistakes endless fog banks for the real world, and structures frozen out of conscious experience for the real "mother-ground" of the sciences. For that is what the "constitution" of all things, natural and cultural, comes to signify. Not content with a limited procedure, with its proper sphere of usefulness and application, Husserl sought to outflank naturalism by injecting the cardinal principle of idealism into his argument at crucial points.[9] Having made an undeniably important advance in methodology, and with some impressive descriptive results to show, Husserl pressed on to the generalization of a universal philosophy. He should have known how to draw the line for an ancillary, subordinate discipline, and how to live and work in cooperation with "naturalistic" workers, on a basis of mutual respect, on which he could then afford to insist. Not only did he "miss" the real world; at times he even despaired of attaining the realm of phenomenology itself. In a moment of humility (in his "Author's Preface to the English Edition of the *Ideas*"), he saw with right that he would never set foot on the "promised land." Only he never really knew why. That has been made clear.

---

9. In keeping with characteristic passages in the *Ideen,* Vol. II, p. 297, for example, where he speaks of experiencing subjects as giving meaning to nature, and argues that if spirits were eliminated from the world, that there would be no nature; and there is an explicit idealistic commitment in the *Formale und Transzendentale Logik*. According to the "cardinal principle," consciousness is the universal condition of being.

## Chapter VII

# THE LIMITS OF SUBJECTIVISM

## A. THE MEANING OF "TRANSCENDENCE"

It has been seen that the concept of experience has proved tenuous enough to be used in support of widely divergent philosophies. No one would care to be placed in the position of denying the findings of experience. It is therefore of the first importance to establish its locus and to determine its nature so clearly that abuses will be made difficult, if not impossible. In recent philosophical literature the theme of "Experience and Transcendence" has been a prominent one, for it has been evident that a philosophy of experience must face the problem of dealing with what is "beyond" experience. For the most part the discussion has been unsatisfactory, and in some cases the trend of thought has been fantastic and ridiculous. This is merely one aspect of a general antiscientific, irrationalistic tendency which, because of its numerous representatives in so many countries, threatens to be a serious danger to the cause of clarity of thought and soundness of action.

The first facts to establish about experience are: (1) *where* experience is; (2) *when* experience is; (3) the *causal conditions* of experience; (4) the boundaries of experience; (5) whether there is meaning to the talk of transcendence, or of something "beyond experience." Clear-cut answers to these questions would surely undermine, and, indeed, render baseless an extensive philosophical literature, and embarrass well-entrenched professional interests in the larger field of philosophy.

In answering these questions, one should never lose sight of the "basic fact" for all philosophical reflection of man's recent development in the physical universe. Ernst Haeckel's formulation of the various "cosmological theorems" in his *Riddle of the Universe* (1899) was an effective statement about the various stages of the evolution of the earth and man, and it remains decidedly pertinent for philosophy. The "cosmological theorems" should be followed by a corresponding set of "cultural theorems," so that the philosopher may always be reminded of the dependence of man on conditions causing cultural evolution—economic, social, and psychological, as well as material factors of the environment. The implications for the idealistic thesis concerning the primacy of the mind have been seen. The central position accorded to the *"cogito"* in French philosophy must certainly be affected by such considerations of fact. It may well be largely true that to undermine faith in the primacy of the *"cogito"* is to assail the honor of France, but one should not shrink from that unhappy eventuality. Furthermore, all the important findings of the special sciences which are concerned with man and nature should be borne in mind by the philosopher. The growing knowledge about the nature of thought processes; the status of the soul, which, like the luminiferous ether, is now a discarded hypothesis; the grounding of values in actual social and psychological realities; the study of actual types of men, primitive and historical; and also a sound knowledge of methodology: these are some of the things which might help greatly in preventing false and unbridled assertions about man and his world from passing for profound insights. Many recent and present writers on philosophy may be charged with egregious ignorance of these very important, pertinent matters. The errors which crept into the phenomenological movement, and especially the great proliferation of existentialist philosophies, might otherwise have been as difficult to market as, say, purely imaginative and unfounded physical views which disregard the findings of the physical scientists.

Terms come and go in philosophy. Some of them have their day without much fanfare. At times, a term comes into great prominence as a rallying point for important interests. For the past, one thinks of reason, freedom, and even of experience, with its "inner" and "outer" dimensions, and its idealistic or realistic variants. Diverse causes could thus be served by supposed appeals to "experience."

Just now, the term "transcendence" is prominent in many countries. It is a term with which to conjure; it frequently has a vague, emotional appeal; and it is a focal point for obscurantism and anti-intellectualism—but, also, a name for a concept in phenomenological inquiry, which, with all the necessary safeguards, may measure up to the requirements of intellectualism. Even in the latter case, however, it has come to serve a dubious purpose, for what should have been a strictly methodological concept of transcendence before long turns out to be a term of disparagement for a "merely" naturalistic or factual realm.

The term "beyond" is as intriguing as it is useful. When the environment is sufficiently perplexing, or embarrassing, one must press "beyond" it. But the goal is not apt to be something attainable, at least in this life. That would only serve to prolong the embarrassment. It must be mysterious and unattainable. In "respectable" quarters it must be an article of faith, and at least a noumenon.

Before deciding to leave the world, even philosophically, one ought to emulate Kant in taking another look at the world of experience. Kant's example is commendable, even though his arguments and analysis are not at all cogent. His discussion of the ground of the distinction between phenomena and noumena is open to all the objections which an idealistic theory must face, and which it cannot successfully meet. The general mind required for Kant's theory of knowledge is no more than a fiction. As an explanatory device, it might be entertained as a possible construction, but it would always be regarded as an empty construction, with no empirical evidence to support it, and hence as purely gratuitous.

In some cases, a more sympathetic understanding would seem to be called for. Thus, "transcendence" may refer to the limits set by human taboos, inhibitions, prejudices, or vested interests. "Freedom" then lies in the "beyond." Under a dictatorship that may be one of the few possible devices for conveying the aspiration of deliverance. The obliteration of freedom makes it to be all the more precious as an ideal. Since the political conditions do not permit mention of any of the freedoms in the concrete, freedom in the abstract becomes a rallying cry, an ideal, and it is conveniently located in the "beyond"—it is "transcendent." It is understandable that sophisticated scholars could derive solace thereby in recent Argentina.[1] The vague, emotional suggestiveness of the term makes it possible to reach a larger number of people. Historical modes of opposition to dominant repressive interests have

1. Professor Reulet's treatment of it is a case in point. Cf. A. Reulet, "Being, Value, and Existence," in *Philosophy and Phenomenological Research*, Vol. IX, No. 3 (March, 1949), and the present writer's discussion, "Professor Reulet on Being, Value, and Existence," same journal, Vol. X, No. 1 (September, 1949).

at times taken devious routes. Perhaps the present illustration indicates the best use to which the concept of the "beyond" has ever been put. If it is connected with mystery, the reason can easily be one of practical necessity. It is unfortunate, however, that scholars so often fail to understand what they are really doing, and resort to antiscientific rationalizations of their plight.

Quite apart from the direct questions to be answered about experience, questions which are designed to establish its locus in a real sense, is the methodological treatment of experience with the real world "bracketed." Experience is now "pure" experience, reflective experience with the "thesis of existence" suspended. "Transcendence" in its basic sense now means the world of "natural" things; and the natural world seems so lowly from the new perspective. In the search for certainty and for perfection, the philosopher is to free himself from the entanglements of the real world. Following the "radical" reduction, he is to engage in "constitutive" activities. How could a sound theory of reality result thereby? It is "essentially" impossible to derive the realm of real existence from the "reduced" realm of consciousness. The phenomenological procedure is valuable in providing a preparatory device for clarification, and an aid in the analysis of experience and in conceptual reconstruction. If developed apart from the causal methods of the sciences and all the other scientific procedures, it could never yield a theory of reality. Only a complete methodology is capable of that achievement.

## B. THE "RIDDLE" OF TRANSCENDENCE

Husserl's posthumously published book, *The Idea of Phenomenology*,[2] is a revealing document. Written several years before his *Ideas* of 1913, it presents an early formulation of the "reduction." Husserl states that the "transcendence" of knowledge presents a serious problem when one begins to reflect about the possibility of knowledge. All natural knowledge, whether prescientific or scientific, is described by him as transcendent "objectivating" knowledge. In his characteristic way he declares that natural knowledge "posits" objects as being, and that it claims to know facts which are not "truly given" and "immanent" in it. Is this a fair statement about natural knowledge? The term "posit" belongs in the post-Kantian tradition, and to speak of knowledge as "positing" existent objects is understandable if the point of view is idealistic. The naturalist, however, *finds* objects, and he recognizes himself as one object-complex among other object-complexes.

Continuing his analysis of transcendence, and along with it, of "immanence," Husserl proceeds to distinguish between two meanings of the terms, which, he points out, tend to be confused early in epistemological inquiry. On the one hand, there is the contrast between the "immanently given" in the sense of being contained in a cognitive experience, and the *transcendent* in the sense of an object of knowledge which is not contained in the act of knowledge. The question then becomes: how can the experience get beyond itself? On the other hand, there is quite a different kind of contrast between immanence and transcendence: one can grasp a meant objectivity in immediate

---

2. *Die Idee der Phänomenologie*, edited by Walter Biemel, Haag, Martinus Nijhoff, 1950.

evidence, one can "see" it immediately; and, in contrast to this direct existence, there is the meaning or positing of something which is not itself seen. This is "transcendence" in a second sense. The question then arises as to how knowledge can posit something as being which is not directly and truly given in it.

Transcendence therewith presents the initial problem of the critique of knowledge for Husserl. He seems convinced that it is the riddle which stands in the way of natural knowledge and stimulates new inquiries. In the phenomenological critique of knowledge, one may not make use of any "pregiven" transcendence. If one does not understand *how* it is possible for knowledge to meet something transcendent of it, he also does not know *whether* it is possible. The scientific grounding of a transcendent existent is not accepted as a solution, because all mediate proof goes back to immediate evidence, and the immediate already contains the "riddle."

But care should be taken not to be walled in by a show of words, to avoid overextending the artificial device of pure reflection. The critique of knowledge must recognize the cognitive relation on the level of "outer" experience as involving the knower and the known. It is unwarranted to begin by abstracting knowledge, and then to find transcendence to be a riddle. The "riddle" evaporates when the real character of the immanence-transcendence distinction is recognized. It is indeed a problem resulting from the adoption of the phenomenological procedure—a methogenic problem; and the riddle disappears on naturalistic grounds. It is an error to inject into the naturalistic view a distinction proper to an opposing view. The *inductive* problem of judging about objects which are not immediately "given" should be

divided into two types: the naturalistic inductive problem
of inference to facts by way of generalization; and the
pure, abstractive epistemological problem, beginning with
an artificially isolated knower who is detached from all
natural and cultural conditions, to infer "transcendent"
things which are not immediately present. This queer
knowing being was born at a definite time and place; he
has feasted on the world, and has profited by his social
system. That does not prevent him from asking, in the
critique of knowledge, for the evidence of an existing
world; and he should not be thought forgetful if he seems
to slight his parents or his wife when asking for the
evidence of an "other ego."

To return to Husserl's argument: he is concerned with
establishing his basic thesis that epistemology can never
be built up on the basis of natural science of any kind.
The line of thought is clear enough. In order to understand how knowledge of transcendence is possible, one
must somehow *see* the relationship of knowledge to the
object of knowledge. Since this is held to be impossible,
we are to alter our own course and perform the "reduction" to pure consciousness. The problem of how transcendent knowledge is possible, and, more generally, how
knowledge in general is possible, can never be solved,
in his view, on the ground of pregiven knowledge of
transcendence, or even on the basis of the exact sciences.
It is nonsense, in his opinion, to try to explain possibilities
through logical derivation from non-intutive knowledge.
As he states it: "Even if I may be completely certain that
there are transcendent worlds, and even if I may allow
all the natural sciences to be valid, I cannot borrow anything from them."[3] The "epistemological" reduction must

---

3. *Op. cit.,* p. 38.

accordingly be performed, i.e., all transcendence is to be eliminated, or to have the index of indifference, of epistemological nullity—an index which says: the existence of all these transcendences, whether I believe them or not, does not concern me here, it is not my concern here to judge about them, they are "put out of play."

The need for the phenomenological reduction is supported furthermore by the contention that the pure *cogitatio* is absolutely given, in contradistinction to the givenness of an external thing in outer perception. In Husserl's words, "The transcendence of a thing requires that we place it in question. We do not understand how perception can meet something transcendent; but we do understand how perception can meet something immanent, in the form of reflective and pure immanent perception, of the reduced type."[4] One may have an appearance in view which refers to, or means, something not given in the appearance itself, so that there may be doubt about its very being. But if the seeing itself is meant, and nothing but that which is grasped in seeing, then it does not make sense to doubt. This is regarded by Husserl as a finality, "an absolute self-evidence." As for that which is not self-evident, the problematical, he speaks of the "mystery" of transcendent meaning.

In this way, Husserl reacts against "psychologism," "anthropologism," and "biologism," which were conspicuous (and, unfortunately, erratic) in the allegedly scientific philosophies in the scholarly world at the time. That they were erratic was forcefully established by Husserl in his *Logical Investigations*. That there could have been a much superior scientific philosophy, even on that level of scientific achievement, is undoubtedly true; and it could be

---

4. *Op. cit.*, p. 49.

shown that it was not necessary to resort to a philosophy of immanence because of the inadequacy of the scientific philosophies of the time.

The idealistic premise latent in Husserl's doctrine of transcendence is clearly seen in a passage appended to his lectures on *The Idea of Phenomenology*,[5] in which he asks about the evidence for the assumption of "things outside me." Can they be assumed on the basis of outer perception? He writes: "A simple glance grasps my environment of things up to the furthest fixed stars. But perhaps that is all a dream, a sensory illusion. Such and such visual contents, such and such apperceptions, such and such judgments, that is the given, all that is given in a genuine sense. Does perception have any evidence for the *contribution*[6] of the transcendence? But as for evidence, what is it but a certain psychical character? Perception and character of the evidence, that is the given, and why something should correspond to this complex is a riddle. I say then perhaps: We *infer* transcendence, through inferences we pass beyond the immediately given, it is in general a contribution of inferences, to ground the non-given by means of the given. But if we leave aside the question, how grounding can make such a contribution, we can answer: Analytic inferences would not help, the transcendent is not implied in the immanent. Synthetic inferences, however, how could they be other than experiential inferences? That which is experienced offers grounds of experience, that is: rational probability-grounds for that which is not experienced, but then only for that which can be experienced. But the transcendent is on principle not experienceable."

---

5. *Beilage* II, pp. 81 f.
6. Italics the present writer's.

In the next appendix,[7] Husserl states that the relationship of knowledge to something transcendent is unclear. He reasons that if the essence of this relationship could be given, so that we could *see* it, then we would be able to understand the possibility of knowledge. Since, as he holds, this requirement cannot be fulfilled for transcendent knowledge, the latter is impossible.

These passages show how far Husserl has moved from the simple facts of natural experience and knowledge, and how he operates with idealistic limitations and dogmas. When he asks about the existence of things "outside of me" he begins with a false abstraction, which may be called the "error of isolation" (although this style of beginning would not be objectionable if it were recognized explicitly as artificial, for what it is and for what it can achieve). The "possibility" that the starry heavens might be an object of a dream, or of illusion, may be dismissed as of interest to philosophical freshmen alone. If the stars are dream objects, then so is the entire subjective realm, apart from the actual, direct content of a passing experience. The supposedly past experience may also be illusory, a trick of the memory. Thus one could not claim anything absolutely. To speak, as Husserl does, of transcendence as a contribution of perception, and of evidence as a psychical character, is to betray an idealistic bias. This could be, but is not, justified in connection with a special procedure, to see what it can yield for the critique of knowledge. Instead of that, it is advanced as contributing the basis for the only possible critique of knowledge— "pure" knowledge and "pure" immanent experience. Certainly perception is of prime importance in the experience of transcendence. But transcendence is there, and

7. *Beilage* III, pp. 83 f.

was there before the perception, before all perceptions. It will be granted that evidence has its "psychical" aspect. But it requires the presence of the objectivity that is involved. Hence it is more than a "psychical character." The "evidence" which is restricted to a "psychical character" can only be one aspect of evidence, or one type of evidence. The evidence of an expected eclipse of the sun involves the natural, "transcendent" world. It is no riddle that something—the physical objects—should correspond to the perception. A riddle exists, but only for a short time, if there is nothing to correspond to it. The existence of transcendent objects is simply a fact, and the alleged epistemological riddle is due to the ingenuity of a sophisticated philosopher in erecting a definitional wall between his truncated experiences and the events of the physical universe.

When Husserl states that the transcendent is not implied in the immanent, he errs doubly. In the first place, there can be no immanence really, for there is no such thing as being "in the mind," whether it be Locke's "empty cabinet" or any other kind of long-discarded receptacle. To speak of "retiring to immanence" really is to be guilty of an illicit *metabasis*, for the idea of a transfer from the real to the artificial "pure" realm is absurd. In the second place, the talk of immanence is justified only as applying to a critical, reflective procedure, as suspending existential beliefs and viewing everything "from the point of view of immanence," i.e., in "pure reflection." Such a strictly controlled procedure could not allow for a "metaphysics of immanence."

It can only be argued that the transcendent cannot be experienced on principle if the direct experience of an individual is meant, in one sense of the term "transcendence," meaning "something beyond my immediate field of experience." That is really the problem of inductive knowledge. If, however, the term transcendence names the objectivity meant in and by the experience, the denial of the knowledge of transcendence would be equivalent to saying that the object of experience cannot be experienced. It would incur the error of treating an artificial construction as the total reality. This leads to the conclusion that transcendent knowledge is impossible. If "pure" reflection, for which all belief in transcendence is suspended, comes up against this impasse, why not resort to a more complete reflection which knows how to preserve all the findings of natural experience, and also how to evaluate the special findings of "pure" reflection.

The purpose of the subjective approach of phenomenology must be borne in mind at all times. The problem-situation and goal which it is designed to meet must be recalled. The alleged unsatisfactoriness of natural perception, the contention that it is impossible to construct a satisfactory philosophy on the basis of the sciences, the argument that we may not "presuppose" transcendent facts, on the one hand, and the positive desire for certainty, absoluteness, and completeness, on the other hand, lead to the methodological isolation of the knowing self, and to a beginning with artificially detached experiences. *In reality,* however, there can be no isolated self, *in reality* there can be no *cogitationes* without their causal conditions, there can be no mind without a body, without a brain, there can be no survival without direct relationships with an environment, and no environment without the natural ("transcendent") world which comprises it. *In reality* an outer perception cannot be treated apart from the stimulus, and an "inner perception" similarly involves causal conditions as well as the meant object. Does one merely *suspend* beliefs, or existential theses, in performing the reduction, in order to make possible a more thorough-going reflective inspection of the process, structure, and validity of knowledge? Or does one operate with a tacit metaphysics from the outset, so that he is predestined to make an idealistic landing after an epistemological flight which begins with the demeaning of the naturalistic-scientific view of the world and its methodology? This question is unfortunately entirely fair, as shown by Husserl's further development of his method; and it is all the more important in view of some of the grotesque and even dangerous developments which have clouded the philosophical atmosphere of so many countries in our time, under the name of existentialism.

## C. THE NEED FOR COMPLETE REFLECTION

The early draft of the "reduction" provided by *The Idea of Phenomenology* cannot be defended on the ground that it is merely a preliminary "breakthrough," to use Husserl's own expression, applied to his initial development of a phenomenological philosophy. It has been amply shown that the later and more fully mature formulation, while certainly more incisive and detailed, reveals similar weaknesses. With an increasing lapse of time since his sojourn among "naturalistic" thinkers, he comes to speak more pointedly of an independent, "absolute" realm, which is not established logically or evidentially. Had he not lived in such a protected, insulated environment—had he, for example, frequented the New York Philosophical Circle and been exposed to frontal objections to his position—he would hardly have thought it unnecessary to justify his idealistic premises, as a major undertaking. The formulations of the *Ideas* of 1913, which have been examined, help to show why the concept of transcendence could not but play an ill-fated subsequent role.

In contrast to "immanent being," which is "absolute," the world of transcendent "things" is held to involve actual consciousness, and not merely a logically conceived consciousness *("auf Bewusstsein . . . angewiesen").* This is expressed pointedly with regard to the initial stage of the "reduction" in the posthumously published "Paris Lectures" of Husserl.[8] "An object exists for me, that is, it is valid for me in accordance with consciousness. But this validity is only validity for me so long as I presume that I could confirm it, that I . . . could provide experiences and other evidences, in which I would be by it myself, as though I had realized it as *really there.*" On the "egological ground" of the phenomenologist, existence and determinate being have no other meaning than being on the basis of possible confirmation. True being, whether real or ideal, "has meaning only as a particular correlate of my own intentionality." But "the being of a real thing is not a mere *cogito* of a single perception which I now have. The perception itself and its object in the 'how' of intentional givenness refers me by means of the presumptive horizon to an endlessly open system of *possible* perceptions as such, which are not invented, but are motivated in my intentional life, and can lose their presumptive validity if a conflicting experience annuls it."

In his *Ideas,* Husserl contended that the realm of pure consciousness which is achieved by his "radical reflection" is not a part of nature, because nature is only possible as an intentional unity motivated in it through immanent con-

8. Cf. E. Husserl, *Cartesianische Meditationen und Pariser Vorträge,* edited by S. Strasser, Haag, Martinus Nijhoff, 1950, pp. 23 f. The "Paris Lectures" were delivered at the Sorbonne on February 23 and 28, 1929, with the title "Introduction to Transcendental Phenomenology."

nections. This "middle period" thesis may be compared with the later discussion of this point in his *Cartesian Meditations*.[9] As Husserl states it, I and my life remain undisturbed in my "validity of being," no matter what happens to the world by way of being or non-being, no matter how I may decide about that. The ego and ego-life remaining after the *epoché* is not a piece of the world, and if it says: 'I am, *ego cogito*,' that no longer means: I, this man, am." But, further: Just as the reduced ego is no piece of the world, so conversely the world and every mundane object is not a piece of my ego, is not immanent in my conscious life. "This transcendence belongs to the sense of everything mundane, even though it can only obtain the entire meaning which determines it, along with its being-validity, from my experiencing, my actual perceiving, thinking, valuing, doing." If this transcendence of an "irreal" inclusion in consciousness belongs to the meaning of the world, "then the ego itself which it carries in itself as a validating meaning . . . is called *transcendental* in the phenomenological sense." The assumption in this reasoning is simple enough to hold up to view. If I suspend all beliefs concerning a transcendent world, my inner experiences of the presumed world cannot be said to have a locus in the world; and if all scientific judgments which are based on the realm of nature are placed in abeyance, the residual ego cannot be the objectively determined self of anthropology and naturalistic psychology. We also get away from biology, including physiology. The reader may be tempted to ask whether the phenomenologist gets away from breathing. Unfortunately, he also requires a

---

9. *Op. cit.*, pp. 64 f. This work was first published in a French translation, *Méditations Cartésiennes*, trans. by Gabrielle Pfeiffer and Emmanuel Levinas, Paris, Librairie Armand Colin, 1931.

reasonably pure atmosphere, and, in fact, a reasonably balanced state of the physical universe. But, enough of this palpably obvious confusion. In striving to establish something so radically new that no one could get on a common basis with him, Husserl took his place in the official German academic tradition (the *geheimrätliche Tradition*), determined to outdo his predecessors in the achievement of a pure, inner philosophy.

In order to recognize the limitations of subjectivism, Husserl would have had to make use of a more complete reflective view than he had at his disposal. To reflect upon reflecting, and so on *ad infinitum,* need not yield any new results, i.e., beyond the stage of making sure that the phenomenologist has been faithful in following out his own precepts. A *complete* reflective procedure must recover the natural and cultural "dimensions" of inquiry, in addition to the phenomenological "dimension"; and the phenomenologist must be seen as historically conditioned. Thus, Husserl might have been able, finally, to see himself as dismissing Berkeleyan idealism, while being nevertheless tacitly inclined toward assuming the cardinal principle of idealism by way of correlating existence and consciousness. It would have shown him how he mistook his own methodological talk of the "constitution" of reality for the *real* reality, which is existentially independent of our cognitive processes, and is properly described as naturalistic in character. It would have explained his frequently expressed antiscientific feeling, usually expressed as opposition to the *philosophy* reflected by the sciences of his time. It would have revealed him in his role of absolutist and eternalist, as making dogmatic claims for essences, or the "eidetic" realm. It would have shown him to be a true son of the first *Reich,* as one who accepted its privileges and class distinctions. And yet, on the good side, one cannot deny the beneficial effect of an attempt to carry through a "radical" suspension of beliefs. It may well be an indispensable stage in all sound philosophical procedure, both because of its own special descriptive merits, and as facilitating universal openmindedness and a thoroughgoing readiness for final understanding. Only it must be applied strictly, and embraced to the most general science of method.

## D.  DOUBT AND CERTAINTY

### 1. The Cartesian Procedure of Doubt and its Phenomenological Use

The subject matter of phenomenolgy is viewed as independent of the natural world order for the purpose of the analysis. The experiences with their "intended" objects are the theme. Husserl states[10] that what is "intentionally" indicated in the apperceptive horizon of a perception is not possible but *certain*. That can always be said of the *present* experience. Can it be said of "inner" experience as a whole? This question is best answered in connection with the Cartesian method of doubt.

Because of its adoption by Husserl as a device for defining the field of transcendental subjectivity, special interest attaches to the Cartesian procedure. The latter is open to serious objections, as is well known. If the purpose were to ascertain how far one could proceed in doubting without contradiction, the answer would have to be, to a solipsism of the present, and hence passing moment, with the past moment already doubted as soon as one reflects upon it. The experience of doubt which occurs "now" is indubitable; but a new "now" takes its place,

---

10. *Erfahrung und Urteil,* p. 105.

and the old one is "not now," which makes it dubitable. Unless absolute reliance can be placed upon memory, or an absolute mind with a fixed structure is provided, or some equivalent principle is allowed, the Cartesian procedure is utterly fruitless. What Descartes did with his method is of historical interest merely. There is a tradition among idealists to admit that what Descartes established was a "thin truth," while maintaining that it is the "important truth" (*viz.*, the "certainty" of the "I doubt" which cannot be doubted, or of the mind). Nietzsche's words in *Beyond Good and Evil*[11] may be recalled: "There may even be puritanical fanatics of conscience, who prefer to put their last trust in a sure nothing, rather than in an uncertain something."

On the other hand, the Cartesian method of doubt may be appropriated in quite a different way, and "doubt" be instituted as a means of inspecting the "normal and natural" assumptions of the mind. It is really the phenomenological substitute for doubt, and now means "suspension." The attempt to achieve a universal suspension of judgment or belief takes the place of the fruitless method of doubt. The general "thesis of existence" which underlies normal experience, and every element of assent or denial in cognitive experience, are placed in abeyance, in order to serve as the subject matter of reflective analysis. The suspension affects beliefs pertaining to other human beings, and oneself as a psychological subject. What is the advantage of this method? And does it provide certainty, in the sense of indubitability?

For one thing, it delimits a distinctive domain for philosophical inquiry. The detached reflective procedure, according to which every object in the world or in human

---

11. *Beyond Good and Evil*, New York, Tudor Publishing Co., 1931, p. 9.

society, or every item in experience and knowledge, is treated as a correlate of a particular experience of an individual experiencing being, with the "existential" thesis suspended, determines the initial stage of the reflective analysis. This stream of experience is indeed the result of a social-historical process, and it could not be inspected without the prior existence of society and a long tradition. That "naturalistic" truth must be recognized. Can the phenemenological residuum resulting from the *logical* analysis be said to be "certain"? Not in the Cartesian sense, or, rather, in the Cartesian sense rendered consistent, if one seeks to determine an endless domain in that way. Without assumptions of uniformity the latter cannot be established, and therewith is sacrificed the ideal of certainty. In other words, it appears that if certainty is to be realized, then nothing is realized; for one must be restricted to a passing now, which allows no basis for generalization and objectively valid determinations.

If one proceeds to determine the "essential" structures and laws of experience, viewed from the subjective perspective, he may claim to be able to discern, to intuit something "general" and thus to have obviated the difficulty of the passing stream of nows. But he can only do that by assuming that every general structure persists, by a principle of the "conservation of generals," analogous to the "conservation of simples" of Platonic and Leibnizian fame. Can *that* principle be made a matter of intuitive evidence? And even if it could, would not another principle of conservation be required, in order to make it continue to be valid—a principle of the conservation of conservation principles? And must not that principle in turn be established by direct vision? And so on, *ad infinitum?*

As a matter of fact, the direct discernment of general structures must be accepted as an important feature of experience. So far as the question of certainty with respect to the occurrence of events is concerned, however—i.e., certainty of anything beyond the specious present, or the content of the "now"—it appears clear that although a perception of a general structure may be termed a "general" perception, it must always be instated anew. Only the passing general perception is "certain" in the Cartesian sense. Thus, "essences" are no better off than particular sensory objects, *so far as this criterion is concerned.* While phenomenologically real (i.e., appearing in experience), the idealities (concepts, forms, relations) which are "read out of" experience are said to have a nontemporal kind of "being,"[12] which is, strictly speaking, no being at all. The term "exists" is really nonsignificant for them, unless one refers to the experiences in which they are thought or meant.

To hold that the "essential" structures, which are conceptual in character, are "prior" to the real order of existence, is to commit a fundamental error of confusion. The conceptual forms are really derived; they are "ideal," in the sense that they are the results of a *process of idealization,* of identification. The events of the existent world are prior to the abstractions of the conceptual order, in the sense of temporal precedence, and also in the sense that they alone can be spoken of as "existent." It is maintained therewith that "to exist" means to have a space-time locus in terms of physical reality.

This position is not at all met by the distinction, so often referred to, between what is "first for me" and what is "first in itself." With reference to man, the physical

---

12. Cf. Husserl, *Erfahrung und Urteil,* pp. 309 ff.

process of becoming is "first," because man is such a latecomer in cosmic history. To argue for "logical" precedence, in the sense that structures or essences are prior to existent events, is to reify abstractions. Nothing that one can establish with regard to the logical relationships of concepts may alter the facts of the relationships in time.

Husserl has maintained (in his *Formale und Transzendentale Logik*) that the formal laws of mere noncontradiction become conditions of the possibility of truth. That such principles are necessary for ordered discourse will be granted. But one cannot legislate for the facts of reality by an appeal to general principles, which are either inductive, and thus presuppose reality, or analytic, with no inherent reference to reality. The metaphysical problem in question cannot be solved by an "essential" analysis and an appeal to "essential" insight, for the required evidence is lacking, and in the nature of the case must always be lacking.

The metaphysical problem can only be treated on a naturalistic-inductive basis, and whether there is anything permanent in the world is a conclusion to be reached and not a settled fact as a point of departure. In short, the pure reflection procedure of phenomenology can only draw a metaphysics out of its procedural hat if it has already been inserted there—which is strictly forbidden by its own precepts.

Even if human beings should disappear, the determinations of the "essential" structures of perception, phantasy-experience, negation, etc., would remain valid as representing determinations of possible types of experience. They are "certain" while being experienced, and valid independently of experience. Such knowledge cannot be used as a means of compensation for those that suffer in the changing world of experience, any more than pure mathematics can be so used.

In the present discussion attention has been devoted to such examples as Husserl himself cites—conceptual forms clearly derived by a process of ideal abstraction. It is not implied therewith that reality fails to exhibit general relations or patterns of order.

## 2. Husserl on Descartes

Husserl has taken Descartes very seriously in a historical as well as in a systematic sense, and he has repeatedly discussed his significance as a pretranscendental- phenomenological philosopher.[13] In the last publication to appear during his lifetime, "The Crisis of the European Sciences and Transcendental Phenomenology," he describes Descartes as the "primal instituting genius" of modern philosophy. He finds in the first two Meditations of Descartes a depth which it is difficult to fathom, and which Descartes himself was so little able to appreciate that he let go "the great discovery" he had in his hands. This exaggerated opinion of the importance of the Cartesian *Meditations* is obviously due to Husserl's own aims. In the complete structure of Descartes's thought, as well as with respect to his influence, his works on the principles of philosophy and methodology are surely not to be subordinated to the *Meditations*. On the contrary, they deserve a greater emphasis. The *Meditations* served their historical purpose

---

13. Cf. Husserl, *Méditations Cartésiennes*, Paris, 1931, and *Die Krisis der europäischen Wissenschaften und die transzendentale Phänomenologie*, a portion of which was published during Husserl's lifetime in *Philosophia*, Vol. I, 1936, pp. 77-176. The entire work, edited by Walter Biemel, was published in the series *Husserliana*, Haag, Martinus Nijhoff, in 1954. Cf. Aron Gurwitsch's discussion of that work in *Philosophy and Phenomenological Research*, March, 1956 and March, 1957.

for Descartes, allowing him to settle accounts with the traditional Church philosophy in a conciliatory manner. For us they have a different function. It is a good thing to carry through a method of doubt periodically, as a means of freeing one's mind of fixed beliefs and dogmas, and of re-examining one's own philosophy. It is also useful as a means of achieving the universal suspension of belief *("epoché")* with which a philosopher must begin his meditations on a first philosophy. In Husserl's hands the procedure of "suspension" is certainly different from anything Descartes envisaged or intended.

But it must also be observed that another "dimension" of reflection must be added to the suspension *(epoché)* of Husserl. It is necessary to view the thinker "longitudinally" as well as "cross-sectionally," and to see him in his place in society and history, as responding to motives prompted by his social system. Reflection which neglects the causally determined order of culture is one-sided and empty in a most important respect. *Complete* reflective analysis thus goes beyond "pure" reflection. It does not face the hopeless problem of making application to reality, so that it is not enmeshed in a dilemma, the alternatives of which are a subjective detachment from reality, or the "constitution" of reality out of pure subjectivity. The complete method of reflection does not neglect any items of established knowledge, least of all the basic fact of man's place in nature and society.

As Husserl depicts Descartes's method, it is a requirement for philosophical knowledge that it be "absolutely founded," and that it be based on a ground of immediate and apodictic knowledge which in its evidence precludes all conceivable doubt. Furthermore, every step of "mediate" knowledge must be able to achieve such evidence.

The radicalism of the Cartesian procedure requires that everything be "placed in question"—the validity of all previous sciences, as well as the prescientific and extra-scientific "life-world"—and this is the historical beginning of a "radical critique of objective knowledge." The role of the Descartes-who-anticipates-Husserl is thus a clearly defined one, even if the historical Descartes was much more modest and far less thoroughgoing in his endeavor. With the fervor of Meister Eckhart, Husserl describes the original Cartesian motive in the following words: [14] "through the hell of a quasi-skeptical *epoché*, to penetrate to the entrance to heaven of an absolute rational philosophy, and to build that up systematically." The ego that performs the suspension or *"epoché"* is not included in the latter's scope. Here one finds the sought-for apodictic ground, which absolutely excludes every possible doubt, for a universal doubt would annul itself.

As Husserl views the procedure, "the" world is transformed into a mere "phenomenon," into my "ideae." "Here we have an absolutely apodictic sphere of being, under the title of 'ego,' and not merely the one axiomatic proposition *'Ego cogito'* or *'sum cogitans.'* " Husserl adds another "remarkable" result: Through the *epoché* (i.e., "method of doubt" regarded as a "suspension" of judgment) I have reached that *sphere of being* which on principle precedes everything that can conceivably be for me as its absolute, apodictic presupposition. Or, as maintained by Descartes: I, the performing ego of the *epoché*, am alone absolutely indubitable. All scientific, "mediate" foundations must therefore be led back to a single absolute, primal evidence. Husserl seems to forget, in his complete

14. *Die Krisis der europäischen Wissenschaften und die transzendentale Phänomenologie*, 1954, p. 78.

feeling of assurance, that there is no *real* "sphere of being" discovered by or for Descartes, beyond an Archimedean point of reference for philosophy, with respect to its "evidence." It is fundamentally a device for universal questioning, for descriptive analysis, and for possible philosophical construction. Evidently what the present writer sees in the *epoché* is not identical with what Husserl sees. The present writer's understanding of it makes it to be a different kind of procedure, devoid of pretense and dogma, and with a firm intention of preventing idealistic metaphysical capital from being made out of it. Any aid in making possible the delineation of a universal field for descriptive analysis is to be greeted. The *epoché* itself will not make all experience and knowledge the subject of investigation, but it does contribute toward that end, in its peculiar way. The suspension of all belief and judgment distinguishes it as a *philosophical* field for investigation.   The philosophical inquiry overlaps the regions chosen by the special sciences, but it does so in its own way. It does not presume to go into the fields of the special sciences, but orders them and their basic concepts and principles within the total structure of a world view.

For Husserl, the ego is not a residuum of the world, but rather "the absolutely apodictic positing, which is only possible through the *epoché*," through the "bracketing" of the entire "validity of the world." Descartes's admission of the soul, for example, is therefore subject to criticism. Although he is credited with beginning "a completely new kind of philosophizing which seeks its foundation in the subjective," Husserl criticizes him for not seeing that the ego, as it is discovered in the *epoché* as being for itself, is not "an" ego that can have other egos outside itself. Descartes evidently did not see that all such distinctions as I and you, inner and outer, first "constitute" themselves in the "absolute ego." As judged from Husserl's perspective, Descartes did not see "the great problems—to 'ask back' systematically from the world as a 'phenomenon' in the ego, in which really exhibitable immanent contributions of the ego the world has first received its being-sense." It is quite certain that Descartes would not have been able to understand this criticism during his lifetime, and probably not for an additional century and a half. Has "the world" really received its "being-sense" in that way? Or is it as viewed *phenomenologically* that one *considers* it in that way? The shifting to metaphysical language, and, in general, the use of pictorial, question-begging expressions, are indicative of Husserl's actual intentions. The Cartesian "radicalism or freedom from presuppositions," which was intended to lead genuine scientific knowledge back to the final sources of validity and thus to ground them absolutely, was held to require a carefully defined subjective procedure, which meant going back to the knowing ego "in its immanence." That is, in other words, the "transcendental sphere."

## E. THE TRANSCENDENTAL DIMENSION AND THE TREATMENT OF HISTORY

The term "transcendental" is one of the most objectionable terms derived from the speculative tradition. Its adoption in the context of a descriptive philosophy of experience makes it possible to exploit its original reference to purely reflective knowledge-experience for purposes of idealistic metaphysics. Husserl uses the term "transcendental" in a very wide sense, to name the motive of "asking back" or retrospective inquiry concerning the "ultimate source" of all cognitive functions, of all self-reflection of the knower. There are clearly differences of view on the nature of the alleged "ultimate source"—for example, among continuators of the Holbach-Feuerbachian, or dialectical materialist, type of philosophy, and among representatives of the natural and social sciences. From Husserl's point of view, such "dogmatic" thinkers are really not philosophers at all. Unfortunately for him, however, he is not at liberty to remake the history of philosophy, however freely he may operate in interpreting it with respect to his own aims and deciding motives.

The meaning of "transcendentalism" in the present context is understood more clearly in contrast with "objectivism." As Husserl states it,[15] objectivism operates on the ground of a world that is self-evidently given through experience and asks about its "objective truth," about that which it is in itself. For transcendentalism, however, the "being-sense" of the pregiven life-world is a *subjective structure,* is the "contribution" of an experiencing pre-scientific life. As for the "objectively true world" of science, that is a structure of a higher level. Transcendentalism maintains that only a radical, retrospective inquiry going back to *the* subjectivity which ultimately brings about all world-validity, to the nature of the contributions of reason, can make the objective truth "understandable" and reach the final "being-sense" of the world. Hence it is not the being of the world in its unquestionable obviousness that is "first in itself." That which is "first in itself" is *subjectivity,* which "gives" (or "pregives") the world. Expressed in this way, with the world itself and not the "world-meaning" given by subjectivity, the thesis of transcendentalism is a sheer dogma, which is characteristic

15. *Op. cit.,* p. 70.

of the writings of Husserl's last period. The methodological reasons for the subjective frame[16] have been long forgotten, and Husserl has come to believe that there is an actual process of meaning-giving at work, amounting to creation. He is careful to point out the danger that this subjectivity be construed as man, or as a psychological subjectivity. His error is on a different level, and is so far-reaching that it involves a reinterpretation of the entire philosophical tradition.

The central problem of Husserl's "radical transcendental subjectivism" is formulated as one which concerns the relationship of the ego and its conscious life to the world of which the ego is conscious, and whose true being the ego knows in its own cognitive structures.[17] The evidence of the method of positive science is not held to be deceptive, nor are its contributions held to be merely apparent ones. His point is that this evidence itself is made to be a problem, that the method of objective science is based upon an unquestioned "deeply concealed subjective ground." The "philosophical illumination" first shows the true sense of the contributions of positive science, as well as the true "being-sense" of the objective world, to be transcendental-subjective in character (103). The "concealed" dimension of the transcendental is held to be really brought to view. The realm of experience that is "opened up" in its infinitude becomes a field for "a methodological philosophy of work," and that is intended to provide the ground on which *("von diesem Boden aus")* all conceivable philosophical and scientific problems of the past are to be put and to be decided (104). The pretense

---

16. The principle of the "primacy of the self," or of subjectivity, is taken over by the existentialists, where it usually appears "as though shot out of a pistol"—unheralded, unjustified, unclarified.

17. *Op. cit.*, p. 101.

of this contention is so unwarranted that it hardly seems likely that Husserl could have realized concretely what he was asserting. Even if one could allow him the possibility in principle of handling all past philosophical problems in his way, it is preposterous to boast of a method for deciding all scientific problems. That could only be done by shutting one's eyes to them, or by dissolving them in intuition, which phenomenology as a descriptive method cannot do. Husserl had practiced his unchallenged monologue too long, and had combed over his self-consciousness to such an extent, that to him the term "everything" came to mean only the set of correlates of his consciousness.

The treatment of history—intellectual and general—carries the basic pattern of the discussion to its final consequences. The history of philosophy, ever since the appearance of the theory of knowledge and the serious attempts at a transcendental philosophy, is portrayed by Husserl as a history of mighty tensions between objectivistic and transcendental philosophy. Why that is so prominent in intellectual history, he does not venture to explain; nor would one expect that it could be done with this type of analysis. In the form of the issue of materialism *vs.* spiritualism this "inner split of philosophical development" has long been familiar. Husserl does not specify and apparently does not recognize the issues involved by the traditional opposition he portrays. The actors in the drama are nameless. He does not apply a historical method in the usual sense, his aim being to make comprehensible the "teleology" in the historical becoming of philosophy and to "clarify" ourselves as its carriers. That is not to view the process "from without," as though the temporal stream in which we ourselves have become were "a merely external, causal succession," but "from within."[18] He is interested in a critical understanding of "the total unity of history—of *our* history." We have our function "as heirs and co-carriers of the will-direction going through it," and we owe that to a "primal instituting which is at once a post-instituting and transformation of the Greek primal instituting." In this is found to lie the "teleological" beginning and the true birth of the European spirit in general.

It would be difficult to say less about history and to miss its real nature more than Husserl has done here. He had long ago lost contact with concrete historical facts. True, he mentioned such facts as Torquemada and the Inquisition in his last period; but, for his philosophical purposes, he had forgotten the real facts of history, which are also sordid, and which make impossible the carrying-through of a "teleological" point of view of this kind. One need not, however, go to the sweat and blood of history to make a demurrer. By attending to the history of philosophy itself, any claim to the alleged unity of aspiration can be broken down. The conflict between objectivism and transcendentalism is, to be sure, a con-spicuous one. But the issue is defined in terms of Husserl's own philosophizing. That interpretation goes on within the limits of a subjective inquiry. The "elucidation of history by a retrospective inquiry concerning the primal instituting of the aims which bind future generations in so far as they live in them in sedimented forms, but can always be awakened and criticized in a new liveliness"— that kind of inquiry is the self-reflection of the philosopher about his aims and his relations to his spiritual prede-cessors. The point is, again to make alive, in their

18. *Op. cit.,* pp. 72 ff.

"concealed" historical sense, the sedimented concepts which are the basis of his private and nonhistorical work. Toward that end one must free oneself from all prejudices (prejudgments), including one's own "self-evidences," recognizing that prejudices are elements of unclearness deriving from a traditional sedimentation. A "historical reflection" of this kind is thus a self-reflection (a "deepest" self-reflection) designed to give a self-understanding of one's aims.

If there is a historical origin, a "primal instituting," then it appears to Husserl (and this is not proved) that there is also, essentially, a "final instituting." The spirit of the inquiry requires that there be complete clarity concerning the truth, by a method for which every step is apodictic. Philosophy thus becomes an "infinite task." The present discussion shows how Husserl has derived from post-Kantian idealism as well as from Descartes.

But Husserl insists on turning away from the "self-interpretations" of the historical philosophers. Because of his carefully defined subjective procedure, he feels that he is superior to his predecessors, in being so reliable in his own self-inspection. (It should be noted, however, that Husserl never "inspected" himself with respect to his actual economic, social, and political place in German society, either under the monarchy, to which he later looked back with regret at its passing, or under the Weimar republic. To the extent to which such "meanings" should have entered even his pure reflective consciousness, the self-inspection of the latter is empty.) Only in the "final outcome" (or "final instituting") is the aim revealed, only from that point can the unity of all philosophies and philosophers be revealed, and an illumination be gained, in which one understands the past thinkers as they never could have understood themselves (74). Whether Husserl considered in detail the consequences of this "unity," which would amount to the amazing proposal to "unify" Catholics, materialists, and "whatnotists," is doubtful. Not that a unified theory of intellectual history is impossible: it is indeed possible to account for the development of ideas in relationship to the various conditioning factors of history—social, economic, scientific, religious, etc.—by means of a well-integrated logical theory, in which due "weight" is given to the various factors. The situation is quite different for the subjective point of view, however, and even the most liberal use of the process of suspension of judgments and "bracketing" of real events cannot achieve the desired unity. The causal-genetic explanation of intellectual history endeavors to account for conflicts, and not to render them unreal, or merely mistaken, where-as the subjective demand for unity misses the actual historical significance of the conflicts. It appears that Husserl removes his view from any possible refutation by facts. The peculiar truth of such a "teleological view of history," he states, can never be decisively refuted by the citation of documentary "self-witnessing" of earlier phil-osophers; for it is shown alone in the evidence of a critical total view, which displays a meaningful final harmony behind the "historical facts" of documented philosophies and their "apparent oppositions."

This view of history not only promises to be sterile but threatens to be dangerous, in the "wrong" hands, just as the misuse of the concept of "eidetic (essential) intuition" led to bizarre results of a mystical kind. At its best, it shows all past thinkers as leading toward, or away from, the "clarity" which Husserl sets up as *his* ideal of reflec-tion. With Husserl as the "final institutor," who can deny him the right to interpret his predecessors in a way they never could have achieved?

Even if it were a successful venture, within well-defined limits, the aim of "self-understanding" as portrayed in the *Crisis of the European Sciences* could not be defended as the sole aim of philosophical reflection. The question of the use of the "pure" analysis provided by the subjective method, for the solution of theoretical and practical problems, including practical social problems, must always be considered. "Pure" reflective analysis has been found to be useful, especially in the philosophy of logic. But there are also shortcomings and dangers, if one forgets the real place of the knower in nature. Only when used in cooperation with other logical methods, and with the special sciences, can such dangers be obviated. For practical social problems, however, the subjective procedure is completely nugatory. A philosopher who refuses or neglects to take account of the pressing practical problems of his day (the well-known ones: capital and labor, imperialism and war, etc.) incurs the cardinal error of making his reflection "empty" in a most important respect He may believe that he is grand and noble in his flight from reality, in his absorption in an honorific realm of pure ideas, removed "in principle" from the "lowly" world about us. But that action may be construed as a renunciation of the obligations one has toward society as well as himself. The neglect of practical problems may also take the form of vagueness or generality of language, even from a professedly naturalistic point of view. To discuss a philosophical theory of value and define justice without explicit reference to property relations is surely to commit the error of "emptiness."

Whether one becomes an active participant in social

and political movements or not, it is evident that, *qua* philosopher, one cannot afford to disregard the actual content of social experience. One's conceptual work will not suffer thereby; one will not cease to be a philosopher for so doing. Quite the contrary is the case. Instead of avoiding all social problems and becoming a "pure" specialist solely, and instead of tacitly falling in line with a "safe," conservative tradition, he becomes a philosopher most worthy of the name, one who sees in philosophy a mode of response to important problems in all fields of experience, social as well as physical and purely conceptual.

## F. MISPLACED SUBJECTIVISM

The philosopher who undertakes descriptions of states of anxiety, fear of death, etc., may be making a contribution which could just as well be made by a psychologist. Such findings are to be distinguished from the philosophical standpoint with which they happen to be associated, as in the case of the so-called "Philosophy of Existence," in terms of which certain human attitudes are construed as "basic categories." What develops is a kind of "misplaced subjectivism," in which the limited virtues of a strict subjectivism tend to be lost. The danger then arises that there may be a false weighting of human states and attitudes in the total picture of man in relationship to his world. The dogmatic use of what may be called "generic determinations" in describing man (which man? which group of men? which historical periods?) is characteristic of existentialism. It is a surprising dogmatism, especially so in view of the body of scientific knowledge concerning man. In carrying through certain limited descriptive studies of a structural, "essential" type, it must not be presumed that man in his real nature is portrayed thereby and that man is fully or adequately considered. To know the "real" man, it is necessary to have the results of historical, statistical, psychological, socio-economic, etc., studies. The descriptive analysis of the experience of dread, or of a state of anxiety, does not entitle one to characterize men in general. In other words, a clear-cut line must be drawn between the "essential" descriptive and the factual orders; and, again, between the former and the philosophy of human existence, with its basic values. Description is *per se* acceptable, if it is correctly executed. The evaluation of a systematic philosophy of human existence requires an examination of all purported factual statements with respect to the evidence. A philosopher must not be allowed to issue statements as though he were an unrestricted oracle, and particularly by means of a language which strains at accepted usage beyond the breaking point. These observations apply to Max Scheler as an exponent of a "philosophical anthropology," to Martin Heidegger, especially on the linguistic side, and to their fellow existentialists.

All the types of experience with which the existentialists are concerned, including types which are of interest in psychiatry, can be investigated by means of a strictly controlled descriptive method, which is designed to take account of all regions of experience, and all attitudes, in its way. That all the conditions bearing causally and genetically upon the existence of the knower and his attitudes should also be considered, has already been set forth.

## Chapter VIII

# MAX SCHELER AND THE SPIRITUAL ELEVATION OF MAN

## A. ANTINATURALISM ON ALL FRONTS

It will be pertinent to consider one of the most interesting figures in the larger phenomenological movement. Max Scheler (1875-1928), who regarded himself as a "co-founder" of phenomenology (a designation never adopted by Husserl), has had a widespread influence far beyond the limits of that movement, all the way from religious and social thought to the Nazi ideology. Much of Scheler's work could hardly survive critical inspection, but it must be reckoned with practically. Unquestionably a gifted man who read extensively, and reacted to some of the major issues of his time, Scheler nevertheless does not compare favorably with Husserl from the point of view of logical standards and devotion to descriptive inquiry.

Like so many philosophers of his generation, Scheler reacted to nationalistic interests. If there had been an international prize for the greatest nonsense attainable by a philosopher in the World War I period, Scheler could have vied with Bergson for that distinction. Bergson, in an article in the *Hibbert Journal* in 1915, "Life and Matter at War," portrayed a mechanical system of unification with science at its service, represented by Germany, as opposed to "the unity which comes from within by a natural effort of life." The aid of the American industrial system, with its emphasis on science, "mechanism," and "materialism," could only add an element of paradox to his philosophical phantasy. As for Scheler, who may in truth be included among the ideological precursors of the Nazis,[1] his case would have been a strong one, supported by such judgments as the following characterization of the French and the English. The Frenchman, says Scheler, is inclined to add something in the expression of his hate, whereas the Englishman is inclined to take something away; and that accounts for the fact that the Frenchman "abreacts his hostility" readily *(sich leicht aushasst)*, whereas the Englishman in the course of time is more likely to "store up hostility" *(eher einhasst)*.[2] Obviously, the advantage of "essential" pronouncements is seen in the way in which they set one free from the tedious process of studying the facts.

Prominent in the religious world (Scheler had a Catholic period), as well as in the phenomenological movement, in which he was especially concerned with the philosophy of values, he also promoted the cause of a "philosophical anthropology" and stimulated interest in the "sociology of knowledge." It can be said that he had a seminal mind, even though he did so much to smudge his insights, in the interest of an all-sided opposition to naturalism. His conception of a "philosophical anthropology," which was given popular expression in his *The Place of Man in*

---

1. Cf. V. J. McGill, "Scheler's Theory of Sympathy and Love," in *Philosophy and Phenomenological Research*, Vol. II, No. 3 (March, 1942). It was fortunate for Scheler that he died before the accession to power of the Nazis, for no ideological elements of agreement would have saved him from the racist charge of "impurity" and the relentless program of genocide.

2. Max Scheler, *Die Ursachen des Deutschenhasses: Eine National-pädagogische Erörterung*, Leipzig, Kurt Wolff Verlag, 1917, p. 45.

*the Cosmos,*[3] amounted to a plea for the spiritual elevation of man. It was intended to provide an alternative to the account of man painstakingly and progressively achieved by the special sciences. The result is familiar in terms of the religious tradition.

The "sociology of knowledge" envisaged by Scheler, while indebted to the historical materialism of Karl Marx and Frederick Engels, turns out to be a kind of non-Marxian Marxism which is acceptable academically. In the course of his discussion, Scheler makes explicit reference to Marx.[4] He declares that, in the last analysis, it is the *being* of men with respect to which all their possible "consciousness," "knowing," and the limits of understanding and experience are directed. But he is careful to add the qualification that the "being" of men does not refer to their economic, "material" being, which he inaccurately takes to be the view of Marx. In other words, the Marxian principle which "holds" for Scheler turns out to be in part non-Marxian, and so does the Marxian principle which he rejects. Marx's doctrine of the "world-historical" mission of the proletariat is characterized as "messianic"; and the "conscious class-philosophy which the German Karl Marx first sought to create" is called "a nonentity (Unding) in itself."

In Scheler's *Formalism in Ethics,*[5] there is ample opportunity to note the importance attached to the Marxian philosophy and his interest in combating it. Aware of the

3. *Die Stellung des Menschen im Kosmos,* Darmstadt, Otto Reichl Verlag, 1928. Cf. the present writer's discussion of that work in *Philosophy and Phenomenological Research,* Vol. XIV, No. 3 (March, 1954).
4. Max Scheler, *Versuche zu einer Soziologie des Wissens,* München und Leipzig, Verlag von Duncker und Humblot, 1924, pp. 6, 37, 77.
5. *Jahrbuch für Philosophie und Phänomenologische Forschung,* edited by E. Husserl, Halle, Verlag von Max Niemeyer, Vol. I, Pt. II (1913) and Vol. II (1916).

general significance of historical materialism, he goes so far as to cite some of the facts usually used to support it (or, if not historical materialism itself, then the "undeclared" historical-evolutionary method). Thus, in the development of religious belief, there is a clearly discernible relationship between the characteristics of the idea of God and the social conditions.[6] In his publication on the sociology of knowledge,[7] he refers to Marx, and to Sombart's criticism of Marx, and he states: "It is first in the epoch of high-capitalism . . . that the epoch enters in slowly, which can be designated as relatively mainly 'economic', and whose laws of motion Marx not only "forced up" naturalistically to 'historical materialism', but also falsely generalized to the entire universal history. Only thus could 'all' previous history become for him a consequence of economic class-struggles." Scheler regarded Gumplowicz and Gobineau on the one hand, and the Rankians and Neo-Rankians on the other hand, and finally the "economicism" of Marx, as representing one-sided thought-movements. In his view, all these tendencies become an erratic "naturalism," and are rejected by him, as such. Above all, Scheler is an implacable foe of naturalism.

The concept of a "work-world," presented in his early work on *The Transcendental and the Psychological Method*,[8] should also be examined in the context of historical materialism. By the "work-world" Scheler understands the common, recognized work connections of human culture. It is not "a datum evident in itself," but a "well-founded phenomenon," of basic importance for the theory of knowledge. Maintaining that neither the

---

6. *Op. cit.*, Vol. II, pp. 160 f.
7. *Op. cit.*, pp. 30 ff.
8. *Die Transzendentale und die Psychologische Methode*, Leipzig, Felix Meiner, second edition, 1922, pp. 180 f.

transcendental nor the psychological method is able to do justice to the problems of philosophy, Scheler proposes a "noological"[9] method, which attempts to unite the methods of transcendental philosophy and transcendental psychology. The basic concepts are the "work-world" and "spiritual life-form."

The spiritual life-form, in Scheler's view, cannot be conceived as a developmental product of psychical facts. Spirt is the "X" which made possible the work-world. Since the work-world is enriched more and more in the process of human history, he maintains, it is not possible, at any time-point of history, to determine the concept of spirit once and for all with regard to its content. Scheler's formulations are as opaque as the concept of spirit is evasive, as illustrated by his final "thesis": The sole mark of the concept of spirit properly valid for a definite stage of humanity consists in this, that through it the work-world, by whose causal reduction it is found, is closed; or, expressed otherwise, that the spiritual activity, which led to the selection of the work-world out of all that is merely "past," preserves itself as identical with that spiritual activity, by which the work-world on its side has become possible. This thesis may well be beyond truth and falsity.

Nevertheless, Scheler showed himself adept at deriving thought motives from the intellectual atmosphere of the time. Although a bitter foe of Marxism, naturalism, and evolutionism, he was shrewd enough to try to appropriate some of their insights and truths. Securely entrenched in his world of desiccated essences, and perfumed by spirit in his "noological" view of culture, such insights were

---

9. Eucken's term "noological" is used for the method favored by Scheler, in contrast with psychological procedure.

safeguarded against all "naturalistic" mischief. In that respect it resembles Husserl's conception of a "life-world," which is also a vague kind of affair, naming something that is "given," or "pregiven." There could not be much life left in it, after the application of the transcendental reduction. Neither is it capable of much application, especially to actual human problems. Scheler's "work-world" is an adroitly chosen term, which could only be made significant from the naturalistic point of view. There can be no talk of work without workers; and whether there are employers or slaveholders will depend upon the historical period in question. In Scheler's hands, and within the chosen limits of his theorizing, the vague concept of a "work-world" remains an unfulfilled promise.

The formulation of the issues of "ethical relativism" and "ethical skepticism" provided another mode of attack on naturalism and evolutionism. The battle was fought on all fronts, including ethics and cultural philosophy as well as the theory of knowledge and logic. In the latter fields, Husserl led the procession with his attack on "psychologism" and the principle of thought-economy. Scheler was most conspicuous in the ethical controversy, but far less successful. Aiming positively at the establishment of an autonomous science of "pure logic," Husserl's efforts were justified, in so far as an idealized formal logic must be treated in abstraction from actual psychological and "naturalistic" conditions. But only in part, as a "truth logic," in contradistinction to a restricted "validity logic," ultimately involves dependence on the real world, to a greater degree than Husserl conceived it to have. His conception of a "truth logic" was too remote from the psychological and social origins, and real applications; whereas his conception of formal logic suffered because of its "absolute" basis, with "necessary" insightful premises. If Husserl met with difficulties through overemphasis of the realm of the "pure," it was to be expected that Scheler would incur still more trouble in the field of human values, where relatedness to human beings enters into the very content of every value-proposition. Even if one were to renounce "human ethics," following Scheler, the more generally conceived values would have to involve relatedness to some kind of organic beings and their needs or interests. One would otherwise be left with abstract essences, which is in fact what Scheler came to, with a redeeming "spiritual" setting.

Scheler's conspicuous participation in the antinaturalistic movement in the first decades of the present century is shown in his work on the *Phenomenology of Feelings of Sympathy*.[10] He had already rejected the view that the act of love can be explained as a "complex" or as a "product of development" of simpler spiritual elements. He charges the naturalistic theory with overlooking the "originalness" of "spiritual" and "holy" love as well as of "inspirited individual love." Not that they are wrongly explained: these "facts," as Scheler calls them, "are not seen at all," and naturalism is "blind" to them. He argues that it does not see the *phenomena,* in which a stratum of acts and values comes to appearance, which not only overlaps our factual organization of life, but the essence of all life, indeed (in "holy love") even the essence of all psychical order. It is in his view completely indifferent, on which stage of development of human history it occurs; and it is also a matter of indifference, whether it comes

---

10. Cf. *Zur Phänomenologie und Theorie der Sympathiegefühle und Von Liebe und Hass,* Halle, Niemeyer, 1913, pp. 81 ff. Now available in English translation is Scheler's *The Nature of Sympathy,* New Haven, Yale University Press, 1954.

to appearance in many people or in a few. He is confident that if the naturalistic theorist really saw the phenomena of holy and "spiritual" love, he would also see at once, that they cannot be explained and derived from any conditions which belong to the vital sphere and love. Despite the fact that naturalism is capable of embracing "emergent" qualities in its view, Scheler contends that it is the very point of view of the naturalistic theory which "makes it blind" to the fact that in the course of development of life and humanity, completely new acts and qualities appear. These qualities "appear essentially by leaps," and never as gradual developments, which are in principle possible for the bodily organization of living beings. It is difficult to understand Scheler's charge that the "point of view" of naturalism prevents it from seeing that, in the course of vital development, new and "deeper" stages of being and value can appear. "Deeper stages of being" would be best treated by a person unburdened with scientific information. In Scheler's opinion, the phenomenon of "holy love" is not to be invoked through any "experiment" or through education. That removes it effectively from critical inquiry, at least of a "naturalistic" kind. Its absoluteness and value level are held to be determined by its "inner phenomenal nature," and not with respect to practical human aims.

Scheler calls attention to cases of "holy love" in which pain and death were endured willingly. Others "freely" adopt a life of poverty, not as an "evil," but as "a radiant lover and bride," as in the case of Francis of Assisi. Naturalistic ethics, according to Scheler, can only interpret such cases in a very few ways, either as a "perversion" of the healthy drive of life, or as a "life-hostile" direction of feeling and striving, or as *"ressentiment."* But Scheler's apparent critical success is based upon a hasty and incomplete list of explanatory possibilities selected from the general naturalistic literature.

When Scheler argues[11] that the idea of "absolute monogamy" is never to be derived from the naturalistic presuppositions, and that sexual love must be regarded as a kind of love which is peculiarly qualified spiritually *(rein seelisch),* in order to give absolute monogamy a "phenomenological foundation," one is tempted to draw a curtain of charity over the entire performance. It is Scheler's aim to make its validity independent of the "accidental equipment" of the human organism, and to have it hold for worlds in which such conditions may be different.

But why the insistence on "independence" of the organism, it will be asked? Relatedness to an organism, and to a society, is essential to values, if anything can be said to be essential. The fear of relativism appears to be merely an evasion on Scheler's part, and a defense against a naturalistic truth in the interest of a supernaturalistic position. The apparent attempt to carry through an analogy in the field of values with Husserl's treatment of "pure logic," which had its region of justification, shows the danger that exists in not clearly recognizing the proper limits of phenomenological analysis. The terms "phenomenological" and "phenomena" ("failing to see the phenomena") become verbal instruments capable of screening devious operations, in the hands of a standpoint partisan.

For Scheler, "Marriages are made in heaven" has a deeper meaning in terms of essences and essential connections. It is only "a mythological expression of the fact

---

11. *Zur Phänomenologie und Theorie der Sympathiegefühle,* p. 87.

that the monogamous marriage is based on the possible existence of a context of essence, which exists between two individuals (masculine and feminine) as such, in so far as they are conceived as essences, and not as first identifiable through these real bodies." He holds that divorce is a false concession to existing historical relations, and is in conflict with the essence-connection founding marriage.

The naturalistic theory, as Scheler views it, undertakes to derive love from "blind" drives, after first obtaining the concept of value on the basis of the relation of a value-indifferent object to a present striving, in itself "blind." But love and hate, according to Scheler, "found" all other kinds of value-consciousness (feeling, preference, value-judgment). In brief, every essence strives for what it loves, and opposes that which it hates, and not conversely. He speaks of an "insightful phenomenological basis" for the theoretical propositions he presents. Who will be persuaded thereby?

Scheler's critique of naturalism proceeds assumptively and fallaciously: assumptively, because he assumes as real and as unanalyzable in naturalistic terms such "phenomena" as "holy love"; and fallaciously, because he gives what purports to be an exhautive set of "naturalistic" explanations, including the Freudian approach, but fails to give the strongest explanation. He neither does justice to the explanations he cites, nor gives the best possible one. The favored term "blind" ("blind drives," "blind striving") is an example of the way in which assumptive terms can be used to falsify an opponent's position, and to predetermine the outcome.

## B. AGAINST EVOLUTIONISM, HUMANISM, AND HUMAN ETHICS

In his discussion of naturalism and the philosophy of evolution,[12] Scheler does not seem to realize that even well-founded points of criticism against Spencer and other vulnerable evolutionists do not suffice to discredit or undermine the principle of evolution itself. Scheler manages to find his way into some of the concepts of the evolutionary philosophy, particularly as conceived by Spencer, and to point out weaknesses here and there. Scheler derived new wind for his spiritual sails from the alleged failures of evolutionary philosophy and science. The excesses and failures of the evolutionary philosophy need not be defended. That movement had its virtues, however, in the great impetus it gave to the undertaking to account for all aspects of man and the world, without residuum. Defects in the evolutionary sciences have been progressively corrected *within* the field of scientific thinking. The existence of inadequate science can only act as a motive for the improvement of science, and not as a directive toward the fideistic apologetics of Scheler.

In the first part of his "Formalism in Ethics," Scheler discusses[13] the error of regarding the "relations of adaptation" which exist between organism and environment, as one-sided adaptations of the organism to its environment, or also of the environment to the organism, as a certain kind of vitalism views it. Both of them are viewed as dependent variables of the life-process, which occurs in

---

12. Cf. Max Scheler, "Der Formalismus in der Ethik und die materiale Wertethik," *Jahrbuch fur Philosophie und Phänomenologische Forschung,* Vol. I, Part II, for the first part of this work, and especially p. 561 n.; also, *Jahrbuch,* Vol. II (1916), for the second part of this work, pp. 136-163, and especially 147 ff., 156 ff.

13. *Jahrbuch,* I, 2, pp. 560 f.

a unified manner. Completely erroneous, Scheler continues, is it to regard the adaptation as adaptation to a
"dead nature," instead of to the "environment"—as though
the astronomical sun belongs to the object, to which a
worm, for example, has to "adapt itself!" This example is
poorly chosen, since adaptation to nature in general is
certainly unavoidable. Why pick out the sun as an
example? As a matter of fact, the example proves to be
a boomerang, for the apparently far-fetched and ridiculous
example turns out to be the great source of earthly energy,
required not only by the worm, but by everything else
as well. This fact was fully recognized by Spencer, and
graphically portrayed in all its significance for the earth
and man, in his *First Principles*.[14] It would have benefited
Scheler had he taken the trouble to read Spencer fairly
and understandingly, instead of driving peripheral and

---

14. Herbert Spencer, *First Principles*, New York, D. Appleton and Company, 1907, pp. 203 f. Spencer writes: "If we ask whence come these
physical forces, the reply is . . . the Sun's rays. Based as the life of
a society is on animal and vegetal products, and dependent as these
are on the light and heat of the Sun, it follows that the changes
wrought by men as socially organized, are effects of forces having a
common origin with those which produce all the other orders of
changes we have analyzed. Not only is the energy expended by the
horse harnessed to the plough, and by the labourer guiding it,
derived from the same reservoir as is the energy of the cataract and
the hurricane; but to this same reservoir are traceable those subtler
and more complex manifestations of energy which humanity, as
socially embodied, evolves . . . Sir John Herschel was the first to
recognize the truth that the force impelling a locomotive, originally
emanated from the Sun . . . Solar forces millions of years ago expended on the Earth's vegetation, and since locked up in deep-seated
strata, now smelt the metals required for our machines, turn the
lathes by which the machines are shaped, work them when put together, and distribute the fabrics they produce. And . . . economy of
labour makes possible a larger population, gives a surplus of human
power that would else be absorbed in manual occupations, and thus
facilitates the development of higher kinds of activity . . . ."

tangential blows at his thought, and choosing a few vulnerable spots long recognized in the critical literature.

Scheler makes much of the danger of arriving at a false "anthropomorphism," by way of making the environment of man to be the environment of the other kinds of organism. Their relations of adaptation are in his view tested with respect to this *human* environment, which is not at all their own environment. Scheler argues that the "environment" of the worm or of fish, for example, is not at all "contained" in the human environment, and he holds that the environments of the different kinds of animals are always to be determined by a particular procedure. Spencer's biology and theory of knowledge are criticized on the ground that the whole world of organization is related to the world of man, and that the change of level of organization is supposed to be reduced to the mere adaptation of organisms to this "environment." Scheler concedes that a common "object of nature" is basic to all the external "environments" of living organisms, including man. But he holds it to be an error, to regard the common nature-object as determined in the categories and forms of the manifold, which are necessary for the mechanical conception of the phenomena of nature. He does not undertake at this point to decide which categories and forms are constitutive for it, and leaves it to his next book, on "Work and Knowledge," to discuss this question more fully.

Numerous errors and shortcomings did indeed creep into the general area of evolutionary thought. But it is to be doubted if even a single well-trained scientist ever makes the mistake of confusing environments. In his eagerness to slay the evolutionary monster, Scheler went so far as to provide it with the necessary fallibility. He must have been aware of the way in which anthropomorphism and anthropocentrism were exposed as fallacies in the evolutionary literature. In all things human, there is always the danger of anthropomorphism, even in the more fundamental and abstract reaches of thought. That Scheler himself is no paragon of logical virtue in this respect is abundantly shown by his cult of spirit and his efforts toward elevating man above the rest of nature by means of a link with a divine being. He is so anthropomorphic, in an individualistic sense, that he sees his own errors in others.

The full impact of Scheler's anti-evolutionism is seen in his discussion of "the relativity of values."[15] This discussion begins with the explicit rejection of "every so-called 'human ethics.'" "Humanity" is only *one* object among other objects, in which we apprehend values, and whose values we judge. Hence, he concludes, it is not in any form the "necessary subject" of this apprehension of value. Neither can it be called the "principle" of value-appraisals in the sense that good and bad would be that which furthers or hinders the "developmental tendency" in it. Scheler charges the modern theory of evolution, which represents man as the result of a natural process of development of life on earth, with having made impossible the idea that peculiar psychical or physical natural agencies are active in "man" as "man."

Scheler finds the "peculiar essentiality" of moral values through feeling. They are not found differently "in" or "by" man than are arithmetical, physical, or chemical propositions and laws. Man *qua* man provides the place and the opportunity for the emergence of values, acts, and laws of acts which can be felt, but which are entirely

---

15. *Jahrbuch,* II, pp. 136 ff.

independent of the particular organization and existence of this human species. Scheler goes on to observe that a freely falling man could also be used to prove the law of falling bodies.

This gives Scheler a way to meet the critical objection that there are really no universally accepted values. He reasons that, so far as the evidence and the objective validity of our apprehension of values are concerned, it is a matter of complete indifference, whether all members of this species possess them, or whether there are, for example, races and peoples who have no such moral insight. It is also a matter of indifference, on which stage of the historical development of humanity such acts of value-apprehension come to appearance. The main thing is, in his view, that wherever they are, and to the extent that they are there, they and their objects obey laws, which are just as independent of inductive experience as are the propositions of color- and tone-geometry. He thinks that our previous knowledge of the probable kind of origin of "humanity" (in the natural sense) makes it even probable that the moral qualities and acts do not correspond to any "general human" potentiality. Scheler is convinced that all our positive knowledge about the origin of man does not support the view that the human species is descended from one and the same animal level. He thinks it probable that the various races go back to different varieties of animals, which are the common ancestors of the human species and the primates. This "polyphyletic hypothesis" of human descent is used to support the view that man is divided into a plurality of races. He regards it as probable, therefore, that within certain races, there are kinds of acts and kinds of value corresponding to them, which actually occur, but without being found in the rest of humanity. This is taken to hold not only for the values and the acts, in which they are apprehended, but also for the norms which guide us in our practical activities. But the "essential connections" of the moral values are not affected by these considerations. The "objective material value-ethics" of Scheler does not preclude a diversity of norms for different races.

Scheler's strategy is clearly outlined by him. He is concerned with completely eliminating the view which regards the concept of value as relative to man, and so with removing the basis of "human ethics." This leaves him in a more agreeable situation, with two alternatives, one of which he manages to find vulnerable. Either the moral values and laws may be reduced to values which are relative to life, ultimately to such considerations as adaptation, inheritance of the useful, and the particular organization of man and his environment; or there appears *within* humanity—it does not matter at which place of its being and its "unfolding"[16]— an entirely new kind of essence of values and acts, in which man begins to take part in a realm which Scheler calls "superhuman" and in its positive sense "divine." This realm is supposed to carry in itself qualities and connections which are independent of and placed above all values and connections given *within* the general vital realm.

Spencer and Nietzsche are cited as representatives of the first alternative. The ethical values and laws are regarded as special cases of the values and laws of life. As Scheler views the issue, the moral values are either *less than* or *more than* something merely "human"; they cannot be specifically human. This forces the issue into

---

16. Scheler's choice of the term "unfolding" rather than "development" is noteworthy here.

a manageable form. All that remains to be done is to discredit the one alternative, and it is possible to argue for a "superhuman" type of ethics. Scheler's target is really "humanism" in general, beginning with the Renaissance period of humanism. His remarks are significant, in that they not only show his objective, but also the one-sided use to which he puts scientific knowledge. He notes that in the humanistic period there was neither a theory of the evolution of life, including man, nor an exact knowledge of the "enormous inequalities" of the human races, and there was no ethnography and science of history "built up upon the insight into these differences." "Man" was supposed to be something firm and stable; the concept of man was idealized, and real men were supposed to correspond to that concept. This is held to account for the "pathos" of the "general human," "humanity," "the truly human," etc., to which, since Nietzsche, Scheler suggests, the "merely human" and the "all too human" have begun to be opposed.

What should be done to correct this "all too human" condition? Scheler's stand is clear enough: essences, insights, eternal and necessary connections, spirit, "superhuman" ethics, and theology.

The two alternatives which Scheler so ingeniously provides should be reexamined. It is easy to set up examples of ethical views as the expression of the existing scientific trend (in this case, the evolutionary philosophy), and to give the appearance of undermining the latter because of the inadequacy of such views. Three questions must be borne in mind, however: (1) Are the relevant scientific theories and facts correctly represented? (2) Are logical conclusions drawn from the facts which are cited? (3) What should be done to correct any deficiencies that may exist in the scientific grounding of moral values? Should one look to further scientific progress for improvement, or turn away from the scientific conception of man to a "philosophical anthropology" and theology?

What objection could there be to a "human ethics"? Is it that one shrinks from its consequences; or simply that one is committed to fideism? We are frankly human-centric in our conception of values. By goodness we mean human goodness—at the most. One may speak of "human goodness" in general, and really mean "class goodness" or "individual goodness." But the goodness of the antelope or of the crocodile is not considered for a moment, unless it be in relationship to human needs or interests. To this extent we make a willful choice at the very beginning of our theorizing about values. It is not honest to pretend that one is talking more broadly about values, even to the point of finding a metaphysical locus for value in all things, including the cosmos "writ large," and to act in accordance with a narrow, human-centric code of value, usually narrowed still more by one's class status, and certainly determined by one's cultural heritage. Neither is it honest to take the line Scheler does, to become interested in "essences" apart from factual occurrences (actual enjoyments, insights, and needs), and to find that such values are "valid" even if there were no world. The analogy with mathematics, especially geometry, seems to make such a view plausible. But, let us ask, (a), is there a sound analogy between the two; and, (b), even if that were the case, has the correct conclusion been drawn?

(a) For the first, it must be recognized that there is a greater degree of freedom of construction and of idealization in geometry, than in thinking about values. The basic units (point, line, etc.) can be defined in different ways, and the assumptions can be changed. The situation is quite different with values, however. If human values are meant, one should look to the best founded values for examples. A basic value may then be defined as a satisfaction of a basic need. Is anything gained by asking us to "apprehend essences"? In this case, it is better to ask a physician about the proper satisfaction of, say, the need for food, than to resort to "ideation" and to attempt an authentic sketch of the "essential relations" involved in the value situation "satisfying the need for food." Such a vacuous procedure need do no harm, of course. The question is, whether it can be profitable. On the other hand, there is some degree of resemblance between geometry and an objective value theory; their propositions are objectively binding, and they hold subject to certain assumed conditions. The differences between the two cases must be borne in mind, however, for there is a certain amount of "free play" and "arbitrariness" in the case of formal thinking which is absent in the field of actual reality, where one is bound to and by the facts.

(b) What conclusion can be drawn from the comparison between geometry and value theory? The independent validity of the geometrical propositions is due to the hypothetical nature of the reasoning. So long as the axioms and definitions hold, the theorems are valid, and they are independent, in that sense, of any matters of fact. If the axioms are changed, different theorems result. But they, too, are valid independently of the world, so long as the same axioms are retained. There is a parallelism to be noted with value theory, but it does not turn out to be the parallelism supposed by Scheler, for two reasons—Scheler's understanding of geometry, and his conception of "eternal," "necessary" essential forms in ethics, which just have

to be "felt," or into which one just has to have "insight."
If geometrical theorems are binding, that is on a hypothetical basis; and if ethical propositions are binding, that,
too, is on a hypothetical basis. The geometrical propositions are "timeless" in their reference: the points, lines,
etc., never occur *as such* anyway. But the ethical propositions are time-bound; they refer to human beings with
needs, organic and cultural. The range of application of
ethical propositions depends upon their abstractness and
generality.

Long ago, Socrates faced quite a problem in interpreting
the nature of concepts. That is understandable. They became fixated as "ideal forms" in a special metaphysical
realm, and they were chained down to objects as their
"essences." Those who are interested in establishing
principles and norms as "superior" to all earthly conditions have always found it convenient to exploit concepts
metaphysically. The prominent *functional* interpretation
of concepts in recent philosophy should have removed
the ground from under such attempts, but it appears that
in philosophy it is not sufficient to undermine or even to
refute an antiquated doctrine. It lives on in the proverbial
thousand forms, so long as there are motivating forces to
keep it alive.

To recall Scheler's thesis: Man *qua* man provides the
place and the opportunity for the emergence of values,
etc., which can be felt, but which are entirely independent
of the particular organization and existence of the human
species. It may be recalled that Scheler added the suggestive thought that a freely falling man could also be used
to prove the law of falling bodies. Are human beings as
incidental and, really, as irrelevant to moral values and
their principles or laws, as they are to physical laws? Again,

one must be on his guard against the danger of false analogy. No man can violate the law of falling bodies. But any man could violate an ethical law, no matter what it may be like. Of course, one faces the difficulty of securing firm definitions here. Let us assume for the sake of the argument, to illustrate the difficulty, that the ethical law be one which declares that all men must and do seek their own happiness. It might then be argued that even a person who commits suicide actually seeks to find his "happiness" in that way. If ethical definitions were merely a matter of Procrustean procedure, there could be no general agreement, and no objectively binding knowledge. The analogy with mathematics, physics, or chemistry is less helpful than a comparison with the descriptive findings about man which are provided by medical and social scientists. A good deal can be said about the actual nature of happiness in a given culture system, and with respect to given individuals. Laws of actual behavior and generalizations about human needs must be formulated carefully, with due regard to changing cultural conditions and individual differences. Such generalizations are by no means independent of "the particular organization and existence of the human species." Neither are the *prescriptive* propositions of medical men, as to what is "good for" a person.

Is this also true of the propositions of the moralist? They necessarily refer to the particular organization (needs for food, fresh air, exercise, etc.) and social existence (meaning cultural activities: music, painting, literature, sports, etc.) of the human species. Scheler's efforts to depreciate science and to provide a means of emancipating the philosophy of values from the humdrum cares of our bodily and social existence prove to be as futile as they are pretentious. The phenomenological language to which he resorts does not obscure the main drift of his text, which is a kind of confession of faith.

Examining the doctrine of the "struggle for existence" for its historical development,[17] Scheler observes (without giving any references to the literature) that there is a transference of concepts from one realm to another. It is in his view very characteristic that this doctrine transfers concepts from the existing social relationships ("civilization") to the nonhuman life-world, and in so far as it has been applied to man, it is based on the application of concepts derived from the modern western-European-industrial civilization to the forms of more ancient mankind. From the observation of the workers' and human struggles for wages and food associated with English industrialism, and the dogmatic belief in the poverty and niggardliness of nature, there arose the idea of a necessary competitive struggle of human beings for their food, and along with it the doctrine expressed by the Malthusian "law of population." This idea, Scheler states, was carried over by Darwin to the entire organic nature. It is a curious thing, to see Scheler fear that the doctrine of the struggle for existence, as a necessary condition of progress for life, might be simply a "projection" of specific historical human relationships into the whole of organic nature. Scheler supposes that Darwin, "whose central interest was in struggle," which he saw as a struggle of human beings about him, and also as opposed to the plant and animal world, never consciously and sharply presented the problem to himself. This problem concerned the relative importance of the tendencies toward mutual solidarity and support, as compared with the principle of struggle which is based upon egoism and the preservation of existence.

---

17. *Op. cit.*, pp. 147 ff.

In Scheler's opinion, organic nature basically has different characters than those attributed to it by Darwin. The more far-reaching the criteria used, Scheler thinks, the more significance does the principle of solidarity gain over that of struggle. Hence he concludes that the total aspect of life is "inwardly solidarity and unity, outwardly struggle and disunity." It would be difficult to find any real illustration of this formulation in human history, or in the animal kingdom, for that matter. The alleged "inner unity" is simply a part of the build-up of the spiritualistic structure at which Scheler is constantly aiming. He believes that the subordination of struggle to solidarity is illustrated by the living things (plants and animals) known to us. The different forms of nourishment of both realms, he thinks, rule out a struggle, or at least make it a secondary matter; and he notes that the form of nourishment of plants conditions that of the animals.

Could this be carried over to classes in human society, so that if one class "conditions" another, "solidarity" is supreme over "struggle"? Were it not for the factor of intelligence, that might prove to be the case, although how human society arrived at the given point of class development would be an enigma without prior intelligent behavior. Hence the supposition is pointless.

Much more characteristic of Scheler than his self-appointed role as the savior of the animal kingdom from the projection of the evil practices of men, and the savior of man by elevating him above the animal kingdom, is his use of the concept of "transcendence." If the primary tendency of life is not the adaptation to a given "milieu," but rather to transcend every given "milieu," to extend and conquer it, then, Scheler maintains, the principle of struggle can only enter into activity to the extent to which this original tendency stagnates, and in its place the mere tendency to adaptation to a given "milieu" predominates. To the extent to which this is the case, Scheler admits, a struggle for the "good things" of this "milieu" is a necessary consequence, but to the extent that it is not the case, the life-unities, as they develop and enlarge their "milieu," make that struggle superfluous or limit it, and are able to live alongside one another in the great whole of the universe.

It is necessary to test Scheler's formulation by some plain facts, not only of biology, but also of history. The great boa is hungry and lies in wait at the water hole. The animal which it crushes after a brief struggle yields its existence for the sake of the boa. Does "unity" supersede "struggle"? It is the boa that enjoys whatever "solidarity" there is, in this case. To be sure, the basic physical laws are not upset by a struggle in the biological realm. But it would be absurd to use them as a support for the alleged "solidarity." It must be borne in mind that there is a physical equivalent for every instance of struggle, so that "solidarity" would either have to be located still "lower," which is impossible, or "higher," which is meaningless. How is it with social classes, and with the nations of the world? Under certain circumstances, say in the case of the early American Indians, a tribe could move on to new hunting grounds, and so avoid a clash with rival tribes. In modern industrial society, however, does the progressive expansion of a country necessarily mean that either it can live peacefully alongside other countries, or that the classes within the country can coexist peacefully? Scheler did indeed allow himself a great deal of room for his formulation—"the great whole of the universe"—which is much more convenient than the sad limitations on this earth.

Thus, his formulation must be referred by him to a divine power, if it is to be tested. No doubt that is precisely what Scheler intended. It would seem that the German clamor for *"Lebensraum"* found an early expression in Scheler's sensitive consciousness.

One of Scheler's reflections on the principle of the relativity to life of moral values, which he pauses to record, is noteworthy. If this principle should be accepted, could man keep the value which is ascribed to him by biological ethics? If by "life" we understand only the *earthly* organic world, then, Scheler's scientific information leads him to believe, without a doubt the laws of nature set an end to it. Just as individuals and species are affected by death, earthly life itself is powerless in the face of its ultimate doom. From the cosmic perspective, earthly life with all its works lasts a mere second.

One school of thought, which is quite foreign to Scheler, would be led to regard this "mere second" as infinitely valuable to those concerned with their brief happiness, and they would expect success in exhorting people to make the most of their limited opportunities. Not so Scheler: he takes the opposite view, and in so doing, he makes a rather mischievous assumption which cannot fail to be damaging to the religious cause he professes to serve. Thus he reasons: If the earthly organisms were not merely carriers, in which life comes to appearance with its own laws, and if it consisted only in the properties and activities of these organisms, then it would be a strange demand, for the ridiculously small extension of that "world-second" in which life endures, which may be obtained through the so-called "moral actions" (i.e., the "life-furthering" actions) and the avoidance of immoral actions, to demand the giving up of so much vital and sensuous happiness, which is a consequence of the ethical norms. The thought of the destruction of life would in this case also include the suspension of all moral values, an idea which, Scheler contends, evidently contradicts all consciousness of the meaning of moral values.

It is amusing to note how Scheler confuses the brief "cosmic second" of earthly life with an impending disaster to living beings *from their own perspective;* and also how he assumes that human beings faced with a finite horizon of activities would derive more sensuous enjoyment by violating "ethical norms." Are "ethical norms" so far removed from human enjoyment that one goes against his inclinations in adopting them? Or is the necessity of subordinating desires, and even suppressing many desires, clearly called for in the interest of the greatest possible enjoyment? Scheler's antinaturalistic position alone would prevent him from admitting the fact that widespread suppression is not necessary; but his confused, "standpoint" reasoning would make it quite impossible anyway.

Scheler argues that the standpoint of biological values cannot justify the proposition that man is the most valuable being in nature, unless it be a matter of merely anthropomorphic self-love. Even his capacity to construct a civilization is not enough to change this biological judgment, in Scheler's view. It may be observed, simply, that it is not necessary for a naturalistic philosophy of values to go to the extreme of enthusiasm for a unilinear evolutionary view, and to regard man as "the most valuable being." At this point the naturalistic moralist need only declare frankly that he is talking about human values. A comparison with values of other organic beings is not in question. That is not the case for Scheler, however, for he is able to continue his sniping at vulnerable moralists in the broader evolutionary movement. Spencer is always conveniently at hand. After trying to show that man cannot on evolutionary grounds prove his moral supremacy, Scheler undertakes to do so from another point of view. With the aid of a "philosophical anthropology," he provides man with the necessary equipment, not only to elevate him above the beasts, but also to place him securely in the lap of God. This is amply borne out by Scheler's text.[18] He reasons that if it is not biologically tenable, to declare man to be the "highest valued" of living beings, then the proposition can only gain an objective meaning by laying down *other* values than the biological as the "highest."

This brings Scheler to the goal of his discussion. It is his thesis that when we evaluate "man," we actually *presuppose* values which are independent of vital values—the value of the holy and the spiritual values. "Man" is said to be only "the highest being" in so far as he is the carrier of acts which are *independent* of his biological organization, and in so far as he *sees* and *realizes* values which correspond to these acts.

The exact nature of this alleged "independence" must be clarified: is there no causal relationship with the biological organization of man, or with man's physical nature? That would be impossible without a sheer, dogmatic affirmation of "faculties" or "substances" in man which are completely independent of his physical and biological equipment. That it would be necessary to "go the whole hog," and to "spiritualize" not only man but the whole of nature, or else be faced with insoluble problems, is amply shown in the history of philosophy by the spiritualistic philosophers and the patchwork efforts to "solve"

18. *Op. cit.,* pp. 156 f.

the mind-body problem. It is also evident from the history of philosophy that even the most ingenious spiritualistic philosophy can simply be rejected *in toto,* as having assumptions with no evidential support for them. But these considerations offer no deterrent to Scheler, whose view of the history of philosophy operates within a limited German professorial tradition of idealism.

Scheler uses the term "presupposition," in the sense of a necessary, unavoidable assumption which is forced upon us. Thus he states that only with the presupposition of the value of the holy and of the spiritual values as independent of and superior to biological values, can man be the most valuable being. He speaks of a "surplus of spiritual activity" as an emergent feature of man, so that it appears as though a fissure were opened in man and his history, in which an order of "acts" and "contents" (values) superior to life came to appearance, and at the same time a new form of unity of this order, which we regard as "personal" and whose bond is love, with pure justice founded upon it. The idea of this "form of unity" as the last carrier of the value "the holy" is called the *idea of God,* and the persons belonging to it and the order are called "the realm of God." Now, says Scheler, we come to a "remarkable" result therewith: "man" himself, regarded as the "highest valued" earthly being, as a moral being, can first be apprehended and phenomenologically observed with the presupposition and "in the light" of the idea of God.

There is not the slightest semblance of justification for this "remarkable" result in the present context. Scheler's mode of exhortation does not seem to be in any need of evidence. In his view, when correctly seen, "man" is the *tendency,* the *transition* to the divine. He is the bodily being which intends God and is the "breakthrough point" of the realm of God, in whose acts the being and value of the world are first constituted. In opposition to the "anthropomorphic" conception of the idea of God, Scheler finds that it is on the "theomorphism" of its noblest examples that the sole value of its "humanity" is based. The "intention" of man beyond himself and all life is said to make up his essence. Essentially, man is defined as a thing which *transcends itself and its life.* The "kernel of his essence" (man also has a *Wesenskern!*), apart from all particular organization, is that movement, that *spiritual* act of self-transcendence. But this, says Scheler reproachfully, is mistaken by "human" ethics as well as by "biological" ethics. He thus takes his place among the heads of the philosophical procession for which "transcendence" is the key concept linking man and the "beyond"—or the "above." His conclusion, he states, is "the result of philosophy." It is evident, however, that he is always aware of the existence of naturalism, his chief foe and target. But presumably that is not "philosophy."

From the failure to determine a strict, essential boundary between man and animal, when the problem is viewed biologically, naturalism and its foes (as represented by Scheler) draw different inferences. For naturalism, man is only a higher animal, and his spirit as well as moral insight are products of animal development. The error in this view, according to Scheler, consists in the assumption of a unified biological concept of "man" instead of recognizing the biological indefinableness of man. The motive for overplaying the "failure to determine a strict essential boundary between man and animal" is clearly seen in the eagerness to make "man" indefinable biologically. With the aid of psychology and the social sciences, it is quite possible to delimit "man," and the answer to the alleged indefinableness of man biologically is a workable definition for the social realm. The evolutionary philosophy includes the social as well as the biological in its scope, and it is unwarranted to restrict it to the biological as such.

From the alleged absence of a biological essential concept of man, Scheler concludes that the sole essential boundary and the sole value-boundary which come in question between the earthly beings, which are alive, do not at all lie between man and animal, who systematically and genetically represent a continuous transition, but rather between person and organism, between spiritual being and living being. Therewith, he submits, at least the problem of "the place of man in the whole," which no ethics can evade, is clearly indicated. He is not only opposed to "the false attempt" on the part of certain philosophers to "impute erroneously" to man as a natural genus, specific "potentialities" for morality, reason, etc., but also to the addition of an immortal soul-substance. He goes so far as to deny explicitly the *meaning* of such attempts. The matter rests, however, with the "explicit" denial. That is sufficient for fideists, who do not look for logical demonstration, but who quarrel with one another's assertions and protestations, by means of counterassertions and counterprotestations. It is unnesessary for Scheler to explain what he means by "meaning," or to go into the question of scientific evidence.

It is Scheler's view that, within the continuous evolution of animal and man, here and there (hence, not necessarily "everywhere") acts of a certain essence and their laws, values of a certain essence and their connections,

come to appearance, which belong on principle to a super-
biological order. They are supposed by him to be sufficient in number to permit us to "surmise" the being of
a world of values, which may here and there "flash"
into the human environment, but is not of biological
origin.

This is to be taken in connection with Scheler's theology.
There is the belief, already noted, that man is the carrier
of a tendency which transcends all possible values of life,
and whose direction is turned toward the "divine," or,
more briefly, he is a God-seeker. But it is not the idea
of God in the sense of an existent, positively determinate
reality, which is presupposed, when the essence of man is
to be "intuited," but rather only the *quality* of the divine
or the *quality* of the holy, given in an infinite fullness
of being.

Scheler managed to snatch numerous insights from
the atmosphere of his time, if not from the scholarly
literature, but what he did with them was another matter.
Unlike Husserl, he was hardly naïve with respect to the
social and religious movements of his time. He noted, for
example,[19] that the God of Mohammed had something of
the character of a fanatical and sensuous sheik, and that
the God of Aristotle had something of a self-sufficient,
contemplative Greek scholar. Similarly, individual, more
concrete expressions of the Christian idea of God, if one
considers the observable religiosity of the peoples and not
merely the dogmas, have something of the peculiarity of
character of these peoples, and also change in accordance
with their historical stage of development. The Christian
God of the young Germanic peoples has something of the
appearance and sentiment of a German duke (in the

19. *Op. cit.*, p. 160.

strange language of Scheler, "something of the blue-eyed appearance and of the blue-eyed *Gesinnung* of a Germanic duke"); etc. Scheler did not consider the question of the place of his religious philosophy in his culture system. He lacked the method and understanding for such a self-inspection, just as all other "phenomenologists" *(per se)* lack it.

In his religious philosophy, in the present context, he disregards the question of the sources of positive religious knowledge, and the characteristics added to religious ideas because of the historical nature of the people in question. He is concerned with showing that there is an *a priori* value-idea of the "divine," which does not presuppose any kind of historical or inductive experience, and does not even have the existence of a world and of an ego as its foundation in any way. His main contribution to theology is thus offered by way of a "phenomenology of the idea of God," which he wishes to be distinguished sharply from the subjective, romantic "feeling conception" of religion as advanced by Schleiermacher.

A philosophical movement which could include men as different as Husserl and Scheler could only be a rather loose kind of collocation. And yet they responded to similar motives, and they aimed at the same targets to a large extent. The differences between them were largely differences in the degree of logical precision, general intellectual refinement and integrity, and degree of devotion to theoretical ideals. Scheler was inferior in all respects. He had a good opportunity to correct the one-sidedness of Husserl's philosophy by greater attention to practical, especially social philosophy. But there he failed miserably, displaying a singular talent for filching fruitful insights from the literature of social science, and rendering them worthless within the frame of his reactionary philosophy. For the rest, his talents never glittered more ominously, than when he anticipated degenerate ideas of the "philosophy" of the coming *Third Reich* of the Nazis.

## Chapter IX

# THE NEW IRRATIONALISM
## A. THE INFLUENCE OF HUSSERL'S SUBJECTIVISM

The widespread influence of Husserl appears to be all the more remarkable when one considers that he really stood alone. Nevertheless, he did not discourage the diversified types of scholars who attached themselves to the larger phenomenological movement. A number of negative characteristics were common to all of them: they were opposed to naturalism and materialism; they were critical of the philosophies based upon the special sciences; and they were opposed to Marxism. Positively, however, there was little unanimity of opinion. There were "realistic" and "idealistic" phenomenologists, religious and non-religious members of the movement, rationalists and fideists. Although Husserl held Professor Pfaender of Munich to be a "dogmatic metaphysician," the latter played a prominent part in the phenomenological movement. Husserl's assistant in the First World War period, Edith Stein, joined the Carmelite Order, and wrote books in the Catholic tradition. Although she was put to death by the Nazis, her writings have been preserved, including the recently published work on *Finite and Eternal Being*.[1]

---

1. Edith Stein, Teresia Benedicta a Cruce O. C. D., *Endliches und Ewiges Sein*, Louvain, E. Nauwelaerts, and Freiburg, Verlag Herder, 1950. This is Vol. II of Edith Stein's *Werke*, edited by Dr. L. Gelber and P. Fr. Romaeus O. C. D.

If Husserl could not be held responsible for the vagaries and foibles of Scheler, he was also in no way to blame for the extraordinary length to which the "Philosophy of Existence" went in the direction of antirationalism and irrationalism. At the worst, Husserl himself could not resist the temptation to advance a general philosophy of transcendental idealism, i.e., apart from his attitude toward the natural sciences and naturalism, and some rather unworthy arguments. But his main tendency was in accordance with the principles of a philosophy of reason.

The "philosophy of existence," or "existentialism," derives from numerous sources and comprises a diversity of representatives and developments. Martin Heidegger, who had been one of Husserl's close students, is the founder of one type of existentialism; and Karl Jaspers, another initiator in this tendency, was influenced by Husserl, particularly in his earlier work. The writings of Kierkegaard are another prominent source of influence on the philosophy of existence. Gabriel Marcel and Jean-Paul Sartre in France are leading figures in a movement which has already spread over a large part of the world. Although representing diverse philosophies of *human* existence (a more appropriate name than "philosophies of existence"), their varied writings may be recognized as being merely different symptoms in the same general syndrome. They are continuations of the idealistic reaction against a scientific philosophy, and developments of new types of irrationalism or fideism, which constitute the fastest growing movement in numerous countries. If experience recedes in importance and fruitfulness, the concept of transcendence plays a correspondingly bigger role. But by no means does that mean a restoration of the natural world of the sciences.

Adding to the difficulty of defining or delimiting the existential philosophy is the tendency to use the designation in a very broad sense, to name any so-called philosophy of human existence, whether avowedly Christian or frankly atheistic. Thus, St. Thomas has been referred to in the context of existentialism.[2] It is by no means a generally welcome designation, however; and it may be said that existentialism is a title that can be assigned nearly everywhere, but is acceptable almost nowhere.

The thought of Husserl was hardly suited for popular consumption. Like the thought of Plato, it could be much admired, or deeply studied, but could not be a popular thought movement. The comparatively large sale of the Spanish translation of Husserl's *Logical Investigations* is only an apparent exception, for the average intelligent reader in Latin America was not reached. An adulteration by means of a popular movement could alone be expected to reach a great number of readers, under present conditions. The philosophy of existence is a historical parallel to the neo-Platonic and Christianizing tendencies in more than one way. The attention is directed to man's more ultimate hopes, and a theory of human existence is developed which takes account of those hopes in a manner more suited for widespread consumption.

Viewed as a philosophical theory of human existence it does not measure up to the requirements of a strict phenomenology any more than it satisfies the standards of the special sciences. As a philosophical "short cut" it may come to supersede idealism as a general tendency,

---

2. Cf. E. Gilson's article on "The Humanism of St. Thomas" in *Twentieth Century Philosophy*, edited by D. Runes, New York, Philosophical Library, 1943. Gilson writes: "I am convinced that St. Thomas is, if we may use a word in favor today, the most *existential* of the philosophers" (p. 295).

for idealism has shown little capacity for further inventiveness and adaptation. Bearing in mind the conservative and often antiscientific role played by idealism, this is a dubious distinction to assign to the new tendency. The existentialists drew strength from the methodological limitations of phenomenology. The reduction to an individual ego was renounced, with the intersubjective world the point of departure. But that is not the world depicted by naturalism. The premises of subjectivism are still retained, although without the clarity, rigor, and intended methodological purposes of phenomenology. A covert subjectivism takes the place of a methodological subjectivism.

## B.  HEIDEGGER ON TRUTH AND METAPHYSICS

Martin Heidegger was one of the most influential members of the phenomenological movement in Husserl's last period.  Husserl was late in expressing opposition to the danger latent in Heidegger's work, and he even seemed to close his eyes to it at first. Heidegger's influence on his students has been tenacious, and has seemed to survive his inexcusable actions under the Nazi regime,[3] even in the personal feelings of many of them. It cannot be denied that he has promoted obscurantism in his systematic thought. The "Philosophy of Existence" is a type of philosophy which can only alienate one for whom the canons and ideals of logic are meaningful, and especially one for whom the ideal of philosophy as a rigorous

---

3. As the late Professor Fritz Kaufmann expressed it, in connection with a defense of Heidegger (in *Philosophy and Phenomenological Research*, Vol. I, No. 3, March, 1941, p. 359): "Some of us still feel the pain of the wound that Heidegger inflicted upon us in 1933. Heidegger's is a demonic nature." Professor Kaufmann was a member of the Freiburg philosophy department in the period preceding 1933.

science is definitive. It is a strange myth that the "problem of existence" was never recognized before, when one considers the enormous literature devoted to the conditions bearing upon human existence, cultural as well as biological and physical, including man's efforts to know himself and his place in the world. Such a myth can only be rendered plausible by means of a cryptic statement of the concept and problem of "existence," using such seductive terms as "thrownness" and "fallenness." Such terms bespeak their theological significance and can only be misleading in a supposedly descriptive investigation, Heidegger's alleged aims notwithstanding. The monstrous linguistic medium, so painfully evident in the much ado about "nothing" in his *What is Metaphysics?* for example, and the perpetual fog of existentialism could only aid it in being used and perhaps misused for purposes which not even an idealistic phenomenologist could condone.

To many readers of philosophical literature, Heidegger appears to have made great contributions to philosophy. But to those who have taken the trouble to read his writings with logical standards in mind, he has very little to offer, and he rates primarily as a pretentious verbal philosopher. He has taken care to create severe linguistic barriers between himself and his readers, which serve to make plausible the claim to untold profundity and novelty. It will be instructive—and quite disillusioning—to examine some of Heidegger's more audacious writing carefully.

## 1. The Importance of Nothing

Let us first look at Heidegger as he appears in his inaugural lecture, "What is Metaphysics?"[4] As with the traditional spiritualists, it appears that science must be circumscribed, and the philosophy based upon science must be exposed as fundamentally untenable. The sciences appear in Heidegger's consciousness to be hostile forces, and obviously something must be done about that. Thus, he asks: "What essential things are happening to us in the foundations of our existence, now that science has become our passion?" To write of science in this way is to betray an antiscientifc bias; it is to disclose the writer as ignorant of the actual extent to which science has become dominant, and to suggest the rejection of the general consequences of the scientific method, while accepting the practical fruits of scientific progress. It is only an ill-informed outsider who will speak of the "disrupted multiplicity of disciplines," and of the "root of the sciences in their essential ground" as having "atrophied." The pictorial expression "root of the sciences" and the vague mooning about an "essential ground" of the sciences are indications of overweening presumptuousness with no scientific knowledge back of it. One should speak of "evidential grounds," or of "methodological rigor," or of "social-historical motivation," and the like, rather than of "essential grounds."

Although Husserl reacted against a naturalistic philosophy reflecting the sciences, he had at any rate considerable scientific knowledge to his credit—in mathematics, physics, astronomy, and psychology. The same could not

---

4. Cf. Martin Heidegger, *Existence and Being*, with an introduction by Werner Brock, Chicago, Henry Regnery Company, 1949: four essays by Heidegger, including "What is Metaphysics?" and "On the Essence of Truth," translated by R. F. C. Hull and Alan Crick.

be said of Heidegger, so that his antiscientific utterances operate on a distinctly lower level.

It is precisely the special sciences of man which provide information in great detail about man's nature and development, and the possession of that information might have greatly altered Heidegger's fanciful notion of man's "pursuit" of science. As he states it: "In this 'pursuit' what is happening is nothing less than the irruption of a particular entity called 'Man' into the whole of what-is, in such a way that in and through this irruption what-is manifests itself *as* and *how* it is." Man's central position in the "what-is" appears to Heidegger to be an obvious truth, rather than an unwarranted anthropocentric (or idealistic) dogma. One could not otherwise account for his further statement that "the manner in which the revelatory irruption occurs is the chief thing that helps what-is to become what it is." Apart from that dogma, one would surely never succeed in making man's "irruption" to be the condition of "what-is."

This piece of writing by Heidegger is distinguished above all by the metaphysical import attached to "nothing." The discussion of "nothing" is, however, hardly more than a prolonged verbal play; it is pointless, and cannot impress any informed person. To an uninformed person it might indeed look like a display of virtuosity of a sort, with well-controlled elusiveness of meaning. In actual content it is surely "nothing." Heidegger's assumption that thinking is "essentially always thinking about something," so that it acts against its own nature in thinking of "nothing," is at least as old as Parmenides, and as questionable. The discussion of "nothing" is relieved for a moment when Heidegger discovers that "real boredom comes when 'one is bored'." Finally, the reader learns that "dread reveals nothing."

Our human *"Da-sein"* is taken to mean "being projected into nothing,"[5] and this "being-beyond" what-is Heidegger calls transcendence. Because *Da-sein* is essentially transcendent, i.e., "projected from the start into nothing," it can relate to what-is, and can have a self-relationship. Thus, he writes: "Without the original manifest character of nothing there is no self-hood and no freedom." Transcendence turns out to be a murky concept. The "projection into nothing on the basis of hidden dread" is spoken of as "the overcoming of what-is-in-totality: transcendence." Being "is finite in essence and is only revealed in the transcendence of *Da-sein* as projected into nothing."

Heidegger is finally led to the interesting conclusion that "every being, so far as it is a being, is made out of nothing." Now, he observes, "science would like to abandon nothing with a superior gesture." (One wonders which scientists have even heard of this metaphysical "nothing.") But, Heidegger argues, "scientific *Da-sein* is only possible when projected into nothing at the outset." He speaks of "the alleged soberness and superiority of science" becoming ridiculous if it fails to take nothing seriously. Heidegger is not only presumptuous. In his ignorance of science, he imagines that he can speak of its "essential task" in abstraction from its triumphant successes in solving problems. He warns that the essential task of science is not "the accumulation and classification of knowledge," thus falsifying the scientific quest by neglecting all the other phases of scientific activity; and he endeavors to conceal his lack of knowledge of scientific pursuits in detail by assigning to science the task of perpetually discovering "the whole realm of truth." Certainly

---

5. It is to be doubted whether "nothing" would be saved from nothingness if written Nothing, as is often done in sympathetic renderings.

the ultimate goal of complete knowledge will never be forgotten. But it is the immediate, pressing problems of a more restricted sphere which are relevant to human action and which will motivate and absorb us in science. Heidegger's contention that "modern science neither serves the purpose originally entrusted to it, nor does it seek truth in itself" is simply an unwarranted misstatement from which he does not shrink in order to bolster up his irrationalism. Nothing was ever "entrusted" to modern science—least of all by Heidegger's tradition; and there is no such thing as "truth in itself." Heidegger has simply directed imaginary weapons against a nonexistent target, all of which may be very appropriate in connection with his interest in "nothing."

## 2. On the Essence of Truth

The reader has the right to expect something definite from any discussion of the concept of truth. He is not likely to be deceived, or impressed, by anything else. Once he has departed from the shallow intricacies of the language dealing with "being" and "existence," Heidegger becomes quite a different kind of figure. The change is, roughly, from tragedy (a linguistic tragedy, at least) to comedy—or the commonplace. Heidegger asks a good question to begin with (321): "What do we ordinarily understand by 'truth'?" The word truth means, in his words, "that which makes something true into a truth." This is hardly subtle, and not at all new. Much better is Heidegger's subsequent recognition of truth as correspondence, whether of a thing with an idea, or of a statement with a thing. He does not justify his assertion, however, that propositional truth *(adaequatio intellectus ad rem)* is only possible on the basis of objective truth *(adaequatio rei ad intellectum)*. It is interesting to note that "the reduction of propositional truth to objective truth" is called a "theological explanation" (325). The theological notion of creation of the world of things, and of minds as well, hardly requires a "reduction." Such a designation is more appropriate for scientific philosophers.

A promising element in the discussion is the consideration of the view that truth is "the likeness or agreement of a statement to or with a given thing" (326 ff.). Heidegger properly attempts to analyze the meaning of "agreement." By agreement can be meant "identity of appearance" between two coins, for example. Or, the statement "This coin is round" "agrees" with the thing. At this point, Heidegger's acuteness runs away with him, for he finds it necessary to observe that the coin is metal, and the statement is in no sense material; the coin is round, and the statement is not spatial. He is quite right in pointing out that with the coin you can buy something, but that the statement about it can never be legal tender. And yet, the statement "agrees with and is true of the coin." If the agreement is supposed to be an "approximation," then how can such a completely unlike thing (a statement) "approximate" to the coin? Heidegger reasons that it would have to *become* the coin, which would remove the basis for agreement. It follows that "approximation" cannot mean a material likeness between two unlike things. The kind of relationship obtaining between statement and thing is then declared to determine the nature of the approximation. Although this theme has been treated at length in an abundant literature, it is approached as though it were waiting for clarification for the first time. Thus he writes, "So long as this 'relationship' remains indeterminate and its nature unfathomed," all argument about such approximation leads nowhere (327). Obviously, he is the person who has been called to fathom this hitherto unfathomed "relationship."

The matter must not be allowed to appear simple in any respect, for then there would be little to "fathom." The statement "represents" the coin, and states "how it is," "what it is like," in some respect or other. Much more could have been said on this point, but detailed analysis is not the objective. "Representation" is taken to mean "letting something take up a position opposite to us, as an object" (328); and the thing that is "opposed" must "come across the open towards us" while "standing fast" as a thing.

But does one always "*let* something take up a position as an object" when he makes statements? Is this not to ascribe too much autonomy and freedom to man as a knower? The activity of the knower must be duly recognized, but it is also important to bear in mind that the knower is causally conditioned, and that many events in the world force themselves upon him, no matter how unwilling he may be. It is a traditional philosophical disease, to exaggerate the status of the mind in reality, thereby ignoring or falsifying the evolutionary perspective.

In the course of his discussion, Heidegger believes he has disposed of "the traditional practice of attributing truth exclusively to the statement as its sole and essential place" (329). He argues that "truth does not possess its original seat in the proposition." It may be observed that scholars have long known that there is a cognitive side and the side of reality (or of the objects) in talking of truth. The ambiguous expression "original seat" suggests order of time, but also logical or metaphysical priority. In addition to that, "truth" is spoken of as somehow real in its own right. There is a set of truths; there is a concept of truth; but is there "truth" in the sense that the true is the whole? That would be a familiar idea, but it differs strikingly from Heidegger's text because of its clarity and relative simplicity.

Quaint indeed is the question (330): "Whence does the representative statement receive its command to 'right itself' by the object and thus to be in accord with rightness?" Quaint, but suggestive. A command, indeed! He is unable to resist a linguistic coup, when he asks, "Why does this accord *(Stimmen)* at the same time determine *(bestimmen)* the nature of truth?" Had he written in English, that sentence might never have been born. His next step leads him quickly to a major objective. He asks how there can be "an approximation to a pre-established criterion, or a directive enjoining such an accord." Having just invented the "directive," he is free to use it as a means to an end. His answer is that "this postulate *(Vorgeben)* has already freed itself and become open to a manifestation operating in this openness—a manifestation which is binding on all representation whatsoever." But in his confident haste he does not show why it is "binding on all representation." What ulterior purpose may he have in mind when he speaks of "this 'freeing' for the sake of submitting to a binding criterion"? It is declared to be only possible as "freedom to reveal something already overt" and being free in this way is said to point to the "hitherto uncomprehended nature" of freedom. If rightness is to be possible, the line of argument goes, there must be freedom. In short, "the essence of truth is freedom" (330). Heidegger concedes that his version of the esence of truth (rightness of statement) as freedom must appear strange. Instead of attempting to give a precise answer to the question "What is truth?" he equates it to an even more misleading and difficult generality. There is an element of justification in introducing freedom, but it is not the central, or even an important part of the question of the nature of truth.

Heidegger weighs the consequences that might be drawn from "turning truth into freedom." Is that to undermine truth by delivering it up to the caprice of man, "to the whim of this wavering reed" (331)? Truth is now "brought down to the subjective level of the human subject." But all sorts of untruth are ascribed to man. That does not deter Heidegger for a moment, for "this human origin of untruth merely confirms by contrast the essential nature of truth 'as such' which holds sway 'over' man" (332). This truth "as such" is portrayed as imperishable and eternal, and as something that cannot be founded on the transitoriness and fragility of mankind.

This is again a misleading formulation of the truth problem. To say that truth "as such" holds sway "over" man is merely to use pictorial language. There is no truth "as such"— that is merely an abstraction. There are truths, as best illustrated by verified scientific statements, or mathematical propositions, which are said to be objectively "true" or "valid," as the case may be. "Imperishable" and "eternal" are emotionally loaded words. Perhaps one should express them with bated breath, if not with the whites of his eyes. If "objectively true" (or valid) relates to a set of facts (or propositions), it may well be, as Bradley expressed it, that "Once true, always true." Every scientific proposition is subject to possible modification, all the way to possible repudiation. But *if* it is once true with respect to a given set of facts, or a given historical situation, then it is always true with respect to the same set of facts or historical situation.

This is not to found truth on "the transitoriness and fragility of mankind," as Heidegger puts it. Man is to be sure transitory, and he is subject to error. The truths (not "truth") which are established, often with great travail, are "from below," and they do not hold sway "over" man.

Heidegger's next step is clearly indicated. If the essence of truth is freedom, as he declares, and if "essence" is "the basis of the inner possibility of whatever is accepted in the first place and generally admitted as 'known'" (331); then the question must be answered as to how the essence of truth can have "a stable basis in human freedom." It is an obstinate prejudice, in his opinion, to contend that "freedom is a property of man." If truth as such is above man, then the reader would expect that freedom must also be construed accordingly. Conveniently, there is experience of "a hidden ground in man's nature and being, so that we are transported in advance into the original living realm of truth." It now appears that freedom is only the basis of the inner posssibility of rightness "because it received its own essence from that thing of earlier origin: the uniquely essential truth." The term "earlier" is not explained, nor is it pointed out how one thing can "receive its essence" from another thing. If that could be explained, essences might well be rendered more fruitful. Neither is the meaning of "uniquely essential truth" explained. The proliferation of words cannot always be accounted for.

Whatever "freedom" may mean to the average reader— one thinks of freedom defined in terms of the satisfaction of his needs, or with respect to the fulfillment of a plan of action—it has a different meaning in the present context. Here it means "freedom for the revelation of something already overt" (333). Having defined the essence of truth as freedom, Heidegger now asks for the essence of freedom. It would be precarious to attempt to apply his formulation, because the reader would be tempted to think of existing historical conditions (for example, slavery), and to interpret him as suggesting that acquiescence is freedom. But this line of thought, which is at least as old as the Stoic tradition, appears to be on a more abstract, metaphysical level of analysis. His formulation reads: "The freedom to reveal something overt lets whatever 'is' at the moment *be* what it is. Freedom reveals itself as the 'letting-be' of what-is" (333). This is not held to imply indifference or neglect, but is intended to mean that one "has something to do with it," or to participate in something overt. The "ordinary idea of truth," as referring to the correctness of a proposition, is now revised and is traced back to "that still uncomprehended quality," the revelation of what-is (334). What-is reveals itself "as *what* and *how* it is, and the approximation which represents it in the statement may take it for a criterion. Unfortunately for the reader who insists on understanding what he reads, there are no examples of the revelation of "what-is." All the examples that would occur to one would have reference to limited situations in a selective manner.

The common-sense understanding of freedom is demeaned and passed off lightly by Heidegger. Thus he states that "freedom is not licence in what we do or do not do" (334). It is evident from his text that he is aware of the distinction between positive and negative freedom, and of the view that freedom is "a mere readiness to do something . . . necessary." Disclaiming these versions of freedom, he maintains that freedom is "a participation in the revealment of what-is-as-such." As distinguished from the vague, if not vacuous, freedom resorted to by Heidegger, there is the concept of freedom construed in terms of taking one's place in the causal order, where "freedom" may be taken to mean relative self-determination. This conception of freedom would not be paraded as the essence of truth, however. It seems that a specially manufactured "freedom" is required as a prop for the present abstract concept of "truth."

Heidegger writes at times like a prophet. "In this *Da-sein*," he states, "there is preserved for mankind that long unfathomed and essential basis on which man is able to ex-sist (335). Once more, he is the man to "fathom" the "unfathomed." It is also interesting to note that there is an "essential basis" on which man is able to "ex-sist." To suggest food as a part of that "basis" would be an intrusion from the realm of facts. Is it something which the special sciences, natural and social, have missed? Or is it something they could never touch, if only because it is "unfathomable" by scientific means, and accessible only through Heidegger's linguistic usage. Perhaps he is right, after all: an artificially induced linguistic problem calls for special linguistic devices.

With characteristic linguistic thoroughness and determination, the term "existence" is beaten into the desired shape. It does not signify an "occurrence" or thing, or the "presence" of an "existent." Neither does it mean "man's moral preoccupation with himself," in any psychophysical sense. The answer reads: "Ex-sistence, grounded in truth as freedom, is nothing less than exposition into the revealed nature of what-is-as-such" (335). This strange usage need not detain us.

The outcome for man and history is noteworthy: "Only where what-is is expressly raised to the power of its own

revelation and preserved there, only where this preservation is conceived as the quest for what-is-as-such,
only there does history begin" (335 f.). Then there was no
history in the remote past, or, in fact, before the emergence
of philosophy. Reminiscent of the idealistic tradition is
the statement that "only ex-sistent man is historical,
'nature' has no history" (336). Heidegger's "history" is as
distinctive as his "ex-sistence," "freedom," and "truth"—
and practically everything else, in his allegedly fundamentally new and original point of view. Thus he is able
to assert that the initial revelation of what-is-in-totality,
the quest for what-is-as-such, and the beginning of the
history of the West, are one and the same thing.

Speculative philosophers should be given unlimited
freedom to reconstruct "absolutes" to their heart's content. But they should not be allowed to operate arbitrarily
with regard to matters of fact, and especially history. One
kind of history does indeed begin with the posing of
the question of the nature of existence. But there are
other kinds of history—economic, political, and on a
larger scale, biological, geological, and astronomical history. It is to be doubted, however, whether Heidegger's
purposes could be served by such clarity of designation.

It will also be observed how Heidegger places certain
terms in quotation marks—"time," "known," "subject,"
"object," etc. It tends to elevate the reader above such
concepts, and to make him feel a partner in a terribly
searching inquiry. Heidegger was of course anticipated in
this practice by Husserl, who undertook to "question"
everything, placing all presumed existents in quotation
marks. For Husserl, however, it was a matter of an exactly
defined method; whereas for Heidegger, in the present
context, it is a matter of straining to get away from

what he regards as ordinary, fallible, and naïve meanings to an inexpressibly "deep" level.

For Heidegger, "freedom is not governed by human inclination"; and "man does not 'possess' freedom as a property," but, rather, "freedom, or existent revelatory *Da-sein* possesses man." It is evident that there can be no application of this conception of freedom to actual historical conditions, which abound in social conflicts and attempts to change social relations. For Heidegger, freedom is construed as "the letting-be of what-is," and it is supposed to "perfect the nature of truth in the sense that truth is the unconcealment and revealment of what-is" (336). The reader is reminded that truth is not the mark of a correct proposition, made by a human "subject" in respect of an "object." Truth is, for Heidegger, "the revelation of what-is, a revelation through which something 'overt' comes into force." But one cannot deny the legitimacy of the truth concept in connection with propositions, and the distinction between subject and object, or knower and known. That distinction is a real one, and no distinction is more important. It does not imply a metaphysical, or an ontological, difference. Whatever else the term "truth" may be taken to mean, it certainly has this application. In one sense, the knower is a finality, an irreducible fact. He has his ideas, and he is a proposition-making animal. His ideas may be good or bad, adequate or inadequate; and his propositions may be good or bad, true or false. If good, they express correctly the actual state of affairs concerned; if bad, they do not. One may say that a true proposition expresses the truth (more exactly, an instance of truth). It can also be said that some aspect or occasion of the real has been portrayed, rather than "revealed," in most propositions. One must be prepared, however, to allow for hypothetical, possible, and even unreal entities—even for impossible entities—in determining the truth or falsity of propositions.

Despite his nice words concerning truth as the revelation of what-is, Heidegger is compelled to recognize error. It would seem to be difficult to provide for human fallibility on his premises, but he has an effective means in the concept of freedom. Although historical man "lets things be," he "cannot really let what-is be just *what* it is and *as* it is." But the reader is not told why historical man cannot do that. Is it because he does not like "what-is" in some respects, or that he wants to play a role more satisfactory to himself in the "what-is"? As Heidegger states it, "what-is is covered up and distorted," and "illusion comes into its own" (337). His statement that man only ex-sists as the property of ex-sistent freedom, which is the essence of truth, is utterly incomprehensible as it stands. It is thus that he tries to account for man's being capable of history. With distortion and illusion, the essential negation of truth, its "dis-essence," appears. If freedom is not a property of man ("man only ex-sists as the property of this freedom and so becomes capable of history"), then neither is the dis-essence of truth a property of man. The latter cannot "simply arise *a posteriori* from the mere incapacity and negligence of man." In Heidegger's view, "untruth must derive from the essence of truth." Thus it turns out that freedom (Heideggerian freedom) must bear the burden of error as well as truth.

The clarification of "what-is-in-totality" proves to be revealing. It is not identical with the sum of known actualities. Conveniently, where few actualities are known, or where they are hardly known by science, "the manifest character of what-is-in-totality can operate far more essentially" than where the field of knowledge is endless. Heidegger speaks disparagingly of the "proliferation and standardization of knowledge, this desire to know everything. . . ." (339). The setting for irrationalism has been prepared therewith. Man's behavior is said to be "attuned to the manifest character of what-is-in-totality." This "in-totality" appears to us, however, "as something incalculable and incomprehensible." Although this "in-totality" is conceived as ceaselessly determining all things, it cannot, in Heidegger's view, be understood in terms of what manifestly "is," and it remains indeterminable. It is "concealed." In each particular case of "letting be," something is disclosed in its proper relationship, but what-is-in-totality is regarded as concealed therewith. Thus, the exsistent freedom of *Da-sein* involves "a dissimulation of what-is-in-totality," or concealment. This concealment is accorded a fundamental place: as an "authentic untruth," it is "anterior to all revelation of this or that actuality," and also to the letting-be of what-is, which, by revealing, conceals and thus establishes the dissimulation" (341). This basis for irrationalism could only find a sympathetic welcome in anti-intellectualistic circles which had found the simpler bill-of-fare of Bergson no longer effective, if only because it was too easily understood.

The reader is now told that the "dissimulation of what-is-as-such" is a mystery, and that absolute mystery, or mystery as such ("the dissimulation of the dissimulated") pervades the whole of man's *Da-sein* (341). In the great tradition, there has been a place for mystery, especially where theological considerations were involved, and it has been regarded as a mark of wisdom to know when to ward off all rational questions or objections. That "*Da-sein,* in so far as it ex-sists, reaffirms the first and most extreme non-revelation of all: authentic un-truth," is no doubt best left as a mystery. Man errs, says Heidegger; he lives in error. But error is not something into which he occasionally falls; it is "part of the inner structure of *Da-sein*, in which historical man is involved" (345). The wrongness of a judgment, or the falseness of a perception, are regarded as only superficial ways of erring. Heidegger speaks of "the error in which historical man must always walk," and of error as dominating man "through and through by leading him astray" (346). What could "save" man, then, it is fair to ask: Heidegger's metaphysics—or possible future theology? Perhaps it may turn out that his being lost is the condition of being saved, and that the losing of the lost is another mystery. But, then, why should the present writer do Heidegger's theology for him? The point to be noted is that it is not too difficult to learn his style of inventing and manipulating a special jargon, and using words with firm connotations in other senses, with a final resort to mystery when the game has gone far enough.

When Heidegger speaks of being, the reader is reminded of the peculiar use of the term "history." Those who have ears for this word (being) are said to determine man's place in history. This cannot possibly refer to what is generally known as real history, or to real men, whether slaves or slaveholders, bourgeoisie, feudal lords, serfs, etc. They have their places in history, but they do not owe them to their having ears for the word "being." Of course, this is not what Heidegger is talking about, for he declares his attitude to history to be "fundamentally new" (351). He is at his best when dealing with a totality which involves mystery.

When inveighing against "all enslavement of philosophical thought" (349), he appears to be wearing the heroic garb of a defender of the rights of reason. His illustration corrects this impression, however, for he cites "the subterfuge of letting philosophy assert itself merely as an 'expression' of 'culture' (Spengler), as the ornament of a creative humanity" (349). Vulnerable though Spengler was, he had many concrete historical realities in mind. The present objection to Spengler would apply to all scholars who recognize the actual part played by philosophies in history, and the ways in which the various cultural conditions—economic, political, scientific, etc.— act upon and determine philosophy. Such recognition does not necessarily lead to the abandonment of the view that there is a cumulative, constructive element to be discerned in much of the tradition of philosophy.

Taken as a whole, Heidegger's performance in his lecture on "The Essence of Truth" is rather clever and ingenious. He appears in the form of a philosopher, but his role is really that of a theologian. If he does not make philosophy serve theology outright—indeed, he ostensibly makes it autonomous—that proves to be unnecessary, for the outcome is the same. There proves to be an ultimate mystery; man is fallible, and in effect condemned to err; there are concealment and revealment; and there are boundaries to possible scientific knowledge. In short, reason is circumscribed and undermined. Through it all there is an unsurpassed degree of pretentiousness and boldness, which is shown repeatedly in the display of verbal inventiveness. It is noteworthy that Heidegger could have written his lines centuries ago, with the same ease with which he is able to detach himself from the world and favor solitude rather than libraries. It is a curious fact that the reader is not likely to be aware of the complete absence of concrete illustrations or scientific references. Modern science and logic neither deter nor aid him in his attack on the German language. He appears in this lecture as a kind of dialectician who sets up contrasts and plays with opposites in order to exploit them. It is a furious attempt at originality, but is a miscarriage at best. A psychoanalytic type of interpreter would probably be tempted to speak of "the rage of intellectual (or scientific) impotence" as characterizing the style.

It is high time for Heidegger to emerge from his self-chosen role of philosopher and to declare himself. There may be a more appropriate place for him in the religious world. His characteristic language would make the step an easy one. There is a place in his system for a divine being, and original sin could have a metaphysical as well as an epistemological basis. That would give meaning and direction to his peculiar nonevolutionary conception of man.

These remarks are sure to be unpleasant to many of Heidegger's former students. Their self-feeling need not be injured, however. They could have done better in choosing a master, to be sure. It is never too late to acknowledge that fact and to reassess what they think they owe him. In some cases, the "transference" to Heidegger was too effective ever to be shaken by logical considerations, and one is reminded of the words, "Though He slay me. . . ." But the extensive influence of the man, now prominent in many countries, is to be explained culturally, in terms of the reasons for the receptivity of the times to irrationalism.

### 3. Heidegger on Husserl

While still an instructor in Husserl's department at Freiburg, Heidegger enjoyed the reputation of being a rebel, and even a revolutionist. His appeal to the youth seemed likely to surpass that of Husserl. In the minds of many of the student "hearers," that amounted to a victory of the incomprehensible over the imponderable. It was the popular impression that Heidegger pointed the way to release philosophy from its incarceration in the subjective realm. "Being" and "existence" were at least terms which promised deliverance.

A letter to Husserl, written on October 22, 1927,[6] gives Heidegger the opportunity "to characterize the basic tendency of *Being and Time*[7] within the transcendental problem." He supposes agreement to exist on the point that that which is *(das Seiende)*, in the sense in which Husserl speaks of "world," cannot be clarified in its transcendental constitution by recourse to anything that is or to any kind of being. But he does not mean to say that what makes up the place of the transcendental is not something that is. What he maintains is that the problem arises, as to the kind of being *(Seinsart des Seienden)* it is, in which "world" is constituted. This is stated by Heidegger as the central problem of his *Being and Time,* i.e., a "fundamental ontology of existence" *(Daseins)*. It must be shown, in his view, that the kind of being of human existence is wholly different from that of everything else that is, and that it conceals in itself the possibility of transcendental constitution. The latter is described as a central

---

6. Cf. Walter Biemel, "Husserls Enclycopaedia-Britannica Artikel und Heideggers Anmerkungen dazu," in *Tijdschrift voor Philosophie,* Vol. XII, No. 2, May, 1950, pp. 246-280.

7. Heidegger's early and most widely known book, *Sein und Zeit,* I, published originally in the *Jahrbuch für Philosophie und Phänomenologische Forschung,* Vol. VIII, edited by E. Husserl, Halle, M. Niemeyer, 1927.

possibility of the existence *(Existenz)* of the factual self. The concrete human being as such, however, as something which is, is never a mundane real fact, because a human being is never only extant *(vorhanden)*, but exists. Heidegger finds it to be "wonderful" that the existential state *(Existenzverfassung)* of existence *(Daseins)* makes possible the constitution of everything positive. He holds the "one-sided" considerations of somatology and pure psychology to be possible only on the basis of the concrete wholeness of a human being, which as such primarily determines the kind of being of man. That which "constitutes" *(das Konstituierende)* is not nothing; it is something that is, although not in the sense of "the positive."

Heidegger concludes that the question of the kind of being of the "constitutor" himself is not to be avoided. But he is not able to do more than verbalize, in view of the rejection of "positive" existence. To be sure, Husserl's concept of "the purely psychical" is derived from epistemological considerations; and therein lies its special justification and function. To speak of the "ontology of the whole man," and of the "universal" problem of being referred to the "constitutor" and the "constituted," is to substitute a verbal construction for the findings of scientific experience. It is evident that Heidegger has not departed from the Husserlian basis of subjectivism; that he is impelled by what could be a promising question ("what *is* the constitutor, or the subjectivizing investigator?"); that he renounces the question of "being" in naturalistic terms, as involving the causal order; and that with a vague "ontology" of the whole man, he takes his place in the same tradition in which Scheler sought to preserve special prerogatives for man. The evolutionary perspective, from which man is viewed as a risen animal rather than as a fallen angel (as Russell has expressed it), has no place in Heidegger's world view; for the constitutor is not something in the sense of "the positive." Heidegger goes further than the tradition in regarding the kind of being of man as *totally* different from that of all other existents. The human anatomist will nevertheless say truly, in view of the facts of comparative anatomy, that man is indeed an animal. That is not to undervalue the special achievements and virtues of man. It is not necessary to cut off all connections with the animal and natural world, in order to do justice to man's peculiarities, which include praiseworthy as well as blameworthy developments. It would have to be shown how man has any features which could not on principle be discerned by way of the sciences.

Furthermore, is it a fruitful question, to ask about the being of that which is? When Aristotle asked that type of question, it was historically understandable, as he really had more to say that was sound about being *qua* being (little as that was), than about particular kinds of natural being. But we are not in that position. There is a great deal that is said in the sciences about particular regions of being, and almost a blank nothing about being *qua* being.

It is always a desirable safeguard, when referring to the phenomenological reduction, to remind ourselves of its initial abstention from metaphysics. A universal "field" or "region" of experience is presupposed, and not a "being" of any kind, as Heidegger tries to make out. A metaphysical version of phenomenology faces the alternatives, either to abandon all talk of being except as "noematic" (in terms of correlates of conscious processes), which is acceptable for a descriptive discipline; or to face the charge of a contradiction, which no amount of linguistic

skill and subterfuge could conceal, namely, the contradiction of suspending all "being" while tacitly making use
of a being of a totally different kind—transcendental-
constitutive for Husserl, and verbally constitutive for
Heidegger.

Heidegger's question about the kind of being of the
transcendental "constitutor" is really a false one for a
strictly descriptive discipline, on the basis of the "reduction." The "constitution" of the "world" is an artificial
procedure, with "being" in quotation marks. Why should
it be supposed that the transcendental ego has "being"
or "constitutes" being really? *There is only one kind of
being,* although there are innumerable organizations of
it, with an unlimited diversity of properties and types to
be distinguished. As for Heidegger's "being," it is quite
empty, and he properly turns to "nothing" in his metaphysics.

## 4. Husserl on Heidegger: Existence and
## Philosophical Anthropology

Husserl's marginalia, transcribed by the Husserl Archives of Louvain[8] from his copies of Heidegger's *Being and
Time* and *Kant and the Problem of Metaphysics*[9] are
striking evidence of his critical powers, and of his
tenacious faith in transcendental phenomenology.

The question asked by Husserl in connection with
*Being and Time*[10] is certainly pertinent: If we understand
by "that which is" *(Seiendem)* something taken in formal
ontological generality, then the question arises, as to
whether there is an apodictic way from a formal ontology

---

8. Mss. of Husserl, KX Hei 1 and KX Hei 11, Husserl Archives, Louvain.
9. M. Heidegger, *Kant und das Problem der Metaphysik,* Bonn, Friedrich
   Cohen, 1929, inscribed to the memory of Max Scheler.
10. M. Heidegger, *Sein und Zeit,* I.

to a real one. Husserl observes that there are no other concepts of "being" here, and hence not of the "state of being" *(Seinsverfassung);* and he asks, "What does 'basic state of the being of that which is' mean?"[11] Noting Heidegger's expression "the existential comprehension" *(das existenzielle Verständnis),* he asks, "Is that clear?" It appears to Husserl that Heidegger transposes the constitutive phenomenological clarification of all regions of that which is and of the universal, of the total region of the world, into the anthropological. The entire problematics of Heidegger appears to him to be a transfer, so that to the Ego there corresponds existence *(Dasein),* etc., and Husserl states, everything becomes profoundly unclear, and philosophically it loses its value. Heidegger's phrase "ontic state" (or constitution: *Verfassung)* leads Husserl to ask pointedly about its meaning. Again, he observes (with respect to page 14, where reference is made to Thomas v. A.) that there is in Heidegger an element of Thomism *("Also steckt in Heidegger ein Stück Thomismus").* In connection with page 307 of Heidegger's book (second paragraph: "The call of conscience. . . ."), Husserl impatiently exclaims: "Always theological-ethical talk!" With regard to page 363 (1. 3, where mention is made of "the scientific draft of that which is"), he refers to the "vague generalities" of Heidegger; and a passage on page 385 (1. 25, concerning "the transmitted understanding of existence") provokes him to write "Again paradoxical talk." Refreshing also is Husserl's comment, in connection with page 424 (first paragraph), "As though the 'vulgar' conception of time did not have its original right, which does not in the least disappear through the constitutive analysis." Such

---

11. "Aber was heisst 'Grundverfassung des Sein des Seienden'?"

utterances support the conception of phenomenology as a specialized procedure which is portrayed by the present writer as alone defensible.

Some of Husserl's marginalia on Heidegger's "Kant-book"[12] are also well worth recording. Thus he observes that Heidegger goes along with an example of "Kantian unclearness" (apropos of page 189). When Heidegger (on page 199, 1. 11-17) discusses the nature and role of anthropology, as "knowledge of human beings," Husserl is led to exclaim, "That is rather fast and very unclear." The text in question asserts that inasmuch as man does not only occur as a natural being, but also acts and produces, anthropology must also seek to apprehend that which man as an active being can and should "make out of himself." What he can do and should do is said to be based finally on fundamental attitudes which man as such can adopt, which we call "world views," whose "psychology," Heidegger asserts, comprehends the whole of the knowledge of man. Also noteworthy is Heidegger's statement (which may also be "fast" but is by no means "unclear") that in the realm of anthropology are also the concealed "innate potentialities" *(Anlagen)* of man, the differences with respect to character, race, and sex. Evidently he was well prepared for 1933. Had Husserl written his comments after that crucial year, the sinister significance of this passage would have stood out in bold relief.

Heidegger asserts (200) that no time has known less about what man is than the present, and that at no time has man become so "questionable" as at present. He is indebted to Scheler's *The Place of Man in the Cosmos,* to which he refers for comparison with this very question-

---

12. M. Heidegger, *Kant und das Problem der Metaphysik.*

able opinion. An immense amount is known about man, as compared to the scientific level of earlier periods; and the process of understanding man is a progressive one. Only by reading something into man which the special sciences do not pretend to touch, or in which they are not interested because it supposedly transcends the field of science, can Heidegger (as well as Scheler) make room for "philosophical vision," in their sense. Heidegger appears here as a diminutive continuator of Scheler's ranting against science because of its alleged fateful limitations and aimlessness in certain respects.[13] In his view (200), for the new philosophical anthropology, something is only known and understood if it has found an *anthropological* explanation; and anthropology does not only seek the truth about man, but lays claim to the decision *as to what truth in general can signify.* In view of his stand on the various anthropological sciences, which are regarded by him as reducing to "complete indeterminateness" in their idea of man, this would allow a specially fabricated "philosophical" anthropology to decide what truth may mean. In other words, Heidegger, who has inherited the "prejudice" of Scheler, Jaspers, Dilthey, and the rest, as Husserl so very well called it, would act as the official judge for the entire world of scholarship. Never has the presumptuousness of the man stood out more offensively.

Heidegger acknowledges the basic difficulty of a philosophical anthropology to lie first of all in the concept

13. Max Scheler, who spoke of the desired *philosophical* anthropology, wrote: "In a certain sense all the central problems of philosophy can be reduced to the question of what man is and which metaphysical place he occupies within the whole of being, the world, and God." Cp. *Zur Idee des Menschen, Abhandlungen und Aufsätze,* Vol. I, 1915, p. 319. These volumes, in the 2nd and 3rd editions, appeared under the title *Vom Umsturz der Werte,* Leipzig, Der Neue Geist, 1919.

itself, rather than in the problem of achieving a systematic unity of the essential determinations. An anthropology may be called philosophical, in his opinion, if its method is philosophical, say in the sense of an *essential* view of man. The latter aims to distinguish the being *(Seiende)* that we call man from plants and animals, and other provinces of that which is, and thereby to work out its specific essential structure. Philosophical anthropology then becomes a regional ontology of man. Husserl's comment, to the effect that essential determinations are not yet philosophy, indicates that he places this view among the early and undeveloped examples of inquiry in the phenomenological movement.

Obviously influenced by Scheler, Heidegger holds that anthropology can also be philosophical if it determines the goal of philosophy, or its point of departure. He reasons that if the goal of philosophy is the elaboration of a world view, then the place of man in the cosmos must be determined; and if man is the being that is "first-given" and most certain, in the order of foundation of an absolutely certain knowledge, then human subjectivity must be brought into the central place in the construction of philosophy. The method and the results of a regional ontology of man would thus be employed for philosophical purposes. Evidently the place of man in the cosmos is not to be determined once and for all, even "essentially," as might be expected. No doubt a large part of the charm of "philosophical" problems lies precisely in their capacity to survive all treatments of them. The *scientific* question of man's place in the cosmos may well be never answered completely. But if there is any basis for the talk of essences, definitive answers should be possible in that realm. Or don't the essentialists mean what they say?

It develops that Heidegger is not prepared to operate as a rationalist with respect to the essence of man. From the manifold possibilities of delimitation of the philosophical character of an anthropology, there follows, in his view, the "indeterminateness" of the Idea. (Husserl's query was: Why indeterminateness?) The indeterminateness is increased, according to Heidegger, if the diversity of the knowledge of empirical anthropology is held in view. The latter is acknowledged to "lie at the basis of every philosophical anthropology, at least at the beginning."

Aware of the obvious objections to his position, Heidegger reflects that its opponents will be able to refer to the circumstance that man does not belong to the center of "that which is," and that there is an "ocean" of "that which is" besides. In his comments, Husserl asks what the "in the center" means; and he expresses the opinion that the opponents of anthropology as the basic philosophical discipline, who reject an anthropologically founded philosophy as an "anthropologism," will not incur the foolish error of denying the central place of the reflecting man in the "oriented world." For Husserl, at any rate, "central" may be defined in terms of a self-reflecting thinker, with all reality considered with respect to his thought-processes.

When Heidegger (205) observes that Kant, in his *Foundation of the Metaphysics of Morals,* digs away the ground on which he placed the critique at the beginning, Husserl comments: "But also Heidegger." And Heidegger's reference (206) to "an almighty essence" which does not have to ask, "What can I do?" leads Husserl to ask: "Is such an essence essentially possible?"

Husserl's critical stand on the concept of "being" is indicated in some pointed remarks (relating to pages 214 f.). He writes: I can question everything that is concerning its "properties," its "relations"; I can question each one about its "general essence." Are there properties and categories, just as there are dogs and cats; or is there "a problem here which must be put finally," as Heidegger states it? What kind of problem? Directly and evidently judging about that which is " in general" (and not limited to the *mundane,* which, Husserl holds, is not at all the only possible kind of being) I gain the formal ontological as well as the mundane-formal or "material." But despite that I am not satisfied. The subject-relation of consciousness, of knowledge, brings the modern difficulties. They do not concern a mythical "being," but the essence-relationship of that which is in general and subjectivity in general, for which it is. In Husserl's view, this leads to the only reasonable problems of constitution, to "a subjective turning to knowledge and to consciousness in general as contributive," and that means the transcendental as contrasted with psychological subjectivity.

Especially interesting in these remarks are the refusal to limit "that which is" to the mundane; the caustic reference to a "mythical being"; and the frank statement of an essence-relationship of that which is in general and subjectivity in general, "for which it is." At least one knows where Husserl stands. His subjectivism is avowed, and is not concealed by words purporting to refer to "being."

Heidegger's statement (216), that "the question of being as a question concerning the possibility of the concept of being arises on its side from the pre-conceptual understanding of being," leads Husserl to comment on the phrase "concept of being," and on the "understanding of being." (1) It is not concerning the possibility of the concept of being, he remarks, but rather concerning the possibility of putting an end to the difficulties *(Verlegen-heiten)* in which the world as "world for us" involves us, and everything that is in general, as something that is for us; or the possibility of making out that which is in general, which is certain to us in naïve evidence and certain as "in itself," as opposed to the accidentalness of human knowing, in order that "that which is" has meaning (formal and material) for us, and no other one than it has for us. (2) Furthermore, all concepts of "that which is" are obtained in an original, in a self-giving manner, out of the conceiving activity and on the basis of pre-conceptual experience; and naturally also the concepts of "being," in so far as that would have a good sense. But what is here concerned is not the possibility, the essence, the concept being; it is rather the psychological, and by virtue of the difficulties, the transcendental possibility of "that which is" in general as being for us. This involves the constituting subjectivity, still not formulated conceptually and not systematically investigated, and the essence-unity of a lived existent, simply and exclusively for us, with the transcendental contributive subjectivity; and from there a concrete full essence-apprehension of "that which is," which does not leave open any essence-questions concerning that which is in general. But the problem of the treatment of the world on this basis is more serious than Husserl supposes it to be. A partial success is possible, if the problem is circumscribed as an inquiry concerning meaning-constitution, based in the last analysis upon immediate experience. The "world," however, remains a standing problem for phenomenology, because of the tacit hope to make the subjectivistic approach accomplish more than it is able to do, "essentially." The very meaning of "world" requires an objectivistic approach.

Heidegger writes (217): "That which is *(Seiendes)* is known to us—but being *(Sein)?* Are we not overcome by vertigo, when we determine such like, or if we are even to conceive it? In fact, no less a person than Hegel has said that pure being and pure nothing are the same." Husserl retorts that the vertigo comes only from the unclearness of the concept of being. This is borne out by Heidegger himself, when he states that with the question concerning being as such we venture to the brink of complete darkness.

In the course of his discussion, Heidegger finally comes (page 220) to the conclusion that the question, "What is more original than man?", is not an anthropological question; for all anthropology, also philosophical anthropology, have already posited man as man. The problem of the foundation of metaphysics accordingly finds its root in the question concerning the existence in man, i.e., concerning its "innermost ground," and the understanding of being *(Seinsverständnis)* as the essentially existent finitude. Heidegger maintains that the foundation of metaphysics must be grounded in a metaphysics of existence.

Reacting to Heidegger's text, Husserl notes: "Thus, existence *(Dasein)* in man is equivalent to understanding of being"; and he asks, "Is the understanding of being the innermost essence of finitude?" He infers that existence may well be identical with the "understanding of being." To one who, although idealistic, always emphasizes the noesis-noema distinction, such language can only appear to be hopelessly confused, or at most a hopeless form of subjectivism.

It is Heidegger's contention that no anthropology which understands its own questioning, and the presuppositions of the latter, can claim to develop even the problem of a foundation of metaphysics, much less carry it through. The question which he regards as necessary for a foundation of metaphysics, concerning the nature of man, is taken over by the metaphysics of existence. With this, the matter is left in obscurity, with concealment the great foe, and a perspective of endless travail before man. Is *this* the cure for the alleged failure of man to "understand" himself at present?

It is not possible, on the basis of his subjectivism, for Husserl to deal successfully with the problem of finitude and infinitude, which is involved by Heidegger's view of human existence. For Husserl, infinitude is nothing other than the capacity for fulfillment *(Erfüllbarkeit),* or for determination *(Bestimmbarkeit)* in the "and so forth." That is as much as the limitations of his type of descriptive analysis will allow.

For Heidegger, the finitude of existence—the understanding of being—lies in "forgottenness"; and the fundamental-ontological basic act of the metaphysics of existence as the foundation of metaphysics is a "remembrance." Certainly this is a covert form of subjectivism. There is no evidence that it is able to transcend the limits of subjectivism, in order to establish a theory of real being. The impossibility on principle of such "transcendence" is seen clearly in the case of a well-defined subjectivism. That the issue is less obvious in the case of Heidegger is due in part to his failure to acknowledge and follow explicit lines of method, and also to the mass of confused and confusing language employed. But there can be no mistake about the barrenness of the outcome.

## C.  BECKER AND PARATRANSCENDENCE

The linguistic extravagances of Heidegger may be said to have culminated in the vapid straining after unprobed depths which Oskar Becker of Bonn illustrated under the heading of "Transcendence and Paratranscendence," in the 1937 meeting of the International Congress of Philosophy in Paris.[14] A mathematician by training, a close student of Husserl, and then a fascinated admirer of Heidegger, Becker was not without personal ambition and verbal inventiveness.

Examining anew the ancient Greek concept of transcendence, Becker hopefully dissociates from it the concept of "paratranscendence," which he offers to the world for the first time, after "liberating" it from its traditional attachment. Transcendence means, in German, "Ueberstieg," or "Uebersteigendheit" ("passing beyond"). "Paratranscendence" is rendered in German as "Unentstiegenheit." This is not taken to mean that nothing is transcended. The point is, that the "passing beyond" does not occur as in the case of genuine transcendence, where the "things" which are transcended sink entirely into nothing. The reference is of course to Heidegger and his valued findings in his inquiry concerning metaphysics. "Unentstiegenheit" is taken to signify something positive because the prefix "un" annuls the syllable "ent." Thus, that which "gets away" *(entsteigende)* from the existent is to a certain extent caught and held back before it completely "gets away," so that "Unentstiegenheit" is a "dialectical" term. The phenomenon of the paratranscendent is held to be undialectical, however. Wherever a *form (Gestalt)* grows organically and lifts itself out of its surroundings, without leaving its native soil behind, there paratranscendence is realized. Hence paratranscendence is designated above all as the "natural," wherever it appears. The word "nature" is construed as signifying "birth." Now

---

14. *Travaux du IX^e Congrès International de Philosophie,* Vol. VIII, pp. 97-104, Paris, Hermann & Cie., 1937.

birth does not mean being created out of nothing; it is
never "immanence," or remaining in the maternal ground,
but is at the most a certain "inherence," a clinging to it
"with the outermost strands of its essence." Birth is
described as the metaphysical counterpart to Heidegger's
"thrownness" *(Geworfenheit)*. Birth does not signify
"thrownness" in the world, just as it does not mean creation out of nothing. Becker could not resist introducing
the notorious concept of race into his metaphysical reflections. "Basic experiences" such as belonging to a definite
people or race are said to have their place here.

A few excerpts will be of interest. "Not the *being* of
the being 'man' is in question, but his *essence,* more exactly
his *'essencing* essence'. And here is seen the philosophical
nature of our language: we sometimes apply the expression
'essence' not only abstractly but also concretely to man.
But not to every human being: namely, not to a grown
man, but to a child and a young woman. Thus we speak
of a 'small essence' *(dem 'kleinen Wesen,'* the child) and
of a 'charming essence' (e.g., a young girl). A man as a
historical personality *has* indeed an essence (his character),
but he *is* not one. The natural human being still close
to naïve primitiveness is on the other hand an essence
which 'essences'. After speaking of the "paraexistence"
of such a human being, Becker reassures his audience:
"These are not mere words and quibbling." His proposal
to inspect the "primal phenomenon" recalls a familiar
Husserlian precept. The use to which it is put is indicated
by the following passage: "The phenomenon of birth,
which is only to be apprehended intuitively, determines
the existence of an unbroken human being, or more
exactly, the mode of existence of a human being, in so far
as he is unbroken." The old "maternal" powers of blood

and earth are said to be visible in "basic experiences." It is furthermore the blood, "that apparently material but in truth to the highest degree formative and impressing force, which determines the types, the 'kinds' of human beings, the basic forms which are possible for human beings."

The apparatus of "intuition" and "basic experience" is, in this context, just so much pseudo-phenomenological claptrap. It could be simply judged to be comical balderdash were it not connected with Nazism; for there is no accidental connection between Becker's "blood and earth" and the teachings of the Nazis. The ease with which existentialism could accommodate itself to Nazi Germany is noteworthy.

Becker finally comes to a formulation of the "ontological inequation" that "Being surpasses the existent," and its analogue in the domain of essence. The "parontological equation" to which he attains is "The essence is identical with that which essences." In contrast to the "ontological difference" (the usage is Heidegger's)—i.e., the transcendence of being over the existent—there is the "parontological indifference" of Becker, which is the "Unentstiegenheit" of the paratranscendent. A "natural essence" is paratranscendent, and hence is only parontological, and not determinable ontologically.

A final consequence for the determination of the "naturally human" is drawn. "Its mode of living is neither genuine nor non-genuine *(fallen)* existence, neither a gaining itself nor a losing itself. It is rather the absence of every self-being, not in the sense of a privation, but rather in the sense of a total negation, or of an antithetical position equal in rank." Becker is talking about "Dawesen" ("essence-there"), which seems to signify great progress beyond "Dasein" (being-there, existence). The pure "non-genuine" *Dawesen* in all its simplicity is just as "original" as the genuine, original *Dasein*.

What kind of blossoms can one expect to sprout in such an atmosphere? Following Heidegger's retreat to nothing, Becker offers us a rebirth with conditions under which most of us could hardly feel at home. The "nature" which he seeks to rescue through "paratranscendence" is truly a foreign land, not the well-known but much despised "naturalistic" nature; and we must agree with Becker to this extent, that it is best to arrive at it by double negation.

### D.  JASPERS AND THE EVASION OF SCIENTIFIC PHILOSOPHY

Karl Jaspers cannot be said to be ignorant of science. Quite the contrary: a medical scientist of acknowledged standing, he established himself in German philosophy in the 1920's. And yet we find him aligned against the party of science in philosophy. This is clearly shown in his book on *The Perennial Scope of Philosophy*.[15] The concept of transcendence is of very great importance in his philosophy, but it is far removed from the original epistemic transcendence of Husserl. There is transcendence, for Jaspers, "if the world does not consist only of itself, is not built upon itself, but points beyond itself." It is clear to him that "if the world is everything, then there is no transcendence," i.e., in his sense. The tacit reasoning must then be: since there is transcendence, the world cannot be everything, and, by *modus tollens*, the man must be right! But what about this mysterious transcendence: what do we know about it? The former medical

---

15. Translated by Ralph Mannheim, New York, Philosophical Library, 1949. Limitations of space restrict the discussion of the existentialists to a few examples.

scientist goes so far as to state that "we take our life from a primal source that lies beyond the being-there . . . beyond consciousness and beyond mind," and "I know that I have been given to myself in transcendence." The "Absolute" is for Jaspers an article of faith, and is said to "erupt from the transcendent into this world by way of our freedom."

It may be true, as Jaspers maintains, that "man as a whole can never become the object of scientific investigation," and that "man is always more than he knows about himself"—true because of the unavoidable incompleteness of knowledge. The descriptive process may well be endless. But what follows from the recognition of this general fact? More science, and not irrationalism or existentialism, would certainly be called for—more knowledge, rather than faith.

In the course of his argument, Jaspers takes the occasion to approve the interesting if not fruitful cosmic view of Preyer, that the world is a gigantic body of life, and that everything that is not alive is its excrement and corpse. The origin of the non-living rather than the living therewith becomes the problem. Obviously, the evolutionary conception is unwelcome to him, and he is impressed by "mystery," above all by a mysterious "transcendence." The fact that he has become one of the important founders of existentialism is testimony at once to the lowly logical level of that movement, and to the dominant motive of antinaturalism.

### E. MARCEL AND MYSTERY

Gabriel Marcel, who is spirtually related to Jaspers, expresses opposition[16] to the conception of man provided by historical materialism and by the Freudian doctrines. His critique of the sciences and the scientific view of the world makes a place for "mystery." The category of the "purely natural" appears to him to be "pseudo-scientific," and to lead to the atrophy of the "faculty of wonder." His readiness to avow mystery is seen in the "mystery of cognition," which is alleged to result from the circumstance that "knowledge is contingent on a participation in being for which no epistemology can account because it continually presupposes it." To one who is not determined to find the inexplicable regardless of the state of our knowledge, the fact of the occurrence of knowing in the world should be fully evident. There are numerous problems to be solved; but there is no mystery.

To distinguish between a "mystery" and a "problem" is not helpful. As Marcel views it, "a mystery is a problem, which encroaches upon its own data . . . thereby transcending itself as a simple problem." The alleged "mystery of the union of body and soul" is hardly an acceptable example, because it is only the traditionally defined concept of a soul that produces the mystery. The concept of a

---

16. Gabriel Marcel, *The Philosophy of Existence,* translated by Manya Hall, New York, Philosophical Library, 1949. The first of the four essays of this volume, "On the Ontological Mystery," was written in 1933; the second, "Existence and Human Freedom" (Paris, 1946), is a critical survey of the philosophy of Sartre; the third, "Testimony and Existentialism," also written in 1946, presents Marcel's conception of existentialism; and the fourth, "An Essay in Autobiography," is taken from the volume, *Existentialisme Chrétien,* edited by E. Gilson, Paris, Librairie Plon, 1947. For a sympathetic account, cp. W. E. Hocking, "Marcel and the Ground Issues of Metaphysics," in *Philosophy and Phenomenological Research,* June, 1954.

mystery is itself placed beyond the reach of all rational means. Thus Marcel reasons that "in reflecting on a mystery we . . . degrade it to the level of a problem." His aim is "by a way of liberation and detachment from experience" to rise to the level of "the meta-problematical and of mystery."

The starting point of metaphysics, or the general theory of reality, would derive its basis from the findings of the special sciences, for a scientifically oriented person. Marcel, however, regards the fact that suicide is possible as the essential starting point of any genuine metaphysical thought. With a rapid succession of key terms, his thought leads to the religion which he professes. Thus, despair, or "the act by which one despars of reality as a whole," is contrasted with hope, which involves the belief that "there is at the heart of being . . . a mysterious being which is in connivance with me."

Condemning "crass materialism," Marcel shows himself to be primarily a fideist. His appeal will be largely confined to persons who are already convinced believers. Although he has many insights, borrowed and original, there is little evidence of the careful methodological preparation of the strict phenomenologist. It is more helpful to follow Marcel's text with his aversions and inclinations in mind, than by attempting to trace out logical connections. He is against materialism and naturalism, against the scientific view of the world as the basis for a philosophy, against the exclusive use of logical procedures; and he is for a supernatural, for a region inaccessible to reason—in short, for "transcendence" and Christianity. Logical connections are largely conspicuous by their absence, and the pervasive irrationalism is partially concealed by the skillful use of special terms.

## F. SARTRE AND THE AVOIDANCE OF
## MATERIALISM

Responding to mixed motives, Jean-Paul Sartre had an early period of interest in phenomenology, reflecting his period of study in Freiburg.[17] His most ambitious work, *Being and Nothingness,* reacts to influences and thought patterns of Descartes, Hegel, Husserl, Heidegger, and psychoanalysis.[18]

The lecture on "Existentialism,"[19] delivered in Paris in 1945, was an attempt at a popular exposition of the central aim of his philosophy. Although it may not be considered a satisfactory statement of any aspect of his philosophy, it is nevertheless characteristic of his style of thinking.

The declaration that "subjectivity must be the starting point," which is meant to be an alternative statement for "existence precedes essence," aligns Sartre with subjectivism. The entire attempt to elucidate this idea is unsuccessful, however. How can it be said that "man is what he conceives himself to be"? Sartre wishes to point out the self-sufficiency of man and his nondependence on a divine being. He could have done much better to let the matter rest with the denial of a supernatural cause, without going to the extreme of having a kind of mythical "man" who "wills himself to be" and "thrusts toward existence." Sartre's man "hurls himself toward a future." Some reading in the literature of evolution, and especially

---

17. Cf. his writings on the imagination: *L'imagination,* Paris, Librairie Félix Alcan, 1936; *L'imaginaire,* Paris, Librairie Gallimard, 1940.

18. *L'être et le néant,* Paris, 1943; English translation by Hazel E. Barnes, *Being and Nothingness,* New York, Philosophical Library, 1956.

19. English translation by Bernard Frechtman, New York, Philosophical Library, 1947.

of cultural anthropology, might have a salutary effect on his thinking and writing.

It is unsatisfactory and confusing to call the principle of subjectivity the first principle of existentialism if that is taken to mean that "man is nothing else but what he makes of himself." If the reader has grasped this formulation of subjectivity, he is due for a jolt when he learns that the essential meaning of existentialism is "that it is impossible for man to transcend subjectivity."

Evidently Sartre regards the characteristic existentialist terms, anguish, forlornness, and despair, to be too precious to drop under any circumstances. The quaint assertion that "man is anguish" is taken to mean that one cannot help "choosing all mankind as well as himself." Why should this he called "anguish," precisely? Is it because there is so much tension when an avowedly individualistic philosophy overstretches itself to consider the good of society? It is hardly necessary to observe that regard for others, or for humanity as a whole, may be accompanied by just the opposite of "anguish." There may be states of tranquility, or of exhilaration, and agreeableness. If the term "forlornness" is taken to mean that man has to face the consequences of God's nonexistence, Sartre is making a damaging admission by his very usage. A self-sufficient naturalism, a vigorous humanism, a genuine optimism— none of these views would find a place for the alleged forlornness of man. Sartre's strange mixture which he calls existentialism seems to have something for everybody, and the many perplexed people of our time will find it reassuring to know that forlornness is a concept with real ontological depth.

The Cartesian *cogito,* or the subjectivity of the individual, is the point of departure for Sartre. Outside the *cogito,* he states, "all views are only probable." This is not a tenable statement, however, for mathematical (deductive) knowledge is not limited to the *cogito,* and is irrelevant to it. In opposition to Sartre, it may be maintained that one can discover neither himself nor others in the *cogito* (Sartre holds that one discovers both himself and others therein). The purely methodological nature of the "cogito" (pure subjectivity) should not be confused with actual reality.

The disbelief in progress, on the ground that "man is always the same," even in the face of Sartre's obvious awareness of changing social conditions and realignments of classes; the rather confused and vulgar classification of people into "cowards" and "stinkers," with respect to the alleged concealment of their "freedom"; and the vaguely expressed reference to "transcendent goals" which must be pursued by man ("man being this state of passing-beyond"—a typically existential utterance!): these are further points which indicate a woeful lack of clear and systematic thinking. Elements of idealism are seemingly taken from the literature at random, and are thrown together with insights of naturalism and even of historical materialism. Thus, Sartre asserts that "there is no universe other than a human universe, the universe of human subjectivity." Fortunately, the concept of transcendence is at hand, although it hardly suffices to pry him loose from his idealistic encumbrances.

Finally, it may be observed that Sartre is simply wrong when he charges that materialism treats all men as "objects" in a narrow sense, "in no way distinguished from the ensemble of qualities and phenomena which constitute a table or chair or a stone." This falsifying hostility toward materialism is seen in still more extreme form in his essay on "Materialism and Revolution,"[20] with particular reference to dialectical materialism. With a haste born of desire, he rushes at his opponents—materialism in general, and dialectical materialism in particular—but without evidence of the necessary preliminary study, or judicial fairness, either in their presentation or critique. If rage were sufficient, they would be truly torn to pieces, and only "ruins" would remain, as Sartre fancies the outcome of his effort to have eventuated. It is abundantly clear, at any rate: Sartre is a non-materialistic non-fideist; and he has succeeded in bringing down an unusually large part of the ideological world upon his subjectivistic (alias existentialistic) head.

20. J.-P. Sartre, "Matérialisme et Révolution," *Les Temps Modernes,* Vol. I, June-July, 1946. Cf. Sartre, *Literary and Philosophical Essays,* London, Rider and Company, 1955, pp. 185-239.

## Chapter X

# EPILOGUE

## A. SUBJECTIVISM ON THE DEFENSIVE

Throughout its entire development, phenomenology has been the target of criticism, both within and outside the field of professional philosophy. Early critics of phenomenology included Natorp, Wundt, Sigwart, and Maier. Husserl's repudiation of psychologism had an unsettling effect upon many of his contemporaries, and the nature of his positive descriptive program was misconstrued. His transition to a transcendental point of view largely estranged him from a generation of scholars who had been impressed by his *Logical Investigations*. The standard reply to critics was to charge them with misunderstanding. That was applied to writers such as Schlick and Külpe, and to Rickert and his sphere of influence. The criticism of Kreis and Zocher[1] was answered by Husserl's assistant, Eugen Fink, in an essay which Husserl endorsed as expressing his own views.[2] In addition to such intra-idealistic criticism, there were unsympathetic reactions and uncompromising rejections of at least the transcendental version of phenomenology by writers such as E. Zilsel,

---

1. F. Kreis, *Phänomenologie und Kritizismus*, Tübingen, J. C. B. Mohr, 1930; R. Zocher, *Husserls Phänomenologie und Schuppes Logik*, München, E. Reinhardt, 1932.
2. E. Fink, "Die phänomenologische Philosophie Edmund Husserls in der gegenwärtigen Kritik," *Kant-Studien*, 1933, pp. 319-383. Cf. the present writer's discussion of this important essay in his *Foundation of Phenomenology*, pp. 543 ff.

J. Kraft, and W. Koehler.[3] Husserl's interest in eidetic description was interpreted as being an opposition to causal analysis and scientific method; and he was charged with license in the permissible types of description, and with discarding the world in the initial preparatory procedure. Although a number of pertinent questions required answers, the critical writers rarely showed evidence of care in rendering Husserl's thought. In the case of existentialism, the critics have fared better on the whole, perhaps because of its very excesses and extravagances.[4]

The criticism by Driesch,[5] although advanced by a writer whose own position, as a vitalist, is vulnerable logically, is among the more serious reactions to phenomenology. As Driesch sees it, phenomenology as a method becomes a danger when it gets into the wrong hands. Questioning the *a priori* study of essences in the field of

---

3. Edgar Zilsel, "Phenomenology and Natural Science," in *Philosophy of Science*, Vol. VIII, 1940; Julius Kraft, *Von Husserl zu Heidegger*, Leipzig, Hans Buske Verlag, 1932; Wolfgang Koehler, *The Place of Value in a World of Facts*, New York, Liveright Publishing Corporation, 1938.

4. For example, G. Stern, "On the Pseudo-Concreteness of Heidegger's Philosophy," and H. Marcuse, "Existentialism: Remarks on Sartre's *L'Être et le Néant*," in *Philosophy and Phenomenological Research*, Vol. VIII, No. 3, March, 1948; A. Schuetz, "Sartre's Theory of the Alter Ego," same journal, Vol. IX, No. 2, December, 1948; A. Cornu, "Bergsonianism and Existentialism," in *Philosophic Thought in France and the United States*, ed. by M. Farber, University of Buffalo Publications in Philosophy, 1950; V. J. McGill, "Sartre's Doctrine of Freedom," H. J. Pos, "L'existentialisme dans la philosophie de l'histoire," and F. H. Heinemann, "What is Alive and What is Dead in Existentialism?", in *Revue Internationale de Philosophie*, Brussels, Vol. III, No. 9, July, 1949; H. Lefebvre, *L'existentialisme*, Paris, Éditions du Sagittaire, 1946; Marjorie Grene, *Dreadful Freedom: A Critique of Existentialism*, University of Chicago Press, 1948; R. Garaudy, *Literature of the Graveyard*, New York, International Publishers, 1948.

5. Hans Driesch, *Philosophische Forschungswege: Ratschläge und Warnungen*, Leipzig, Verlag Emmanuel Reinicke, 1930.

empirical fact, he criticizes the error of attempting to "deduce" particular things from general, *a priori* concepts. Scheler's *"a priori* intuition" provides a convenient illustration; for according to Scheler, the essence of man can be discerned, and from this "intuition" it can be deduced that men must have sense organs. In Driesch's opinion, that would be justified if it were advanced as a hypothesis. But he holds it to be an error to confuse that which is learned empirically with its possibility as an *a priori* matter.

Apart from the habitual warfare of the schools, the sharpest criticism has emanated from the ranks of the materialists. The question discussed by Naville,[6] "Marx or Husserl?", was pertinent for France at the close of World War II, in view of the element of interest in subjectivism. So far as the French workers were concerned, Husserl would have had nothing to say to them, except perhaps, as he once remarked, that "a working man is worthy of his hire." Although it would be pointless to the extent of being amusing to suggest that subjectivism be of interest to the workers as such, it does not follow that it is devoid of all possible social consequences. For all mankind, viewed ideally, every advance in basic understanding, every technique which adds to our knowledge, however abstract or general, may ultimately have practical value. The usefulness of subjectivism is to be judged in the same way in which the practical aspect of pure mathematics is judged. That it would not in the least suggest the slightest change in existing social relations anywhere may, however, be accepted as a foregone conclusion. More than subjectivism is required in order to solve social problems.

---

6. Pierre Naville, *Les Conditions de la Liberté*, Paris, Éditions du Sagittaire, 1947.

To be sure, Husserl had considered the philosophers to have been responsible for the sad state of the world following from World War I. His reasoning was simple: clear thinking is necessary for sound action; the philosophers are specialists in clear thinking, and they have failed to come to any agreement. But it would have been difficult to impress even a dozen Frenchmen with the proposition that a descriptive subjectivism could be a constructive step toward a happier France.

Ideally, Husserl had a point. But the more widespread adoption of a general logic, conceived as a comprehensive methodology, which would comprise subjective procedures, among other methods, would be far more to the point. Even so, one must be careful not to commit what may be called the "rationalistic fallacy," or "rationalistic dogma," according to which the acceptance of general principles necessarily would lead to the indicated goals. An awareness of the conflicting interests of our complex society, and of the important part played by non-rational factors in influencing human conduct, should enable us to understand why any supposed knowledge of what is right will not necessarily lead us to act in accordance with that knowledge. There would be no general agreement on what is "objectively" right, in any case of conflicting social interests, or of competing national interests.

In the recent Russian literature, Professor Bykovsky has challenged subjectivism in his discussion of "The Deobjectification of Philosophy."[7] Assigning a leading role in the tendency to "deobjectivize" philosophy to phenomenology, he speaks of its "expelling" the entire objective world and all real objects from philosophical inquiry. The result of the "reduction" outlined by Husserl was the

---

7. B. E. Bykovsky, *Voprosy Filosofii*, 1956, No. 2, pp. 142-151.

removal of philosophy from all concern with real things; for the "bracketing" of the world means retirement to the "pure immanence" of consciousness. In agreement with a formulation by Engels (in his *Anti-Dühring*), Professor Bykovsky speaks of the objective study of the most general laws of being and thought, obtained from practical life and experimental science, in order to contrast to it the seeing of "pure essences" by means of intellectual intuition. The basic content of phenomenology is rightly designated as the description and analysis of eidetic types; and Husserl is quoted to the effect that the "sphere of fictions," and not reality, may be taken to characterize the subject matter of phenomenology.

Professor Bykovsky makes reference to the present writer as "trying to avoid the reactionary consequences of phenomenology." Readers of the present volume will note with interest the statement that its author "cannot deny" that there was in Husserl a strong feeling of opposition to the naturalistic approach to phenomena, or to natural-scientific thought. The present writer is credited with sound criticism of the most reactionary representatives of Husserlian subjectivism. His position is declared to be manifestly utopian, however, in that it represents an endeavor to "cultivate phenomenology without raising its fruits." Professor Bykovsky contends that it is unavoidable that a sterile scholastic flower should result on the tree of the eidetic reduction. This is well understood, he adds, by the Catholic neo-scholastics "who toy with phenomenology." Viewing phenomenology as an expression of opposition to philosophy conceived as a scientific world view, he observes that the aim to be free from all partisanship prevents it from entering into the problems of actual life and social reality. Husserl is portrayed as working with the perspective of centuries to come, with non-interference in the great problems of our time the result. This is taken to be a betrayal of the social mission of philosophy.

When Professor Bykovsky speaks of "an endeavor to cultivate phenomenology without raising its fruits," he assumes that phenomenology is to be regarded as a universal philosophy; for otherwise the "fruits" would be limited to "purely reflective" and "essential" descriptions, to a structural study of experience. In view of the present writer's independent position, as set forth on numerous occasions, it could not be said that he proposes to "cultivate phenomenology" as a general philosophy—as though there were necessarily an implicit commitment to idealistic metaphysical principles involved. It does not imply "cultivating symbolic logic" without raising *its* "fruits," if one recognizes symbolic logic as a legitimate and valuable descipline. The charge of unacceptable "fruits" in this case would involve going beyond symbolic logic, perhaps to a formal relativism, or an "escapist" formal philosophy, which restricts the function of philosophy to the consideration of formal relationships. "Symbolic logicism" would be a queer philosophy; and a generalized subjectivism even queerer, i.e., as generalized to a complete philosophy. The present writer has not only made clear the antinaturalistic motivation of Husserl and his entire sphere of influence. Construing phenomenology as a descriptive discipline solely, and as subordinated to a general methodology which recognizes the true place of man in reality, he has also undertaken to direct criticism unsparingly and impartially against the outstanding subjectivists of our time, whether "reactionary" or simply mistaken.[8]

( See Footnote on next page. )

In keeping with the need to view naturalism and subjectivism in their historical form of conflict, the term
"subjective" has been retained for the present. But it
would conduce to greater clarity if it were replaced by the
term "reflective," which would allow for various types, including "radical" reflection. Similarly, all other tradition-
laden terms should be replaced. The positive outcome of
subjectivism as a mode of procedure, in its best examples,
would thus be a contribution to methodology. Holding
firmly to what has been called in the present volume
the "basic fact" for all philosophizing, which is a "naturalistic" truth, there would be no room for unfounded and
illogical metaphysical adventures.

## B. THE METHODOLOGICAL OUTCOME

The conception of methodological and logical pluralism,
which pervades the present writer's work, goes along with
"ontological" monism. The pluralism is twofold: (a) Methodological pluralism signifies that no one type of procedure is to be regarded as the correct method exclusively.
That would be an error as untenable in its way as it
once was to have the syllogism occupy the central place of
honor. An unlimited number of methods, restricted at
a given time only by human ingenuity and the extent of
knowledge, is the response to an unlimited number of
types of problem. The principle of the cooperation of

---

8. Cf. the present writer's "A Review of Recent Phenomenological
Literature," *Journal of Philosophy*, June 19, 1930; "Husserl's *Méditations Cartésiennes, Philosophical Review*, July, 1935; "Phenomenology,"
in *Twentieth Century Philosophy*, edited by D. Runes, New York,
Philosophical Library, 1943; "Aspects of Phenomenology and Existentialism," in *Philosophie*, ed. by R. Bayer, Paris, Hermann & Cie., 1950,
Vols. X and XIV; and *Husserl* (in Spanish), Buenos Aires, Ediciones
Losange, 1956—as forerunners of the point of view presented in this
volume.

methods applies, whether the methods be objectivistic or subjectivistic, "longitudinal" (historical or evolutionary) or "cross-sectional" (conceptual and formal). The use of fictions is indispensable in mathematics, and in conceptual thinking generally. The exclusive use of fictions would be another matter, as seen in the delimitation of an artificial domain for subjective inquiry, and its illicit use for a theory of reality. It is the over-extended use of such a domain for the purposes of a general philosophy that is so objectionable. The use of fictions *per se* is certainly not objectionable. (b) Logical pluralism recognizes the validity and constructibility of a large number of distinct systems of knowledge. In formal science, the idea of a "collective totality" of all the systems of formal knowledge allows for unity and diversity; and a similar pattern applies to the sciences of reality. This is to be distinguished from the rationalistic ideal of a single tree of knowledge, with all the sciences branching out from the one trunk, underlying which are a few "root ideas." In addition to our interest in establishing basic invariant principles, there is the need to recognize the principles which are peculiar to each special system.[9]

The ontological monism which goes along with this pluralism recognizes only one kind of "being" in the last analysis, namely, physical events. It is not necessary to assume other types of "being." The nature and organization of the basic physical units account for different types

---

9. Cf. the "Foreword" to *Philosophy for the Future,* a cooperative volume edited by R. W. Sellars, V. J. McGill, and M. Farber, New York, The MacMillan Co., 1949. Cf. also the present writer's papers: "Relational Categories and the Quest for Unity," *Philosophical Review,* July, 1934; "Logical Systems and the Principles of Logic," *Philosophy of Science,* Jan., 1942; "Types of Unity and the Problem of Monism," *Philosophy and Phenomenological Research,* Sept., 1943; and "On Unity and Diversity," same journal, June, 1946.

of properties and behavior in the inorganic, organic, and cultural realms. This view leaves out nothing that can be descriptively established. Even the most abstract activities of the "pure" reflective (or "transcendental-subjectivistic") investigator may be fully allowed for on this monistic basis. Man is not debased thereby. On the contrary, he feels a greater sense of dignity, earned by the understanding that progress through science in all its forms—natural and formal, empirical and abstract—may eventually enable him to solve all important problems. Therein lies the optimistic outlook of this balanced and logically weighted naturalism.

It will be well, in conclusion, to return once more to our earlier questions about experience. This will amount to reminding us of the basic points of reference for all philosophical inquiry. The locus of experience is found in human beings in their interactions with nature and with one another. The process of experience occupies an infinitesimal part of the cosmos, and it occurs only when there are sentient beings in action. The causal conditions of experience are physical, organic, and cultural. There are certainly "boundaries" of actual experience. Experience is always selective. But this does not imply that there is any "qualitatively" transcendent realm. There is always "more" of the same sort of experienced features, but there is no evidence of a "beyond" which is removed on principle from the world of experience. There is quantitative incompleteness, and not qualitative inaccessibility.

Bearing these elementary points in mind, it is entirely safe to institute special procedures, including the "egological" stage of purely reflective inquiry. The interest is solely in obtaining descriptive results, and there need be no epistemological blunders leading to metaphysical confusion. A further foundation of relevant principles concerning the field of existence and man would rule out or properly place in question the thought of a transcendent source of existence, and existentialist stereotypes of man.

Finally, it is well for philosophers to remind themselves repeatedly of the time-honored functions of philosophy: clarification of basic ideas, periodical synthesis of the chief results of the sciences, methodology, and the continued elaboration of a theory of values. Respect for their scientific colleagues will therewith be emphatically brought to mind, with a wholesome effect on their thinking. If philosophy is to bring wisdom to others, it must not be misled by narrow and unclarified motives, or warped by irrationalism and verbal jugglery, which at times seems indistinguishable from downright lunacy. A lasting bulwark of defense against all falsifiers and traducers of reason is guaranteed by the well-founded prestige of the sciences, and the undeniable interests of mankind.

# INDEX